DESIGN AGAINST RACISM

↓

Creating Work That Transforms Communities

Omari Souza

PA PRESS
PRINCETON ARCHITECTURAL PRESS · NEW YORK

I0801303

Contents

Praise for *Design Against Racism*

"*Design Against Racism* is not only informative and fact-based but also liberates those who have been or are enduring. As a successful interior designer in Atlanta, I've been fortunate to experience incredible opportunities and serendipitous collaborations that have propelled my brand forward. Yet, I recognize that tradition and a lack of inclusion have often constrained my success in Georgia's design industry. Despite being excluded from opportunities, awards, and platforms for daring to innovate, I remain deeply proud and grateful. True success isn't measured by acceptance but by the integrity of one's vision. Anything gained through authenticity and love holds immeasurable value—far greater than any barriers imposed by convention."

→ **Monét Masters-Coats, principal, Forbes Masters**

"*Design Against Racism* is a necessary and timeless resource that examines the historical relationship between design, racism, and inequality. Omari Souza's work empowers designers and educators to challenge oppressive structures and build more equitable futures."

→ **Sophia Little, designer and art director**

"The stories offered in *Design Against Racism* are part high-octane fuel and part expert field guides for designers, educators, and change makers interested in creating more socioculturally honest outcomes to design processes.... *Design Against Racism* presents design as a means to create products, experiences, systems, and new ways of doing that positively shape social realities, counter biased narratives, and dismantle racial biases."

→ **Michael R. Gibson, professor of communication design, University of North Texas**

"Omari Souza takes us on a journey to understand the historical practices and perspectives of the colonial era that have shaped the modern design pedagogy while highlighting the undercurrent of resistance and reclaimed memory from marginalized and forgotten groups.... A small shift in how we teach and practice design can create massive changes in a manner that restores and uplifts all."

→ **Tracey L. Moore, design educator, Prairie View A&M University**

Published by
Princeton Architectural Press
A division of Chronicle Books LLC
70 West 36th Street
New York, NY 10018
www.papress.com

© 2025 Omari Souza
All rights reserved.
Printed and bound in China
28 27 26   4 3 2

No part of this book may be used or reproduced in any manner without written permission from the publisher, except in the context of reviews.

Every reasonable attempt has been made to identify owners of copyright. Errors or omissions will be corrected in subsequent editions.

Editor: Sara Stemen
Designer: Natalie Snodgrass

Library of Congress Cataloging-in-Publication
Names: Souza, Omari, author.
Title: Design against racism : creating work that transforms communities / Omari Souza.
Description: First edition. | New York, NY : Princeton Architectural Press, [2025] | Summary: "An anti-racist approach to design practice based in an understanding of history, a focus on community building, and a commitment to inclusion"—Provided by publisher.
Identifiers: LCCN 2024049040 | ISBN 9781797223582 (paperback) | ISBN 9781797228150 (ebook)
Subjects: LCSH: Anti-racism. | Community development.
Classification: LCC HT1563 .S68 2025 | DDC 305.8—dc23/eng/20250318
LC record available at https://lccn.loc.gov/2024049040

Credits
11: New York American Civil Liberties Union ©Robert K. Chin / Alamy Stock Photo
12 top: ©Chris Lee / St. Louis Post-Dispatch/MCT/ Alamy Live News
12 middle: ©Visions of America, LLC / Alamy Stock Photo
12 bottom left: ©Alamy Stock Photo
12 bottom right: ©Andrew Katz / Alamy Stock Photo
13: ©Alamy Stock Photo
17: Science History Images / Alamy Stock Photo
25: colaimages / Alamy Stock Photo
26: CPA Media Pte Ltd / Alamy Stock Photo
41: FLHC DBAP1 / Alamy Stock Photo
42: AF Fotografie / Alamy Stock Photo
53: Alamy Stock Photo
57: Marion S. Trikosko, *U.S. News & World Report Magazine* Photograph Collection. March 26, 1964
58: Gino's Premium Images / Alamy Stock Photo
60: ©Alamy Stock Photo
67: Science History Images / Alamy Stock Photo
70 top and bottom: ©Alamy Stock Photo
82: Rosemarie Mosteller / Alamy Stock Photo
84: Science History Images / Alamy Stock Photo
87 top and bottom: ©Alamy Stock Photo
88 top: Glasshouse Images / Alamy Stock Photo
88 bottom: ©Alamy Stock Photo
122: Cassini Nazir
144: Omari Souza
147: Peter Horree / Alamy Stock Photo
151: Pictures Now / Alamy Stock Photo
158–64: ©Alamy Stock Photo
189–97: Marryam Moma
200: Lauren Williams
201–5: Austin Prouty
206: Daniel Chichester
208 top and bottom: Daniel Chichester
211: Daniel Chichester
217–18: Texas State University
220–27: Indigo Bishop
231–33: Omari Souza
240–45: Civilla

Part 2: Practice

Part 3: Case Studies

Introduction

Design Against Racism is a historical and philosophical exploration of design and how it fails (and has the potential to serve) underserved communities. This book not only critiques the current field but also provides avenues for people who are omitted from the design process. As a corrective measure and a guide for practices to promote greater equity now and into the future, *Design Against Racism* seeks to spark dialogue and offer suggestions for actions that designers and educators can take to make their practice more antiracist and antihegemonic.

This book is organized around the idea of restorative design—**an approach to design that centers on healing, inclusivity, and equity by addressing and repairing past harms inflicted upon marginalized communities**. Rooted in the principles of restorative justice, it empowers these communities through participatory and co-design methods, allowing them to reclaim agency and lead in creating solutions tailored to their needs and experiences. Restorative approaches to community design, such as co-design and participatory design, actively involve communities in the decision-making process, thereby restoring their power and agency. "Design by" strategies take this a step further by positioning the designer as a supportive partner, allowing communities to take the lead in designing their own solutions. This approach ensures not only that marginalized voices are heard but also that the solutions created are truly tailored to the needs and desires of the community.

The essays in this book unfold the layers of restorative design, unveiling its profound significance in challenging biased narratives, and nurturing healing and reconciliation. Drawing inspiration from restorative justice, this exploration delves into the role of storytelling circles in building understanding, trust, and community; the power of reclaiming histories; and the importance of incorporating diverse cultural content in the shaping of inclusive design environments.

For designers and storytellers, a restorative approach to storytelling requires critical analysis of traditional narratives, consideration of multiple points of view, and examination of power dynamics within the stories. Asset-based framing, which highlights marginalized groups' strengths and positive attributes, can counteract internalized oppression. By considering the portrayal of characters in stories and avoiding one-dimensional representations, designers can promote inclusivity and empower marginalized communities. And by acknowledging the complexities of history, challenging dominant narratives, and embracing a restorative approach to storytelling, designers can contribute to a more just and equitable future. Through these principles, restorative design becomes a catalyst for transforming the design process into a collaborative, community-driven endeavor.

As a backdrop for these practices, we examine the historical context of Western society, marked by the troubling legacy of cultural erasure of Black and Brown communities, a legacy deeply intertwined with the forces of colonialism and Eurocentrism. This history is a stark reminder of the inherent connections between cultural erasure and design. Understanding this connection is paramount to our discussions and endeavors in shaping a future that is worthy of all of us. As we confront the cultural limitations of current mainstream design practice while critically engaging the audience through discourse, our goal is to frame a dynamic and contemporary design practice that draws on lived experiences, storytelling, and culturally situated practices.

What Is Restorative Justice?

This book is shaped by the principles of restorative justice. In *A Kind of Mending: Restorative Justice in the Pacific Islands* (2010), edited by Tess Newton, Sinclair Dinnen, and Anita Jowitt, John Braithwaite's insights illuminate restorative justice as a powerful response to injustice. Braithwaite portrays restorative justice as

> a process in which all the stakeholders affected by an injustice have the opportunity to discuss the consequences of the injustice and what might be done to put them right.... The key value is that because injustice hurts, justice should heal.

Braithwaite explores the principles and values that underpin restorative justice, emphasizing its potential to rectify harm and to heal and empower individuals across diverse cultural and historical contexts.

Museum of Broken Windows, 9 West Eighth Street, New York, New York. Exterior of a political art exhibition by the NYCLU.

At its essence, restorative justice embodies the value of nondomination, with empowerment as its active embodiment. In its most idealized form, restorative justice prevents the state from interfering in conflict resolution between individuals and communities, thus enabling them to regain agency and control over their lives. While forgiveness, healing, and apology are integral to restorative justice, empowerment takes precedence, serving as the foundation upon which the other values effectively manifest (Braithwaite 2010).

Restorative justice centers cultural pluralism, historical pragmatism, and contextual adaptability. Acknowledging that justice is dynamic and that there is no one-size-fits-all solution for addressing injustices that occur in varying temporal and spatial contexts, restorative justice proves versatile. It adapts to the customs and traditions of diverse cultures, enriching societies' understanding of the nuanced ways in which justice can manifest (Braithwaite 2010).

Crucially, restorative justice is not about maintaining an unjust status quo but about healing injustice and reestablishing it as an innate human right. By identifying structural or systemic root causes, restorative justice allows

top: Protesters retreat as tear-gas canisters detonate around them on August 13, 2014, in Ferguson, Missouri. It was the fourth night of unrest in Ferguson after the fatal police shooting of Michael Brown.; middle: Silhouetted National Guard during 1992 riots, South Central Los Angeles, California.; bottom left: Two men throw beer bottles at burning vehicles during riots after the funeral of Freddie Gray, Baltimore, Maryland, April 27, 2015. Gray died from injuries sustained while in police custody.; bottom right: Rodney King riots. LAPD in riot gear file past burning squad car on day 1 of the riots, April 29, 1992.

for comprehensive solutions to often widespread problems, potentially transforming communities and reducing the likelihood of future violence. This transformative aspect extends beyond retribution, addressing the underlying problems that lead to offenses (Braithwaite 2010). Overall, restorative justice promises a future in which empowerment and understanding prevail over domination and retribution.

What Is Restorative Design?

Restorative design, which follows from tenets of restorative justice, is a methodology that is clear and evident in the discourse you'll find within the essays of this book. Although it doesn't currently exist as an acknowledged field, the aim of this book is to make it one. Restorative design consciously disrupts prevailing Western and Eurocentric perspectives while endeavoring to restore and validate the narratives and worldviews of diverse, often marginalized, communities. This approach accentuates the incorporation of nondominant social, ethnic, and cultural groups into the design process, respecting their unique viewpoints and experiences. It entails thoroughly exploring alternative epistemologies and worldviews through diverse storytelling traditions linked to anticolonial and decolonial actions. Within this paradigm, the designer undertakes the role of facilitator, aiming to mend impaired relationships. For example, design projects can address social injustices or develop spaces that facilitate reconciliation and healing. By embracing these principles, design transcends its conventional boundaries and emerges as a vehicle for social change, inclusivity, and empowerment (Braithwaite 2010).

Small American flag at site of 1992 riots, South Central Los Angeles, California.

The concept of design has undergone a significant evolution; as Keith M. Murphy's article "Design and Anthropology" highlights, design was initially associated with "planning" and "drawing," but the term's usage has since diversified. Some have used it to describe how objects are created, for example, the design of a bird's nest. However, this broader interpretation has faced resistance. Today, the term is understood as encompassing both the planning or intention of something and the act of drawing or outlining forms, aiming to explore uncharted analytical pathways and conceptual intersections (Murphy 2016).

Design, as I define it, encompasses **anything artificially created that guides, augments, or curates the human experience**. This broad definition includes wayfinding in airports and grocery stores, the layout of homes and offices, the architecture of worship halls, the furniture we sit on, and even the utensils we use during meals. Essentially, design influences every aspect of our daily lives, subtly directing our interactions with our environment and with each other.

Design intersects meaningfully with anthropology, the study of human societies and cultures, as well as how we form a sense of meaning, cohesion, and order. It does so in three configurations: **anthropology of design, anthropology for design, and design for anthropology. Anthropology of design** refers to a subfield in which design is the subject of ethnographic research. This approach recognizes design as a fundamental human capacity and a source of social order. Acknowledging the sociocultural and political significance of design, this subfield emphasizes the moral implications of human intervention in the lives of others. **Anthropology for design** employs anthropological methods and concepts in the design process. **Design for anthropology** borrows concepts and methods from design to enhance traditional ethnographic approaches.

These configurations underscore the moral implications of intentional interventions in people's lives. The emergence of design anthropology encourages collaboration between anthropologists and designers, blending creative skills with anthropological sensitivity to people's lived experiences (Murphy 2016). This is a relatively recent development. Historically, design did not occupy a central place in ethnographic analysis within anthropology. However, the advent of design anthropology is reshaping this landscape and encouraging anthropologists to collaborate with designers on projects that combine creative expertise with an in-depth understanding of people's lived experiences. The placement of lived experiences at the center of the design process is a radical restorative approach in and of itself.

The Three Fundamental Principles of Restorative Design

Restorative design encompasses three fundamental principles: **encounter**, **repair**, and **transform**. As a whole, this framework aims to tackle underlying sources of harm in crafted artifacts, spaces, and user experiences, as well as within broader systems and frameworks.

Encounter is a cornerstone principle that guides us through the vast landscape of acknowledging harm, restoring identities that have been altered or brutalized by colonizing norms, and amplifying the marginalized voices that are too often left out of larger discussions about the future we are creating as a collective. Of course, while there may be current attempts to malign this phase of the process, many times for the purpose of assuaging "white guilt" or clinging to the status quo, it is pivotal in the journey of future-shaping, which we'll explore in many essays throughout this book.

The essence of encounter compels us to delve deeply into the complexities of understanding the people involved and the historical and social factors that demand restoration. It is a call to break free from the confines of our perspectives, reminding us that, especially in design, our solutions are meant to be crafted for others. Therefore, our awareness must transcend the boundaries of our positions, extending to the viewpoints and needs of those for whom we design.

Within the broad sphere of restorative justice, the encounter phase takes center stage. It is the starting point that brings together all parties affected by violence—a diverse ensemble including victims, household members, wrongdoers, and other community members. Crucially, participation in this process is voluntary and uncoerced, necessitating a genuine commitment to taking complete accountability for one's actions before any meetings around reconciliation can occur. This phase embodies the profound exercise of empathy, demanding that those who have caused harm confront the total weight of the consequences they have inflicted.

The second phase of the restorative design process is **repair**. Restorative design focuses on repairing the harm caused by design education, practice, and research. This harm may stem from the assumption that everyone's story is similar, or the tendency to gravitate toward the loudest story or storyteller. Practitioners within the field of restorative justice use storytelling circles to build understanding, trust, and community. Strategies for repairing harm through storytelling and memory in the design process include listening more, seeking stories from diverse sources, and sharing our own stories.

The stories told about people of color can be trauma inducing, and our challenge is to navigate this racially induced trauma—dispelling myths, being successful despite negative narratives, acknowledging that many of us carry intergenerational trauma, thriving despite trauma, building relationships around trauma, and so on. This trauma does not affect only people of color, but its impact is likely more obvious on them than it is on white people.

Lee Anne Bell, a professor emerita at Barnard College, Columbia University, encourages us to problematize and interrogate stories with embedded racist agendas that rationalize white privilege and the status quo, even in design practice. Unfortunately, design stories may embed these agendas. For example, design stories may be written and told for a presumed white audience, presenting predominantly white, male, heteronormative modes of being and doing while presenting other ways of being and doing as deviant from the norm. Design materials may flatten the stories of underserved groups and communities, using them as props for storytelling rather than telling deeper stories and presenting richer narratives.

The second phase of restorative design necessarily takes us to the third phase, **restore**, whose focus is on developing and sustaining strategies for effecting change through design. At its core, it is a phase that engages marginalized communities in the design process, acknowledging the harm perpetuated by conventional design while aiming to foster inclusivity, empathy, and empowerment through the shaping of new futures.

Restoration is an act of reclamation, and it often occurs through storytelling. Through the stories we tell, we can dismantle harmful narratives, heal the wounds of the past, and bring agency and empowerment to marginalized voices. Restorative storytelling is not only a practice that challenges imperialist and colonialist sentiment; it is also a vehicle for nurturing trust, collaboration, and comprehension among diverse communities. It situates designers and writers as pivotal agents in this process, entrusted with reshaping historical memory by including counternarratives that amplify the voices of marginalized communities.

In this phase we can plumb the depths of oral history and storytelling from various perspectives, and we emphasize why it's so imperative to acknowledge and esteem distinct cultural standpoints and ways of knowing. This, in turn, facilitates a more accurate portrayal of historical occurrences and individual identities. Global forms of storytelling serve as a testament to the potent role of narrative in the preservation of traditions, the contestation of dominant historical accounts, and the advocacy of inclusivity.

Historical narratives can shape our understanding of the world, often perpetuating harmful stereotypes and biases. However, they can also be used to expose the truth and promote reconciliation. The griots of Mali, who maintained oral histories through storytelling, and the African American author and anthropologist Zora Neale Hurston are inspiring examples of storytellers who have used their craft to challenge harmful narratives and reclaim their cultural identities.

By sharing stories that reveal the hidden truths of history, this third phase of the restorative design process introduces a forward-looking dimension to the therapeutic approach—restorative futuring. Drawing parallels with the traditional concept of restoration, this approach involves updating elements to meet current needs and redress past harms. Throughout this book, examples from various artists and designers showcase how restorative futuring can be effectively implemented.

American author Zora Neale Hurston (January 7, 1891–January 28, 1960). Hurston was a prominent African American author, anthropologist, and folklorist, best known for her novel *Their Eyes Were Watching God*, which explores the lives and struggles of Black women in the South in the early twentieth century. A key figure of the Harlem Renaissance, Hurston celebrated Black culture and dialects, and she made significant contributions to preserving African American folklore and oral traditions.

Overall, encounter/repair/restore offers a loose framework for the essays in this collection—delineating our shared histories and mapping a way forward. This path underscores the importance of hopes and dreams in shaping our futures. Overall, we hope to emphasize the world-building capacity of design in restorative futuring and provide insights into leveraging these capabilities.

In essence, restorative design transcends the mere creation of products or services; it is a profound commitment to equity, inclusivity, and social justice. As we navigate the essays in this book, our exploration reveals how the restorative design approach repairs the damage inflicted by past design practices and enriches current processes in the field with insights that we hope will lead to more innovative and meaningful outcomes. Collectively, the authors wish to underscore the transformative power of restorative design, positioning it as a pivotal agent for positive change in both the design landscape and the structures that make up our very societies.

The Organization of This Book

Although I have authored the majority of essays in this book (those that appear with no byline), I have worked with several other design professionals who have contributed their thoughts and ideas in a variety of pieces. The essays in the first third of the book present a series of explorations that establish a historical context. These pieces acknowledge the harmful repercussions of colonialism and Eurocentrism, providing a necessary foundation for meaningful discussions around restoration. They also provide a deeper understanding of the coloniality of power, which contributing essayist George Fourlas describes as a concept that reproduces lingering colonial norms not just in the sociopolitical sphere but in the ways that design itself can emerge from universalist projections tied to Eurocentrism and the fallacy of white supremacy. Other explorations highlight the importance of listening to marginalized voices as a catalyst for innovation, emphasizing the role of empathy and understanding in design.

A major aspect of restorative design is identity reclamation. Thus, interspersed throughout the book are various strategies that promote understanding self. These strategies illuminate the many complex and intersecting layers of identity, encompassing both individual self-identification and the broader recognition of cultural identities. For example, the piece "Positionality: Acknowledging Oneself," by Lesley-Ann Noel, focuses on the importance of acknowledging the multifaceted identities that combine to shape an individual. This understanding is fundamental to the encounter phase and underscores the importance of incorporating one's identity into the design process.

Language and naming are also highlighted as potent tools that shape cultural identities, especially among marginalized communities. These elements have been used as instruments of oppression in colonial contexts, but they can also be harnessed to empower communities. By reclaiming their languages and names, marginalized groups can reaffirm their unique identities and challenge the narratives that have sought to sideline them. In addition, the role of design and education in perpetuating or challenging these narratives is underscored, emphasizing the need for inclusivity and diversity in these fields. Personal experiences with identity and representation in design education further illustrate the importance of inclusivity.

Additionally, the essay "What's in a Name?" explores the importance of titles and monikers. It prompts us to examine people's names and whether they are chosen or bestowed upon them. Drawing from the powerful narrative of Oluale Kossola in Hurston's *Barracoon: The Story of the Last "Black Cargo,"* we witness the erasure of cultural identity through the stripping away of a person's name. Hurston's insistence on using Kossola's original name is a poignant and highly intentional act of reclaiming a piece of his long-discarded identity as an act of resistance against coloniality—as well as a celebration of personal agency and ancestry that has inspired many of the pieces in this book, as well as the approach to an anticolonial, collaborative method of design.

In fact, Hurston's role as a leader and advocate who worked to protect the rights and voices of African Americans serves as inspiration for designers and storytellers, illustrating how we may humanize and preserve the cultural heritage of minority communities. Hurston's remarkable contributions to anthropology, particularly her dedication to capturing the rich culture of Black communities in the American South, underscore the power of inclusivity and representation in design. Her ability to foster trust within these communities and document their narratives, beliefs, dances, songs, and stories is a legacy from which designers can draw to gain insight into the communities for whom they design.

The essays also include transformative strategies for harnessing futuristic visions for design. Shamika Klassen's piece on Afrofuturism as a design strategy explores how Afrofuturism is a powerful tool for self-liberation and agency, allowing Black individuals and communities to imagine themselves in futuristic narratives that have historically excluded them. This approach challenges the status quo by advocating for proactive participation in shaping future material realities rather than being passive subjects. The narrative also delves into Afrofuturism as a creative response to hopelessness, emphasizing its role in transforming circumstances through speculative design. The critical perspective it introduces in design and engineering addresses often-overlooked issues of power, race, gender, and sexuality, promoting empathy by centering those who have been most affected by oppression. By employing Afrofuturism as a design lens, the narrative encourages innovation from the margins, enriching the reader's understanding of a more inclusive and representative approach to design and technology.

The exploration extends to "Africatown: A Space of Liberation and Generational Transformation," which discusses the impact of urban planning on friendships, perceptions of equality, and the potential homogenization of cities. Readers will also gain insight into the invisible forces of architecture and urban design that guide perceptions and interactions within disparate communities.

Kaleena Sales and Zariah Cameron's "Transforming for Workspace and Academic Safety" offers insights into creating safe and inclusive workplaces, particularly for Black employees and marginalized communities. Their essay reflects on the cultural dualities experienced by Black Americans and the necessity of psychological safety in professional environments. Readers will gain strategies for nurturing diverse, inclusive, and supportive workplaces, which are integral to an equitable design culture that fosters the restorative processes delineated throughout the book.

To bring these concepts to life and offer practical illustrations, we also present case studies that exemplify how designers can amplify the voices of the communities they engage with, fostering inclusive and empathetic design practices. The case studies establish a partnership-oriented approach that transforms the audience into active contributors who share power in the design process.

As we journey through the diverse chapters of this exploration into restorative design, the interconnected threads of Afrofuturism, urban planning, and workplace inclusivity weave a tapestry of transformative possibilities. Together, these narratives underscore the broader commitment of restorative design—one that not only repairs historical harms but also envisions a future in which innovation arises from the margins, inclusivity is paramount, and diverse voices shape the design landscape, leading to a more hopeful tomorrow for all.

Overall, design can be a powerful force for restitution, or it can perpetuate the violence of our colonial past while remaining hidden in plain sight. A restorative perspective encourages designers to transcend superficial constraints and consider the broader social impacts of their creations. Design is not merely a means of crafting beautiful objects; it is a powerful instrument that can shape social order and influence the lives of individuals and communities. In this light, designers are prompted to contemplate the far-reaching effects of their work, embracing their roles as shapers of artifacts and social realities (Murphy 2016).

The practice of design can be elevated to new heights by incorporating the wisdom of anthropology, the ethos of visionary thinkers like Zora Neale Hurston, and the principles of restorative justice. This allows design to transcend the realm of aesthetics and functionality, positioning it as a potent tool for effecting social change, fostering inclusivity, and empowering individuals to heal and flourish. Design, thus redefined, becomes a vehicle for the positive transformation of society itself.

References

Braithwaite, J. (2010). "The Fundamentals of Restorative Justice." In *A Kind of Mending: Restorative Justice in the Pacific Islands*. ANU E Press. http://doi.org/10.22459/KM.11.2010

Murphy, K. (July 2016). "Design and Anthropology." *Annual Review of Anthropology* 45: 433–49. https://doi.org/10.1146/annurev-anthro-102215-100224

Newton, T., Dinnen, S., and Jowitt, A., eds. (2010). *A Kind of Mending: Restorative Justice in the Pacific Islands*. Canberra: ANU E Press.

Part 1
History

1.1

The Birth of Eurocentrism and Violent Colonial Conquest

This book explores restorative approaches to design, and it is essential to begin by acknowledging and confronting the detrimental effects of colonialism. Even though the very concept may seem to be connected to bygone eras, it is important to trace colonialism's trajectory through the era of postcolonialism—the aftermath of Western colonialism in which we continue to live and by which our social structures are still largely circumscribed. It describes not just the political and socioeconomic conditions of most of our world today but also the ongoing endeavor of marginalized peoples to reclaim their cultural identities and sense of agency from cultural imperialism and sometimes invisible forms of subordination, including our constructed environments and symbolic vocabularies.

Throughout this book, we'll explore how individuals have begun their own repair by seeking to challenge and move away from Eurocentric practices, aiming to broaden the scope of the design canon by recognizing how our embodied histories affect our constructed environments and our varied approaches to symbolic expression. By understanding the design profession's historical context and its implications, we can work toward dismantling colonial influences and embracing diverse perspectives in design.

In the introduction to their book *Unthinking Eurocentrism: Multiculturalism and the Media*, Ella Shohat and Robert Stam argue that Eurocentrism emerged from colonialism. They trace its debilitating effects, describing how situating European culture as the world's center of gravity perpetuates the idea that only European history and philosophy are worth knowing and remembering as we consider the future of our world at large—as well as who has the power to determine what that looks like for the rest of us (Shohat and Stam 2014).

Image from the German colonization of Togo, 1900s.

To comprehend the impact of this oppression, we must begin with an exploration of European colonialism and occupation. Colonialism is the practice of a nation-state occupying another country and asserting itself as the head of state (Heaky and Da Lago 2014). New laws, systems of education, and religious indoctrination are imposed (Malone 2014), and the means of production are seized, with the occupier exploiting Indigenous labor and resources for economic gain.

Western history books have often sanitized the violence of colonial conquest (Young 2010). The spread of European influence often came at the barrel of a gun, to subjugate the resistance of Indigenous populations. Although the expansion of territory has gone hand in hand with death throughout human history, colonizing European nations were notorious for using force that exceeded the requirements of military strategy. Since non-Europeans were viewed as uncivilized, savage, and, in many cases, subhuman, the customary rules of military engagement did not apply. Colonial forces mutilated, killed, and imprisoned Indigenous people, destroying their property along the way.

A formative event in the history of colonialism, and a significant underpinning of its violence, was the Berlin Conference of 1884–85. At that series of meetings, the leaders of the United States and fourteen European nations crafted a control plan for Africa's resources and trading routes (Uzoigwe 1985), despite the fact that the continent was already inhabited by nations that had existed and flourished for centuries, even millennia. This resulted in the distribution of African land and resources among the European nations, and they achieved the full subjugation of sub-Saharan Africa, with the exception of Liberia and Ethiopia, by 1910 (Young 2010).

As argued by the political theorist Tom Young in his book *Africa*, the full extent of the destruction of colonialism went far beyond the subjugation of the peoples who belonged to the exploited societies and cultures. This was especially true if the colony's resources were needed to bolster private enterprises, which would then increase the overall prosperity of the colonizing nation. After the Berlin Conference, the Congo Basin, for example, was recognized as the possession of its sole owner, Belgium's King Leopold II. One of the Congo's most abundant resources was the natural material needed to make

The Rhodes Colossus caricature portrays Cecil Rhodes, a British businessman and politician, as a dominant figure straddling Africa, symbolizing his role in expanding British imperialism and European control over the continent. Rhodes's vision of a Cape-to-Cairo railroad, the founding of De Beers, and the establishment of Rhodesia highlight his controversial legacy of colonial exploitation and the Eurocentric belief in European superiority.

rubber. With the introduction of the bicycle and, later, the automobile, which used solid rubber tires, demand for rubber rapidly increased.

Leopold resorted to increasingly predatory forms of resource extraction to maximize his returns on the colony's resources. Congolese villagers had strict quotas for collecting rubber; if they failed to meet quotas, the Belgian colonizers would amputate their limbs. The Belgians established whippings, village burnings, and hostage taking as regular enforcement practices. The increase in demand for rubber enriched King Leopold II, but the harsh working conditions were catastrophic to the Congo's population, which declined by at least a third between 1880 and 1930 (Young 2010).

European colonialism and its devastating consequences, as detailed by scholars like Ella Shohat, Robert Stam, Enrico Dal Lago, Karen Malone, Robert J. C. Young, and G. N. Uzoigwe, serve as stark reminders of the profound and enduring impact of Eurocentrism on our global history. We must confront these uncomfortable truths, acknowledging the suffering and exploitation inflicted upon Indigenous peoples in the name of colonial expansion. Today, we strive toward a reality that celebrates the richness of our diverse human experience through a collective understanding and acknowledgment of the atrocities that have torn apart our human family in ways we are only beginning to understand—ways that continue to create bias, conflict, and harm in the realm of design and beyond.

References

Healy, R., and Dal Lago, E., eds. (2014). *The Shadow of Colonialism on Europe's Modern Past*. Palgrave Macmillan.

Malone, S. (n.d.). "The Berlin Conference of 1884–1885 | Africa's Great Civilizations." PBS Learning Media. https://kera.pbslearningmedia.org/resource/6031c3a2-ada9-42b4-8045-52006e2a2b07/the-berlin-conference-of-1884-1885/

Shohat, E., and Stam, R. (2014). *Unthinking Eurocentrism: Multiculturalism and the Media*. Routledge.

Uzoigwe, G. N. (June 1985). "Reflections on the Berlin West Africa Conference, 1884–1885." *Journal of the Historical Society of Nigeria* 12, nos. 3–4: 9–22.

Young, T. (2010). *Africa: A Beginner's Guide (Beginner's Guides)*. Oneworld Publications.

1.2

What Is Eurocentrism? A Historical Perspective on Design

George Fourlas

Eurocentrism—the set of beliefs and practices that treat "Europe" as both a historical constant and the apex of human civilization toward which all humans ought to strive—is the ideological force that drove early colonialism and affords its maintenance through the continued coloniality of power (Quijano 2024). Also called Occidentalism, Eurocentrism functions in tandem with what I describe elsewhere as Orientalist racism (Fourlas 2022), or the negation of those deemed naturally inferior or uncivilized in contrast to the white, "civilized," European, able-bodied, land-owning, Catholic/Protestant male, who epitomizes the pinnacle of human development.

Occidentalism, whiteness, and Europe emerge and exist through this process of negating those who exist outside the in-group. Ironically, Europe as a construct could not exist without the peripheral worlds it has colonized, exploited, subjugated, and denied. Here I unpack the general definition of Eurocentrism through a brief historical critique that aims to (1) denaturalize or provincialize "Europe" (Chakrabarty 2007) as a real and historically constant phenomenon; and (2) show how coloniality, or the lingering reproduction of colonial norms and expectations that were initially imposed in the thirteenth and fourteenth centuries, is itself a form of design that rests on baseless universalist projections.

It is worth emphasizing that Europe is, at best, a political idea and not a fixed land mass. From a geopolitical perspective, it makes the most sense to speak of the political territory currently demarcated "Europe" as western Eurasia; the fact that many are unsure of how many continuous land masses (i.e., continents) exist on the planet (there are six), or that Eurasia is a more appropriate term for the land that extends from Portugal to China, is itself a reflection of the power that Eurocentrism has over the colonized mind. The colonial mindset is an ideology rooted in Eurocentrism, where European culture, values, and territorial definitions are seen as superior and universal, often justifying the domination and exploitation of non-European lands and peoples. Like so many other contingent artifacts of the present, Europe has not always existed as currently imagined—and when deconstructed from a historical perspective, it quickly becomes clear that the idea of Europe is shaky at best (Dainotto 2007). Its material existence is the culmination of labor, resources, and thought that come from beyond itself.

Indeed, the extractivist heart of colonialism, coupled with the denial of that extraction, is captured throughout the twentieth century by such thinkers and activists as Eduardo Galeano (1997) and Aimé Césaire (2001), to name only two of the many critics who made a text like this one possible.

The Eurocentric narrative posits that figures like Christopher Columbus sailed west to find a new route east, purely out of an exploratory spirit, but Columbus's exploration always had a material foundation. The territories now associated with Western Europe were in shambles because the Ottoman Empire controlled the primary trade routes of central Eurasia and almost all of Africa. The "dark" or medieval period in European history was simultaneously the "golden age" for the Ottoman world, as well as various other civilizations that were thriving prior to colonization. The need for an eastern route was a material need, and the resources that were used to fund the Portuguese/Spanish colonial project initially came from the appropriation of non-Catholic wealth and land in the Reconquista period that preceded 1492.

The material motivation for colonization was also ideologically concealed from the beginning, as witnessed in the early pleas of the Spanish clergyman and social reformer Bartolomé de las Casas to the Spanish crown (Las Casas 1992). In his famous defense of the Indians, las Casas argued that the first peoples of the Americas should be treated more humanely because they were not the sort of barbarians who couldn't be converted to Christianity—for las Casas, the true barbarians were "Arabs, Turks, Greeks, and Romans," or those "enemies" of what was becoming Europe (in its imperial construct) who were closest to its fluctuating boundaries. In other words, in his failed attempt to save the First Nations people from the colonial brutality he'd witnessed on the ground, las Casas appealed to the popular myth that colonization was at its core an attempt to civilize the savage other. The response by the Church and crown was a refutation of las Casas's plea, and a reaffirmation of the colonial genocidal norms that were decimating the American continents.

Eurocentrism and colonialism are undeniably intertwined, as both ideologies relied on constructing a false narrative to justify the colonizers' actions and maintain political, economic, and social dominance. Eurocentrism as a worldview not only positioned Europe as the apotheosis of civilization but also conveniently overlooked the inherent brutality of its colonial endeavors—which were hardly the actions of a humane or civilized people. The proponents of colonialism have claimed that Europe emerged from its "dark" age through reason, enlightenment, and hard work—positioning Europe as the paragon of civilization while denying the bloodthirst and cruelty involved in establishing and maintaining this false position.

The Martinican poet, activist, and political figure Aimé Césaire (2001) extends this point powerfully:

> The essential thing here is to see clearly, to think clearly—that is, dangerously—and to answer clearly the innocent first question: what, fundamentally, is colonization? To agree on what it is not: neither evangelization, nor a philanthropic enterprise, nor a desire to push back the frontiers of ignorance, disease, and tyranny, nor a project undertaken for the greater glory of God, nor an attempt to extend the rule of law. To admit once and for all, without flinching at the consequences, that the decisive actors here are the adventurer and the pirate, the wholesale grocer and the ship owner, the gold digger and the merchant, appetite and force, and behind them, the baleful projected shadow of a form of civilization which, at a certain point in its history, finds itself obliged, for internal reasons, to extend to a world scale the competition of its antagonistic economies. (32–33)

Here Césaire is rejecting the ideological myth of colonization—that its goal was to uplift or improve the general condition of humankind—while noting that the heart of colonization is the universal imposition of a singular and provincial system. Though the system that was originally imposed through violent force—liberal capitalism—has since festered and grown in various complex ways, the fundamental characteristics of the colonizers' global design remain entrenched.

The Peruvian sociologist Aníbal Quijano (2007) captured these designs in his invaluable reflections on the coloniality of power and distilled them into several fundamental features. *Coloniality* is the term Quijano deployed to capture the lingering function of colonial domination after direct colonial rule was mostly dissolved in the mid-twentieth century. Colonial domination "fell, above all, over the modes of knowing, of producing knowledge, of producing perspectives, images and systems of images, symbols, modes of signification, over the resources, patterns, and instruments of formalized and objectivised expression, intellectual or visual" (Quijano 2007). Local systems of life were replaced with Western European modalities, which, Quijano noted, were organized (and functioned to organize) according to racial expectations and classifications, but racism is itself a subset of the broader universalist "rationality" that reduces the lived world to oversimplified object forms and atomistic individual "knowers" who engage the objectified world as if they stand outside the relational matrix.

The race/rationality and "objective" individual framework are, in many ways, the wellspring from which the ongoing problem of coloniality convulses; it's a decaying mode, the rot of which continues to poison the lives of most of the world's people. Many still benefit from the power structures that colonization imposed, such that the question of an anticolonial alternative must keep in mind not only the epistemic and sociopolitical features of coloniality but also those who remain affirmatively invested in these decadent systems of supremacy.

References

Césaire, A. (2001). *Discourse on Colonialism*. Monthly Review Press.

Chakrabarty, D. (2007). *Provincializing Europe: Postcolonial Thought and Historical Difference*. Princeton University Press.

Dainotto, R. M. (2007). *Europe (in Theory)*. Duke University Press.

Fourlas, G. N. (2022). *Anti-Colonial Solidarity: Race, Reconciliation, and MENA Liberation*. Rowman & Littlefield Publishers.

Galeano, E. (1997). *Open Veins of Latin America: Five Centuries of the Pillage of a Continent*. Monthly Review Press.

Las Casas, B. d. (1992). *A Short Account of the Destruction of the Indies*. Edited and translated by N. Griffin. Penguin Publishing Group.

Quijano, A. (2007). "Coloniality and Modernity/Rationality." *Cultural Studies* 21, nos. 2–3: 168–78. https://doi.org/10.1080/09502380601164353

Quijano, A. (2024). *Aníbal Quijano: Foundational Essays on the Coloniality of Power*. Edited by W. D. Mignolo, R. Segato, and C. E. Walsh. Translated by D. Frye. Duke University Press.

1.3

Unveiling the White Gaze: The Narrative of Whiteness and Colonial Nostalgia

Language informs storytelling, which informs culture, which influences policy—all of which ultimately transform our phenomenological existence. The stories and messages we consume are as much a part of our lives as eating and sleeping. In design education, students come to curricula using a wide variety of visual languages, but many leave indoctrinated into one singular language, having adopted the rules of "good design," which has become synonymous with Eurocentric aesthetics. A restorative approach to design practice must intentionally create opportunities to reclaim language—especially as we consider that what is visually appealing in one culture may not be appealing in another.

Common beliefs about the origins and evolution of nations often take form through language—particularly through stories. Although these stories may travel orally (as they did in antiquity), the written word has become the formal mechanism for the communication of substantive information. Prior to television and film, novels and newspapers—like the internet and television today—introduced a sense of the simultaneity and interconnectedness of events across different places.

Storytelling is a method by which the prevailing norms and values of a culture can be articulated. This has often been the case with novels, whose characters offer a symbolic understanding of individual psychology and collective ontology (i.e., the nature of being and existence). Novels are couched in revelations about the nature of the individual and of the society in which they live. For example, a bildungsroman (a novel whose central concern is the formative years or emotional maturation of the protagonist) was traditionally envisioned as a distinctly German literary form—one that typically involved heaping dollops of nationalism.

Novels provide readers with the concept of the purposeful movement through time of fictional entities bound together in a narrative whole. However, the act of choosing which narratives are canonically accepted—or more specifically, whether a narrative is allowed to disregard whiteness as a normative ideological center—is a display of power not regularly allotted to the racially subjugated.

Western history books and canonical American fiction focus on the white gaze by normalizing customs and inquiries that are entrenched in whiteness as a prevailing, unquestioned framework. Although the twentieth century afforded us a number of literary examples that went against the grain—from the poets and novelists of the Harlem Renaissance to more contemporary truth tellers like Toni Morrison and Maya Angelou—and we currently enjoy an increasingly recognized crop of chroniclers and fable makers like Marlon James and Ocean Vuong, this inclusivity and expansiveness are precarious at best and under constant assault. The assaulting factors include everything from book bans to the disingenuous tendency to cast a mournful backward glance upon more "universal" stories (as if tales of European monarchy, as in Shakespeare, or depictions of the old feudal cotton aristocracy, as in Faulkner, were ever absent of cultural specificity—or uncontested in their own time).

To add a layer of complexity, nostalgia for the "uncomplicated" days of storytellers from the dominant white culture often sits astride nostalgia for the pristine, bygone cultures of people of color, untouched by colonial influences. Often, in the latter type of narrative, encounters with the "other" are couched in a vocabulary that prioritizes "purity" and "authenticity," almost akin to the armchair anthropologists of colonial times, who simultaneously looked upon their "primitive" subjects with horror and admiration. This narrative device can even be directly tied to contemporary films like James Cameron's *Avatar*, in which the protagonist is a white "freedom fighter" who joins the subjugated humanoid population of the planet Pandora to the degree that he out-natives the natives.

In "Imperialist Nostalgia" (1989), an article by the American cultural anthropologist Renato Rosaldo, the titular concept is introduced as a seemingly contradictory phenomenon. It refers to the sentiment experienced by the agents of imperialism, who lament the passing of cultures or ways of life that they intentionally altered or destroyed through their brazen colonizing actions. The nostalgia arises in the context of imperialism, as individuals express regret that the societies they colonized have not remained unchanged by their intervention. This form of longing adopts an "innocent yearning" posture, conveying the fantasies of those experiencing it while concealing their complicity with the brutal domination imposed by imperialism.

While imperial nostalgia arises from the subjugating powers, colonial nostalgia applies to the people who experience subjugation. Imperialist nostalgia emerged from the colonizers' longing for a romanticized past, during which they exercised control and domination over the occupied territories. It involves a selective and idealized view of the colonial era, disregarding the harm inflicted on the colonized populations. From the reverse perspective, colonial nostalgia represents the sentiments of the colonized, particularly in their longing for certain aspects of the colonial past, even as they grapple with the complexities and repercussions of that period in the present day.

In his work, the anthropologist William Cunningham Bissell (2005) explores colonial nostalgia in contemporary Africa. This sentiment arises from a sense of loss and longing for days shaped by specific cultural concerns and struggles. Bissell highlights how residents yearn for the colonial past as a critique of contemporary urban conditions. In Zanzibar, a local resident expressed profound sorrow over the city's present state, noting that seeing how it used to be would bring tears to one's eyes. This sentiment is widely shared, reflecting a collective sense of loss and longing for the British colonial era. The Zanzibari resident's lamentation is not just a comparison of the city's current state and its past under British rule. It is a poignant expression of the heartache that the sight of the city's perceived former glory evokes, underscoring a profound sense of loss and yearning for a past era despite the difficulties faced during that time. At the time of the essay, Zanzibar was grappling with numerous challenges, including a decline in public services like health care and education. Yet, amid these hardships, the memory of the past, with its perceived order and stability, shines through, highlighting the depth of colonial nostalgia.

Colonial nostalgia and imperial nostalgia are distinct in both their focus and nature. The latter is about the loss of empire, encompassing the decline of national grandeur and international power dynamics. In contrast, colonial nostalgia is about the loss of sociocultural status or the colonial lifestyle, emphasizing an idealized vision of past intercultural relations within the colony. This distinction is crucial to understanding the complex emotions and narratives associated with postcolonial societies.

Both colonial and imperial nostalgia involve romanticizing aspects of an earlier era, but they differ in focus and scope. Colonial nostalgia typically refers to a longing for a specific period when a foreign power directly ruled a particular region or territory. It often involves reminiscing about colonial rule's perceived benefits or stability, such as improved infrastructure, governance, or perceived cultural superiority. Residents may idealize aspects of colonial life while overlooking or downplaying the negative impacts of colonization on the native populations, such as exploitation, marginalization, and loss of autonomy.

In contrast, imperial nostalgia tends to encompass a broader longing for the grandeur, power, and influence associated with a past empire (Lorcin 2013). It can extend beyond the direct experience of colonial rule to include a sense of pride or nostalgia for an imperial power's achievements, cultural dominance, and global reach. Imperial nostalgia may focus less on the specific governance structures or daily life under colonial rule and more on the empire's legacy, glory, and historical significance.

Overall, colonial nostalgia often centers on the perceived benefits of direct colonial rule, while imperial nostalgia encompasses a broader longing for the influence and prestige of past empires. Both forms of nostalgia continue to influence contemporary postcolonial societies. The idealization and longing for a past that involved oppression and exploitation have lasting effects on how people perceive themselves and others. For those who experienced colonization, colonial nostalgia may intertwine with complex feelings of identity, pride in cultural heritage, and the desire for reclamation and restoration. Conversely, imperialist nostalgia can shape colonizers' views of their past actions, resulting in an ambivalent reconciliation of their involvement in historical domination.

These paradoxical sentiments reveal the intricate workings of the human psyche, as well as our capacity for making meaning as we collectively grapple with the legacies of imperialism and colonialism. As postcolonial societies confront their complex histories, nostalgic sentiments remain powerful forces in shaping perceptions, aspirations, identities, and the stories we perpetuate about who we (believe) we are.

Seldom, if ever, have racialized and other types of minorities been depicted as anything other than objects of the white gaze—symbols that expound upon white subjectivity and serve as narrative devices that delineate the progression of white protagonists and historical figures. Alongside literary and artistic choices that center whiteness, society does the same—through laws, policies, institutional structures, and systems that favor and reward whiteness. Whiteness largely determines whose voices are heard, as well as who is seen and in what ways. All of this is invisible to most white people, in the same way that the fact of whiteness is often cloaked from those who hold it as an identity. This is because whiteness (white maleness, in particular) is often referenced as the default.

The term *white centrality* describes how the dominant culture places white people and whiteness at its center, focuses on them, establishes whiteness as the norm, and expects everyone to live by those norms. In *The Enduring, Invisible, and Ubiquitous Centrality of Whiteness* (2022), Kenneth V. Hardy argues:

> Too often, white, heterosexual, cisgender males produce "objective scholarship," where their social location as white and male is strewn throughout the pages they type without any acknowledgment that their position could be a factor in what they see, say, and write. (9)

Whiteness is the ubiquitous atmosphere in which marginalized identities of color are made conspicuous and deemed lacking—outsiders in the environment, which itself is demarcated by an implied whiteness. Thus, although white supremacy tends to be defined under the aegis of hate groups who make their sentiments about minorities volubly known, it is more often expressed covertly or through seemingly innocuous means (e.g., through categories like First World and Third World, which grant superiority to white, Western, Eurocentric norms while subordinating the rest of the world). Whiteness as a dominant ideal prevails through its very invisibility, for the purpose of erasing its influence and the consequences of that influence. In this sense, white people are conditioned to believe that they should be the recipients of special benefits—but seldom are they encouraged to cultivate the self-awareness that would enable them to see that whiteness is the reason for such a belief. This ingrained sense of white innocence is an aspect of the oppression under which people of color live (Sue 2006).

We must understand that our collective storytelling, and the language undergirding it (which includes design vocabularies), is essential for engaging in meaningful discussions about the impact of history on contemporary realities. However, before we can do this, it's imperative that as design practitioners, educators, allies, and activists, we critically examine the implications of our design solutions and the language of the artifacts we create. We must identify, challenge, and unlearn ideologies, aesthetic philosophies, and historical perspectives that perpetuate Eurocentrism and minimize the existence of marginalized communities. This journey of self-examination and transformation is essential in the field of design. Restorative practices that address the collective memory of the past and endeavor to heal suffering perpetuated by imperialism and colonialism can play a crucial role in making room for far more than a narrow selection of stories representing the voices and perspective of the most powerful.

References

Bissell, W. C. (2005). "Engaging Colonial Nostalgia." *Cultural Anthropology* 20, no. 2: 215–48. http://www.jstor.org/stable/3651534

Hardy, K. V., ed. (2022). *The Enduring, Invisible, and Ubiquitous Centrality of Whiteness*. W. W. Norton.

Lorcin, P. M. (December 1, 2013). "Imperial Nostalgia; Colonial Nostalgia Differences of Theory, Similarities of Practice?" *Historical Reflections / Réflexions Historiques*. https://doi.org/10.3167/hrrh.2013.390308

Rosaldo, Renato. (1989). "Imperialist Nostalgia." *Representations* 26: 107–22. https://doi.org/10.2307/2928525

Sue, D. W. (2006). "The Invisible Whiteness of Being: Whiteness, White Supremacy, White Privilege, and Racism." In M. G. Constantine and D. W. Sue, eds., *Addressing Racism: Facilitating Cultural Competence in Mental Health and Educational Settings*, 15–30. John Wiley & Sons.

1.4

What's in a Name?

In *Barracoon: The Story of the Last "Black Cargo,"* Zora Neale Hurston, the American author, anthropologist, and documentary filmmaker, employed the restorative practice of using her subject Oluale Kossola's original language. When Hurston first met Kossola at his home in Alabama, she called him by his African name, even though he also went by the slave name Cudjoe Kossula Kazoola Lewis. Stripping Kossola of his given name was an act of cultural theft intended to separate him from his ancestry and to reduce him to the status of property. If stripping Kossola of his given name was an act of cultural erasure, Hurston's insistence on using his original name was an act of revelation, one that articulated an enduring connection with a piece of his identity that had long been discarded.

Cudjoe Kazoola Lewis (ca. 1841–July 17, 1935), born Oluale Kossola. He was one of the last known survivors of the transatlantic slave trade, captured in West Africa and brought to the United States aboard the illegal slave ship *Clotilda* in 1860. After gaining freedom, he and other former enslaved people from the *Clotilda* founded Africatown near Mobile, Alabama—a community preserving their African traditions and heritage.

Oluale Kossola was born around 1841 in what's now Benin (Broughton 2019). He is known for being one of the last survivors of the transatlantic slave trade. He was captured and brought to the United States on an illegal slave ship called the *Clotilda*. Along with 115 other Africans, Kossola was hidden when they arrived in Mobile, Alabama, in 1860. The ship was sunk to avoid getting caught and was found only in 2019.

In the United States, Kossola and the other captives had to give up their original names for ones that were easier for Americans to pronounce. This was a huge loss for him.

Even though he was freed after the Civil War, Kossola felt that he had lost his home and struggled with his identity (Zimmerman et al. 2018). Kossola was more than just a survivor, though. He became a leader for the African community in Africatown, Alabama, a place created by the freed *Clotilda* survivors. This community had its own rules and kept its members' cultural practices alive, despite the challenges they faced in the Deep South (Hurston 2018).

Kossola's story was recorded by Hurston in *Barracoon*. The book was initially turned down for publication because Hurston kept the subject's words in his original dialect, which was important to his identity and

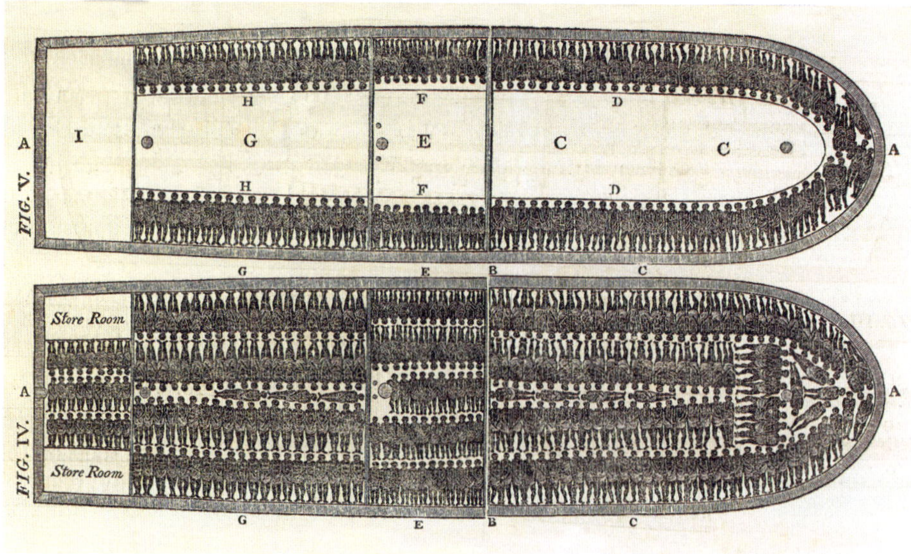

The *Plan of the Slave Ship Brookes*, a detailed diagram of a British slave ship used during the transatlantic slave trade. This infamous illustration, first published in 1787, graphically depicted the overcrowded and inhumane conditions in which enslaved Africans were transported across the Middle Passage. The image played a crucial role in the abolitionist movement by visually exposing the brutal realities of the slave trade to the public, helping to galvanize support for its eventual abolition.

history. By doing this, Hurston made sure that Kossola's true voice and story were kept intact, giving a real account of his life and the experiences of the last Africans brought to America as enslaved people (Zimmerman et al. 2018).

Throughout history, the practitioners of colonialism and slavery have forced subjugated peoples to use the language and names of their oppressors. The question we should consider as designers is whether cultural erasure is inadvertently a part of our practice. Are our methods forcing people to use language and names that are not theirs (as can so often be the case in academic or research-based spaces that adopt jargon and terminology to legitimize the entire process)? Are the insights gleaned from this approach valid, or are there vital nuances that we miss in translation? Is this the most equitable approach? Can we do better? And if so, are we making the necessary efforts to transform our methods into ones that honor the people we are attempting to serve?

By failing to acknowledge and appreciate the humanity and worth of others—which includes the ways that marginalized people self-define and perceive their identities—we actively participate in the harmful process of cultural erasure. It is vital to recognize that a person's identity encompasses a variety of elements, such as their name, accents, attire, religious beliefs, and language, all of which serve as crucial forms of communication. When we ignore or suppress these aspects of identity, we directly affect our own perception and that of historically marginalized communities, influencing the collective understanding of morality, justice, and beauty in ways that render them incomplete and exclusionary. The consequences of denying aspects of individuals extend far beyond mere exclusion; they raise profound questions about traumatic disruptions in the creation of identity, belonging, and acceptance. Exclusion and erasure can be seen as deliberate acts that cause harm, contradicting the very essence of restoration.

The processes by which colonialism and slavery have forced people to adopt the language and names of their oppressors have broader ramifications for how people self-present, as well as on the types of identities that are given precedence and considered "superior." As designers, we must question whether cultural erasure is embedded in our own practices.

Indeed, erasure also applies to physical spaces. In my home city of New York, there once was a community called Seneca Village. This predominantly African American community was located on land that is now part of Central Park, between West Eighty-Second and West Eighty-Ninth Streets in Manhattan. Founded in 1825, it grew into a vibrant settlement of about 225 people by 1855, including African Americans, Irish immigrants, and a few Germans. Seneca Village provided a safe and stable environment for its residents, many of whom owned property. Land ownership, a common path many Americans took to acquire and pass down wealth, was a rare achievement for African Americans at the time. Today, the name Seneca Village is known by few.

The story of Seneca Village is one of conflict and erasure. In the early 1850s, New York City created Central Park to address health concerns and provide recreational space. The chosen site included the land where Seneca Village stood (Central Park Conservancy, n.d.). Using eminent domain, the city forced out about sixteen hundred residents, including nearly three hundred from Seneca Village, to make way for the park. Even though residents were paid for their property, they often felt the compensation was too low, and losing their homes marked the end of their community.

By the early 1860s, Seneca Village had been erased, and its history and residence were forgotten. Recently, archaeological efforts and historical research have begun to uncover and remember this important part of New York City's history, revealing artifacts and stories that show what life was like for the residents of Seneca Village. Despite these efforts, the creation of Central Park remains a powerful example of how urban development can erase significant cultural and historical communities, and their names, from history (Central Park Conservancy, n.d.).

The article "Emotion and Urban Experience: Implications for Design" (2000), by Aušra Burns, argues that we should discuss urban experiences and emotions to understand these phenomena and create designs that fit different social and physical conditions. The article emphasizes the importance of accepting diversity and change in our surroundings, recognizing that today's cities blend physical and virtual spaces, which means designers need to update their strategies and methods.

Designers can and should learn from the different experiences of city residents, understanding that public spaces mean different things to different people. They need to be ready to adapt to unexpected events in the city and understand that informal practices can offer valuable insights. By discussing urban experiences and emotions, designers can improve their understanding and create design strategies matching specific social and physical conditions. This makes it easier to connect aesthetic choices to practical actions in the environment. Ignoring historical events like the destruction of Seneca Village dismisses the emotional connection to space and place (Burns 2000); an approach that acknowledges memory encourages designers to change their perspective, becoming more aware of modern social conditions and more responsible for their actions while appreciating the diversity of human experiences.

For many who fall into marginalized identities, their only space of understanding often comes when translated through a Western lens. A name can communicate an individual's social class and their gender, geographic origin, religion, social group, and ethnic identity through our knowledge of naming conventions within their community. Naming systems are not static; they evolve in contact with the cultures of settlers from within and outside the region where they were first used. Some cultures gift new generations the names of their ancestors, allowing the past to live on through the present.

The act of reclamation often goes hand in hand with an understanding of how marginalized people might "voluntarily" give up their names in order to gain social acceptance and fit into the American imperative of assimilation. Throughout history, individuals have experienced the weight of their names, leading some to alter or adopt different names to navigate social barriers and prejudice. This phenomenon is evident with, for example, the Irish, Italian, and Polish immigrants in early twentieth-century America, who often chose Eurocentric names for their children to enhance social mobility and avoid persecution (Blake 2019).

Research conducted by professors from the University of Chicago and the Massachusetts Institute of Technology suggests that employers discriminate against job applicants based on their names, potentially reflecting implicit racial biases (Leonard, n.d.). In an extensive experiment, professors created realistic résumés for phantom job seekers with common Black and white names. These résumés were sent to thousands of employers in Chicago and Boston. The study found that Black-sounding names were more likely to be overlooked, indicating that employers may unconsciously favor candidates with white-sounding names (Bertrand and Mullainathan 2004). The prevalence of discussions and stereotypes surrounding Black-sounding names, as observed in media and academia, reveals the complex dynamics at play. Names like "D'Brickashaw Ferguson" and "Tyrasciuses" have been subjects of comedic ridicule. This has long been parodied in popular culture; however, regardless of a name's cultural origin, for marginalized audiences, choosing a name is a direct response to erasure and an act of restoration that should be respected.

In the 1960s, Black and white parents tended to choose names for their children that aligned with white conventions. However, a significant transformation occurred in the early 1970s, as many Black parents, particularly those living in racially segregated communities, began adopting more distinctly Black names (Blake 2019). This shift coincided with the emergence of the Black Power movement of the late 1960s and 1970s, suggesting that this influential social and political movement and the accompanying sense of Black pride shaped Black individuals' perceptions of their identities.

The movement stressed the importance of capitalizing "Black" when referring to people of African descent. Changing from lowercase to uppercase showed a move toward self-naming, self-defining, and self-determining, highlighting both individual and group power in shaping racial and ethnic identities. Using *Black* with a capital *B* shows peoplehood, pride, and power, unlike the negative views of *black* as an adjective before the 1960s (Claybrook 2021). The movement aimed to redefine what it meant to be Black in the United States. Capitalizing Black acknowledges the humanity of African people and their descendants, reflecting a fight against the impacts of race and racism. The movement also insisted on capitalizing historical terms like *Negro* to show respect and dignity in naming practices (Claybrook 2021).

Other twentieth-century movements like Black Is Beautiful hark back to nineteenth-century conventions that prioritized the reclamation of African names—or even the assumption of new names to break away from the limitations and indignity imposed by racism. Consider the Black abolitionist and feminist Sojourner Truth, who was given the name Isabella Baumfree at birth as an enslaved woman; Truth's subsequent conversion to Christianity as an adult led to her assumption of a new and powerfully symbolic name. In what she saw as her spiritual calling to spread the universal truth of human equality and share the social ills perpetuated by slavery and other forms of injustice, she expressed her agency and self-determined identity through a fundamental form of identification—her name.

Black identity in the United States has also been shaped by encounters with other cultures that led to new naming conventions—ones that emphasized the right to equality and liberty, regardless of race. In 2019, the National WWI Museum and Memorial organized a discussion featuring the historian Saje Mathieu, the author of *The Glory of Their Deeds: A Global History of Black Soldiers and the Great War*, and the *Wall Street Journal* reporter Cameron McWhirter, the author of *Red Summer: The Summer of 1919 and the Awakening of Black America*. The discussion focused on the experiences of Black Americans upon their return to the United States after serving in France during World War I, and it also commemorated the hundredth anniversary of the Red Summer of 1919, when more than thirty cities across the United States experienced white-supremacist terrorism and racial riots (National WWI Museum and Memorial 2019).

During their presentation, the two authors detailed how African American soldiers who fought in France during World War I had a transformative experience that significantly influenced their views and aspirations. Their encounter with French culture and society exposed them to a different racial dynamic, one in which they were treated with more respect and dignity than they'd experienced in the United States. The African American experience was riddled with segregation and discrimination. In contrast, the soldiers who served in France witnessed African soldiers fighting alongside French troops and were inspired by the idea of equality amid the war.

Exposure to a completely new racial dynamic and the experience of being recognized as heroes and equals motivated them to advocate for their rights and demand fair treatment upon returning home. This heightened awareness led African American soldiers to also return to the United States and incorporate French words, euphemisms, and names for their daughters, all in an effort to challenge their social standing or simply to aspire to be perceived, treated, and embraced as something greater (National WWI Museum and Memorial 2019).

Many such examples abound throughout African American culture and history. One could argue that Cassius Clay's decision to adopt the name Muhammad Ali, Prince's choice to be identified as "the artist," and the preferences of the trans and nonbinary communities to use their chosen names or pronouns all share similar roots in challenging prevailing norms and issuing a clear demand to be seen, treated, and acknowledged as more than the identities assigned to us by the dominant culture.

Respecting and honoring chosen names, dialects, and pronouns is essential to working with others. Pronouncing and spelling names correctly demonstrates care and inclusivity. Sharing stories related to our own names can foster a deeper understanding of one another's cultural backgrounds and help break the ice when working with new collaborators. Discussing the names that individuals would choose for themselves allows for further exploration of personal identity and agency. Publicly embracing the names of our peers in a society that has historically marginalized us affirms our cultural lineage and contributes to validation and healing.

It is important to reflect on the various forms of language used within our groups and societies. We must consider discriminatory language practices and whether there is an ingrained default to English or a disregard for dialects. Encouraging people to reflect on their language usage, as well as their comfort with certain forms of language, can deepen our understanding of cultural dynamics. Honoring instances of code-switching, which is the practice of shifting from one mode of language to another on the basis of social context, is also a crucial aspect of restorative, people-centered design.

This brings us back to Hurston, who drew on her unique position as a Black woman and anthropologist to conduct meaningful research. By embracing her cultural background and identity, she could perceive Kossola not just as a subject of study but as a fellow human being, allowing her to approach her research with sensitivity and insight and to use the restorative practice of incorporating his actual language into the text. Hurston's powerful approach enabled her to both self-reflect and more clearly see Kossola for who he was and how he wanted to be seen.

As Hurston understood, an important part of healing and restoration for marginalized people is the reclamation of their names and identities. In relation to the practice of design, this concept focuses less on the outcome of what is crafted and more on how we interact with and understand the audience we aim to design for. A name rests in and on the edge of language. Just as individuals project different meanings onto public spaces, which can vary widely from person to person, designers cannot effectively create for marginalized audiences without first understanding who they are and what their cultural identities and identifiers mean to them.

Design can either perpetuate erasure or become a catalyst for learning and revelation. Designers and other professionals who've also experienced being socially excluded often face pressure to conform to the dominant culture and downplay their cultural identities if they deviate from the "norm." Thus, we must also pay attention to the possibility of internalized oppression having dictated our practices. Self-erasure not only deprives us of our heritage but also hinders social progress and innovation. Instead, like Hurston, we can consciously honor and stand strong in our identities, placing them at the forefront of our design practice to dignify our cultural past, to restore our own visibility, to emphasize our contributions to society, and to be advocates for all marginalized people who are in a similar process of self-reclamation.

References

Bertrand, M., & Mullainathan, S. (2004). "Are Emily and Greg More Employable Than Lakisha and Jamal? A Field Experiment on Labor Market Discrimination." *American Economic Review*, 94(4), 991-1013. https://doi.org/10.1257/0002828042002561

Blake, J. (2019, June 15). "What It's Like to Be a White Woman Named LaKiesha." CNN. Retrieved June 9, 2024, from https://www.cnn.com/2019/06/15/us/white-black-names-blake/index.html

Broughton, T. M. (2019). "Cudjo Lewis." Enslaved.org. Retrieved June 9, 2024, from https://enslaved.org/fullStory/16-23-106156/

Burns, A. (2000). "Emotion and Urban Experience: Implications for Design." *Design Issues* 16, no. 3: 67–79.

Central Park Conservancy. (2018, January 18). "Before Central Park: The Story of Seneca Village." Central Park Conservancy Magazine. Retrieved June 9, 2024, from https://www.centralparknyc.org/articles/seneca-village

Claybrook, K. (2021, September 10). "Black Identity and the Power of Self-Naming." AAIHS. Retrieved June 9, 2024, from https://www.aaihs.org/black-identity-and-the-power-of-self-naming/

Hurston, Z. N. (2018). *Barracoon: The Story of the Last "Black Cargo."* Edited by D. G. Plant. HarperCollins.

Leonard, J. (n.d.). "Study Reveals Employer Bias Based on Names in Job Applications." University of Chicago / National Bureau of Economic Research (NBER).

National WWI Museum and Memorial. (2019, July 30). "We Return Fighting: Red Summer Remembered—Saje Mathieu and Cameron McWhirter." YouTube. Retrieved June 9, 2024, from https://www.youtube.com/watch?v=XBFmUcr5p4I&t=1380s

Zimmerman, J., Hurston, Z. N., Walker, A., and Plant, D. G. (2018, May 8). "'Barracoon' Brings a Lost Slave Story to Light." NPR. Retrieved June 9, 2024, from https://www.npr.org/2018/05/08/608205763/barracoon-brings-a-lost-slave-story-to-light

1.5

Language as a Tool for Marginalization—and Resistance

Language plays a pivotal role in perpetuating systems of oppression, particularly in the context of slogans that point to hostile rhetoric and legislation waged against minorities in the United States. In recent years, anti-identity legislation has seen a surge in the United States, targeting discussions of systemic racism and oppression. Bills that seek to eradicate critical race theory and LGBTQ+ rights aim to suppress conversations about historical injustices and reinforce power structures built on white supremacy. Language that originally came out of social-justice communities has also been weaponized against marginalized people.

For example, *woke* is a term that originally connoted a Black person who was educated and conscious of discrimination, racism, and the many forms of inequality that abound in American society. However, it has been mainstreamed by right-wing commentators who have sought to use it as a pejorative catchall decrying any progressive ideas that are perceived as harmful. Unmoored from their original intentions, such powerful terms have been co-opted by legislators to perpetuate the lie that discussions about race, gender, and LGBTQ+ experiences are divisive and unpatriotic. Consequently, marginalized communities find themselves continually excluded from the American narrative—as their very identities are construed as deviant or undesirable—and left to question their place and identity in society.

The manipulation of language to uphold systems of oppression is deeply rooted in American history. White supremacy has been ingrained in our nation's systems, institutions, and laws, perpetuating racial hierarchies of white dominance and nonwhite subordination. Even after the Civil Rights Movement, white power structures continued to employ veiled language to maintain control, swapping overtly discriminatory phrasing for seemingly race-neutral rhetoric (e.g., "separate but equal") while preserving the same discriminatory goals.

Anti-identity legislation and the redefinition of American identity have a profound impact on minority communities. African Americans and other marginalized groups face discrimination, biases, and limited opportunities due to linguistic bias. Dialects associated with these communities, such as African American Vernacular English (AAVE), are denigrated, leading to negative stereotypes and discrimination. Studies have also revealed that having a Black-sounding first name has led to racial bias in hiring practices, as well as in housing and concerning the likelihood of fair treatment in the criminal-legal system. We can see that language, especially in relation to identity, subjects already marginalized individuals to unfair judgments and treatment that habitually go unquestioned and are even outright denied or minimized by the dominant culture of whiteness.

But in and of itself, this minimization points to the implicit bias that is often shielded by the function of language as a system that reproduces social norms without drawing attention to itself. Language as expression carries culture (Shakib 2011) and is influenced by our identities and positionality. Our ability to consciously string words together, like magic, conjures our ability to motivate, organize, build, or destroy. Whether written, spoken, or performed, successful expression is rooted in a fundamental understanding and shared meaning. The use of mutually agreed-upon cadence, grammar, dialects, and syntax limits the possibility of misunderstanding, allowing the underlying message to be received and understood clearly. However, it is crucial to acknowledge that "standardized English" is fundamentally based on white conceptions of proper language, despite its diverse usage worldwide as a colonizer's language.

One way that dominant groups work to erase the identity of oppressed peoples is to force them to use the colonizing party's language. Language is often deployed by colonizing powers to invalidate the cultural sovereignty of others, in that oppressed people have often been forced to speak the language of their oppressor and to abandon their own languages altogether (Shakib 2011).

In his book *Black Skin, White Masks*, the Afro-French psychiatrist and political philosopher Frantz Fanon describes colonialism as a nation's attempt to increase its influence over other territories through military force (Julien et al. 2017). During the colonial period, European powers exalted Eurocentrism while maligning Indigenous cultures in much of Asia, Africa, and the Americas. Colonizers imposed their religion, economics, and linguistic practices on the natives. Fanon details how colonization affected the views, values, and cultures of the oppressed populations. The subjugated groups were forced to

Numéro 305 PRIX DU NUMÉRO : 40 CENTIMES 31 Octobre 1885

A. ROBIDA RÉDACTEUR EN CHEF

La Caricature

JOURNAL HEBDOMADAIRE

Abonnements d'un an, Paris et Départements : 20 francs. — Union postale : 24 francs. — Trois mois : 6 francs. — Bureaux : 7, rue du Croissant.

L'ÉPIDÉMIE DE COLONISATION, — par A. ROBIDA

C'est une épidémie. Les Européens des diverses tribus, pris de la maladie colonisatrice, se disputent l'honneur de faire goûter aux nations non cultivées, les douceurs de notre culture. On demande des continents, des archipels nouveaux, des iles et au besoin de simples ilots. Les découvreurs de chaque nation sont en route et promènent à travers les Océans, les échantillons de l'industrie européenne les plus propres à séduire les bons sauvages. Par malheur, souvent la concurrence vient de passer et d'approvisionner les clients en canons, mitrailleuses et autres produits.

"The colonisation epidemic," drawing by Albert Robida, *La Caricature*, cover, Paris, October 31, 1885.

abandon many aspects of their identity in favor of a Eurocentric one, largely displayed through language (which can be further broken down into distinctions between the correct use of the language, in accordance with the education and status of colonized people).

Permitting a colonized culture its own language is to acknowledge its existence, independent of the colonizing nation. And to erase the right to an Indigenous group's own language is to erase cultural sovereignty and to impose ideals that perpetuate a silent, internalized racism that feeds upon the mental and emotional health of the colonized.

Language is indeed a powerful tool to perpetuate systems of oppression and marginalization, as it has methodically shaped American identity to exclude historically marginalized groups. For example, anti-identity legislators have worked to negate attempts to address systemic racism and oppression. Even words like *equity* and other terms couched in the power of diversity, equity, and inclusion (DEI) have been cut to size and deemed anti-American, further narrowing definitions of Americanness (white, male, heterosexual) that remained unchallenged for centuries.

But who gets to lay claim to being American? And if the language of social justice, meant to advocate for the rights of historically marginalized groups, is deemed anti-American, it stands to reason: Language that upholds white supremacy and other forms of chauvinism is being used to reify and justify an American identity that is at its core exclusive and reserved for the privileged few. In fact, according to this worldview, the only way that marginalized groups of people can become American is by assimilating into dominant social norms, largely demarcated by language. Erasure of people of color and other marginalized groups through the norming of language is yet another way to deny oppressed groups the right to self-determination.

However, the flattening of culture through linguistic homogeneity and politically expedient terms that have historically been used for fearmongering and the stoking of division has always encountered resistance. This resistance has persisted through everything from the creation of memorable social-justice slogans to the mainstreaming of colloquial terms that emerge from prominent subcultures helmed by people of color, such as hip-hop.

In fact, hip-hop has long been excoriated by white media and politicians as perpetuating violence, drugs, and provocative behavior among youth. However, it might be more accurate to note that perceived harms may have more to do with the unabashedly political messages that emcees have laced into their rhymes for the last five decades, as well as the social currency that rap has accrued to itself, despite the fact that it has long been viewed as a more debased or illegitimate art form by white society. A *New York Times* magazine article notes the massive influence that hip-hop vernacular has wielded over not just pop-culture lingo but also social movements (Lewis 2023). BIPOC (Black, Indigenous, and People of Color) and white people are being directly influenced by hip-hop's ingenious methods of reclaiming and inverting language—including deft wordplay, the invention of words, and the infamous battle rhymes of freestyling emcees, which demonstrate how linguistic inventiveness can generate more empowering personas that have the capacity to cross over into our assumed identities within our public spaces. So it is little wonder that hip-hop's ascendancy has paralleled a more direct engagement with language as a prime vehicle for new and more equitable ideologies. It's also little wonder that staunch opponents of racial equity are up in arms about it.

Champions and advocates of language as a tool of resistance against cultural imperialism know very well its self-replicating power, which takes hold in the imagination. The creative efforts of people of color and other minority groups have certainly had their fair share of appropriation, but they are also a sign of the creativity and resilience of marginalized people when it comes to challenging linguistic supremacy, which maintains the stranglehold of whiteness (and its accompanying associations with Americanness).

References

Agozino, B. (2017, July). "The View Beyond Looking: Isaac Julien's Frantz Fanon: Black Skin, White Mask." *Karib—Nordic Journal for Caribbean Studies* 3, no. 1.

Julien, H., Pecoskie, J. L., & Reed, K. (2017). "Trends in Information Behavior Research, 1999–2008: A Content Analysis." *Library and Information Science Research*, 39(4), 284-290. https://doi.org/10.1016/j.lisr.2017.11.003

Lewis, M. (2023, August 11). "How Hip-Hop Changed the English Language Forever." *The New York Times*. Retrieved June 10, 2024, from https://www.nytimes.com/interactive/2023/08/11/magazine/hip-hop-language-dope-cake-woke.html

Shakib, M. K. (2011, July). "The Position of Language in Development of Colonization." *Journal of Languages and Culture* 2, no. 7: 117–23. https://academicjournals.org/article/article1379500755_Shakib.pdf

1.6

“I AM A MAN”

Dr. Martin Luther King Jr., speaking at a press conference at the US Capitol about Senate debate on the Civil Rights Act of 1964, Washington, DC.

In 1968, shortly before his assassination, Dr. Martin Luther King Jr. visited Memphis, Tennessee. During this visit, King emphasized the importance of economic equality alongside Civil Rights. He addressed more than twenty-five thousand people at Mason Temple, urging them to demand recognition of and support for impoverished people in Memphis (Brown 2018).

After this speech, on March 28, a protest march took place, with King and the local Methodist pastor James Lawson leading the way. The march and strike were in support of the sanitation workers in Memphis. This action was initiated due to the deaths of two workers, Echol Cole and Robert Walker, and evolved into a protest against the horrible working conditions, low pay, racism, and discrimination faced by the predominantly Black workforce.

During the 1960s in Memphis, many African American migrants had relocated from rural areas in the South in search of better opportunities. However, they encountered continued discrimination and low wages in industries such as manufacturing, domestic service, and sanitation. During the Memphis Sanitation Workers' Strike of 1968, the involvement of white counterprotesters underscored the racially tense climate of the era. These individuals often opposed Civil Rights for Black Americans, reflecting a broader resistance to the Civil Rights Movement that intertwined racial integration with economic and labor rights.

Unfortunately, the March 28 protest turned violent when a cohort called "the Invaders" showed up. The Invaders were young Black activists who were part of the Civil Rights Movement. During the march on behalf of the striking Memphis sanitation workers, they expressed their frustration by resorting to violence and throwing objects. Their frustration stemmed from the ongoing racial injustices and the slow pace of change, which was a common sentiment among younger activists during the Civil Rights era. These demonstrators were often willing to adopt more aggressive tactics over the nonviolent approaches favored by leaders like King (Coleman 2020). Subsequently, martial law was declared by the mayor of Memphis, who called in the National Guard.

The sanitation workers, mostly Black individuals, had been organizing marches from Clayborn Temple, their union headquarters, to City Hall, to protest their unequal treatment. The demands of the striking sanitation workers included the recognition of their union, improved wages, and better working conditions. They wanted the city to address the inhumane conditions under which they worked, to provide proper equipment, and to show respect for their dignity as human beings.

Initially, they carried signs with messages like "Dignity and Decency" and "We Are Together." As the strike progressed, they adopted a powerful symbol: printed placards boldly stating "I AM A MAN."

This iconic phrase, likely created in collaboration with union leaders and the white preacher Reverend Malcolm Blackburn, communicated the urgency and determination of the workers. In fact, the day after the counterprotesters attacked them,

I Am a Man exhibit as part of the National Civil Rights Museum and the site of the assassination of Dr. Martin Luther King Jr., Memphis, Tennessee.

more than two hundred primarily Black sanitation workers marched, carrying I AM A MAN signs. One sanitation worker later explained that the motive behind these signs was to emphasize the humanity of the Black protesters (Brown 2018). For the sake of negotiation, the protesters aimed to challenge the power dynamics of the white gaze.

The design of the placards was straightforward, featuring striking display type and a simple line beneath the word *AM* to underscore the core message of inherent worth. Some workers held the signs on rods (Toppins 2020). The I AM A MAN slogan and its visual representation emphasized the workers' urgent demand to be acknowledged as fully human, and it played a pivotal role in the historic events that led to advancements in labor rights and Civil Rights.

The 1968 Memphis strike was not just a labor dispute but a profound statement against systemic racism and a struggle for human dignity. Central to this confrontation was the powerful slogan I AM A MAN, a defiant response to the demeaning practice whereby Black men were routinely called "boys" by whites in the South. This term, steeped in the history of slavery and segregation, served to emasculate Black men both verbally and symbolically, paralleling the physical violence they often faced, such as beatings, lynchings, and aggressive suppression by groups like the Ku Klux Klan. King, as well as the many workers who were inspired by his example, posed a threat to this ideology, challenging what had gone unquestioned for so long as the natural social order.

Sojourner Truth's legendary "Ain't I a Woman?" speech, delivered in 1851 at the Ohio Women's Rights Convention, is one of the most famous speeches in the fight for both abolition and women's rights. In her speech, Truth, who had been enslaved, challenged the idea that women were too weak to be equal to men (History Channel 2021). She pointed out that she had endured hard labor and tough conditions, just like men, yet was still denied the same rights simply because she was Black and a woman. By repeatedly asking "Ain't I a woman?," she highlighted how Black women were often excluded from the protections and rights that white women fought for.

The Memphis Sanitation Workers' Strike, with its powerful slogan, I AM A MAN, echoes Truth's essential message. Just as Truth demanded recognition of her

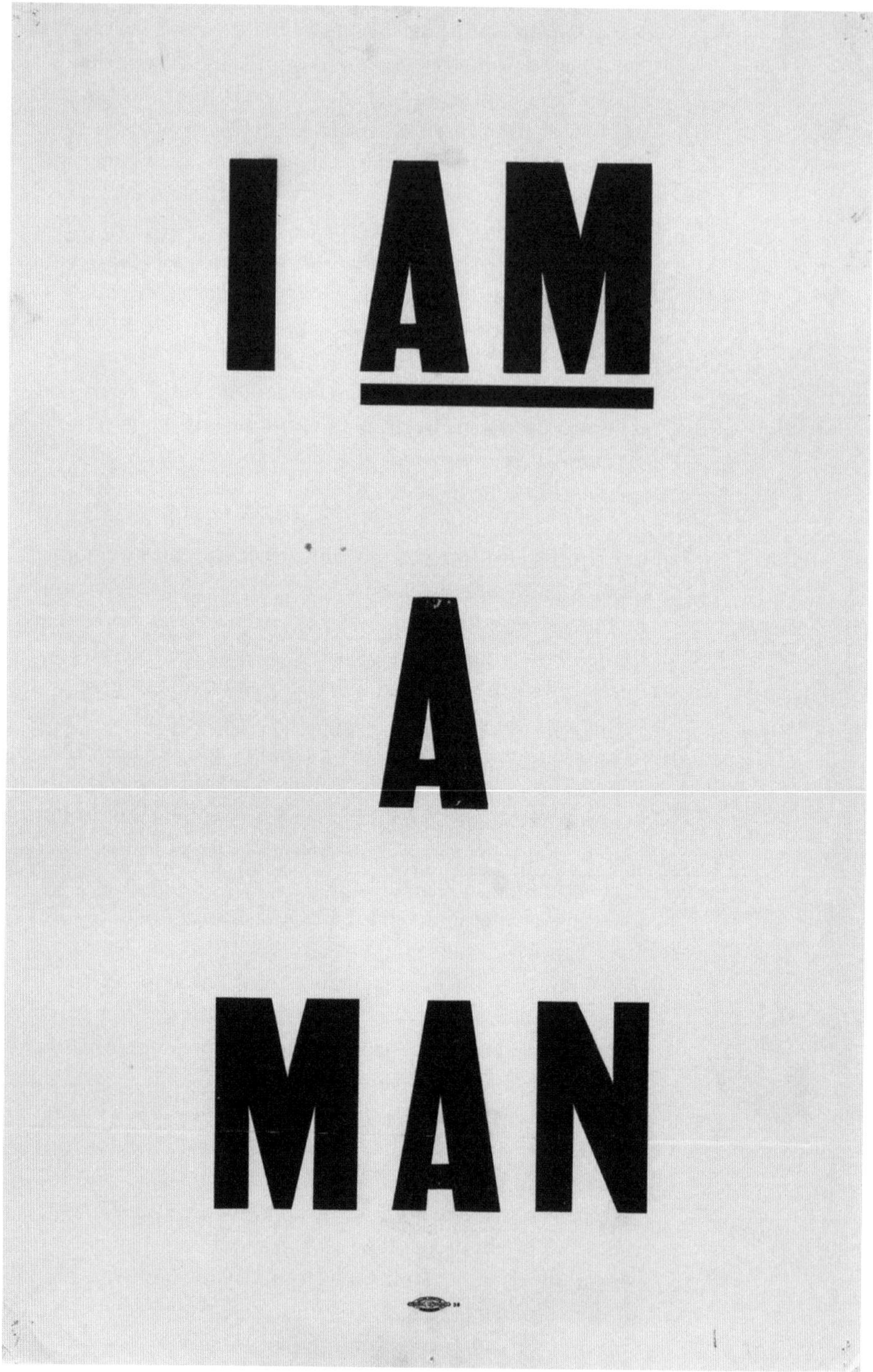

A white poster with black lettering used by Arthur J. Schmidt during the 1968 Memphis March. The poster reads: I / AM / A MAN. A small allied printing label is stamped on the bottom of the front of the poster at center in black ink. The back of the poster is blank.

humanity despite the intersection of race and gender, which had relegated her to a lowly status, the sanitation workers in Memphis fought for their dignity and worth in the face of racism and economic injustice. Both Truth's speech and the strike's slogan called out the unfair treatment of Black people with a powerful rhetorical device demanding that racist hypocrisy be fully heeded and overturned.

More than forty years after the Memphis protests, in 2011, two renowned American rappers, Jay-Z and Kanye West, released a collaborative album titled *Watch the Throne.* The opening song, "No Church in the Wild," delves into profound themes of religion and decadence. The song's lyrics question the ostensibly hierarchical order of the universe. They challenge the notion of a divine chain of being, where God holds ultimate power, followed by kings and then ordinary humans. One line stands out: "What's a god to a non-believer who doesn't believe in anything?" The song suggests that the foundations of authority and power are shaky and untenable, because belief is the ultimate source of power—and belief is something that we have the capacity to question and change.

Reflecting on the violence suffered by King and fellow protesters, one might wonder how the counterprotesters perceived terms like *human*, *king*, *god*, and *non-believer*. This exploration aligns with the writings of Pastor Claude Atcho in his book *Reading Black Books: How African American Literature Can Make Our Faith More Whole and Just* (2022), in which he uses literature as an aid in exploring the challenges faced by marginalized individuals when others refuse to acknowledge their right to exist. Specifically, Atcho uses the language of spirituality and religion, just as King (a Baptist minister) did in his activism, to emphasize the dignity and inherent worth of Black lives.

In his opening chapter, Atcho sheds light on the prevalence and significance of "I am" statements within Christianity. He initiates his discussion by evoking a crucial exchange between God and Moses, recorded in Exodus 3:13–14.

In this dialogue, Moses grapples with addressing the Israelites and conveying his divine mission. He seeks to understand God's name, recognizing its importance in gaining the people's trust and belief. God's response to Moses carries profound implications: "I am that I am." This declaration encapsulates the essence of God's being.

It signifies that God is eternal, unchanging, and self-existent. It asserts that God is not defined by external factors or constrained by limitations but exists inherently within Himself. By drawing attention to this divine dialogue, Atcho underscores the importance of knowing and experiencing the presence of God in order to cultivate self-knowledge, especially in the face of oppression and erasure. The Hebrews' understanding of God as the eternal "I am" instilled in them strength and hope, reminding them that they were not alone in their trials.

Atcho draws an intentional parallel between God's "I am" statements and the I AM A MAN signs carried by protesters. He articulates that the protesters demanded to be seen and recognized as individuals bearing the image of God. They did not merely kowtow to white discomfort by making their message more palatable; they firmly insisted on acknowledgment and respect in the face of systemic injustice that continued to dehumanize them and relegate them to second-class status.

Atcho lays the foundation for further discussions on the power of solidarity and the importance of new constructions of identity that uplift oppressed peoples. He invites readers to contemplate the profound implications of "I am" statements, particularly as they relate to the significance of the I AM A MAN protests in 1960s Memphis.

The 1968 Memphis strike ended with a formalized settlement on April 16, which included a fifteen-cent hourly wage increase, a memorandum of understanding regarding the union's existence, dues checkoff, merit-based promotions, and an end to racial discrimination in the workplace. Although the union did not receive official recognition as the sole bargaining agent, both sides claimed victory as they resolved the dispute (Estes 2000)—which no doubt was expedited by the striking presence of a slogan that would reverberate in the hearts and minds of activists for years to come.

References

Atcho, C. (2022). *Reading Black Books: How African American Literature Can Make Our Faith More Whole and Just.* Baker Publishing Group.

Brown, D. (2018). *I Am a Man: Martin Luther King Jr. and the Memphis Sanitation Workers' Strike.* University of California Press.

Coleman, C. (2020, July 21). Wikipedia. Retrieved June 3, 2024, from https://www.history.com/news/sanitation-workers-strike-memphis

Estes, S. (2000). "'I Am a Man!': Race, Masculinity, and the 1968 Memphis Sanitation Strike." *Labor History* 41, no. 2: 153–70. https://doi.org/10.1080/00236560050009914

History Channel. (2021, May 4). "Sojourner Truth Delivers Powerful Speech on African American Women's Rights | May 29, 1851." History.com. Retrieved August 30, 2024, from https://www.history.com/this-day-in-history/sojourner-truth-delivers-aint-i-a-woman-speech

1.7

Confronting Invisibility

In the opening chapter of *Reading Black Books: How African American Literature Can Make Our Faith More Whole and Just* (2022), Pastor Claude Atcho explores the power and importance of surfacing insights around joy, sorrow, emotional growth, and trauma from stories written by Black people, about Black people.

Atcho's book explores the intersection of theology and literature, engaging with twentieth-century novels and poems by Black authors. Each chapter focuses on a theological concept and its connection to a literary work, fostering a mutual enrichment between the two disciplines. Atcho notes that the marginalization of African American people throughout history has contributed to a major theme in Black stories around the matter of invisibility, which can lead to feelings of sorrow, hopelessness, and despair, especially in the absence of status among the dominant white culture. Atcho (2022) points to the novelist Ralph Ellison's nameless protagonist in *Invisible Man* and his quest to find dignity in an American society insistent on denying his humanity.

At the beginning of *Invisible Man*, the main character reflects on his life's journey and makes a statement that underpins the remaining narrative: "I am an invisible man." This declaration represents his experience of limited freedom and selective visibility, which is further illustrated by his delivery of a speech at his graduation emphasizing the importance of Black humility and subservience in society. For the drunk audience, the idea of social equality is framed as a challenge to the existing social hierarchy that places Black individuals in a secondary class while maintaining whites as the dominant group.

As articulated in the book, the idea of equality had commonly been denounced in newspaper editorials and debates the protagonist had heard in private (Ellison 1995). In contrast, the notion of social responsibility is believed to be a less confrontational approach, placing the onus of social problems and solutions on the Black community itself, irrespective of the origins of these issues. It becomes so successful that the protagonist is invited to perform the same speech to a separate gathering of influential white individuals. However, the situation takes a dark turn when the protagonist is subjected to a series of increasingly violent humiliations. When he finally delivers his speech to the group of white people, he faces intoxicated demands to repeat the phrase *social responsibility*. In an unintentional slip, he utters "social equality" instead, angering the white men.

As Atcho notes, the novel's references to invisibility symbolize the protagonist's marginalized existence and the external constraints imposed upon him by white society, which involve a specific kind of respectability politics whereby the protagonist is granted viable status only when he conforms to white ideals of Blackness. This Blackness in and of itself is a false identity that is not self-determined; by white definitions, it should always be in a state of servility and even gratitude for any meaningful opportunities, particularly those that offer upward mobility and acceptance into the dominant culture. The main character, stripped of even a name and reduced to a generic representation of Black masculinity, is robbed of his agency. Despite his status as an educated man, he is constantly reminded of his subordinate position. He is stripped of his individuality until he recedes into the background completely.

Throughout this narrative, invisibility as a conferred status becomes ironically hypervisible; it is the absence of individuality and agency, and the way in which Blackness is subsumed under the mantle of white ideals becomes glaringly obvious. Invisibility looms menacingly over the Black characters in this book, including the titular man, reflecting the broader struggles that African Americans, often overlooked and unheard in a society that fails to acknowledge their complete humanity, have faced for generations. As the story unfolds, we witness the Invisible Man's defiance of encumbering social norms and follow him on a journey to reclaim his identity and restore his dignity in a world that perceives him as insignificant.

While Atcho's book is rooted in the idea that Black stories have the power to expand our spiritual idioms and our understanding of the ways the Black experience can be contextualized in the broader context of humanity's struggle to find justice and meaning, his examination of Ellison's novel is centered on the importance of visual representation. The chapter on Ellison asks the question: "What does it mean to live as an image bearer when other image bearers try to limit your existence?"

By *image bearer*, Atcho refers to the theological notion that we are all made in God's image, but through sin this image has been distorted and undermined. However,

"Am I Not a Man and a Brother?"

scripture says that because all of us are image bearers, we must accord to one another a sense of dignity and respect. Of course, this very possibility is truncated in Ellison's novel, which reveals both the overt and covert ways in which white people render the protagonist invisible through their refusal to see him for who he is. Atcho (2022) speaks to the power of visual representation by calling into question the "inner eyes" that disabuse individuals of their full humanity.

Visual and symbolic representations of emancipation, manhood, and the Black body have historical roots in abolitionist propaganda. In the late 1700s, the British

Society for the Abolition of the Slave Trade used a seal featuring an enslaved man with a banner stating, "Am I not a man and a brother?" Interestingly, this design, created by white individuals, depicted the figure kneeling, appealing for sympathy. White abolitionists aimed to gain support by emphasizing the universal truth of shared humanity, all while portraying enslaved people in a subservient stance. In contrast, the slogan "I AM A MAN," created by Black activists, presents a different narrative. The protesters carrying those placards stand tall behind a self-authored declaration, asserting their manhood as an undeniable reality and demanding recognition.

"I AM A MAN" connects with another slogan, "A Man Was Lynched Yesterday," displayed on a flag outside the NAACP headquarters from 1920 to 1938. This flag was raised each time an African American person was lynched, serving as a continuous protest against the ongoing brutality of racial violence. Like the placard, the flag used direct language and bold typography to assert Black manhood without adornment. (The NAACP eventually ended the campaign due to eviction threats from the building's owner.)

Both the I AM A MAN placard and the A Man Was Lynched Yesterday flag seem to say that, in the face of attempts to make invisible or to marginalize Blackness, hearty defiance is necessary. Indeed, these symbols and slogans visibly reject enforced submissiveness and directly speak to the systemic racism and violence faced by the Black community. They emphasize the importance of bold, even confrontational, visual slogans, regardless of the discomfort they are sure to evoke among white people captured by the distortions of their own "inner eye."

References

Atcho, C. (2022). *Reading Black Books: How African American Literature Can Make Our Faith More Whole and Just*. Baker Publishing Group.

Ellison, R. (1995). *Invisible Man*. Vintage International.

1.8

How Cultural Erasure Manifests in Children: The *Brown v. Board of Education* Doll Test

It was 1940, near the end of the Great Depression, when two young scholars chose the city of Springfield, Massachusetts, as the testing ground for a poignant observational study. Springfield, a city rich in abolitionist history, not only served as a station on the Underground Railroad but was also home to such abolitionists as Primus Mason and John Brown. Its steady supply of factory jobs attracted diverse residents, and Springfield's public schools were racially integrated by state law; however, racial tensions and inequality persisted. The town housed thirty-two hundred Black residents, roughly 2 percent of the population (Spofford 2024).

White and Black dolls comparable to those used in Kenneth Clark and Mamie Clark's studies at their Northside Center for Childhood Development, founded in 1946

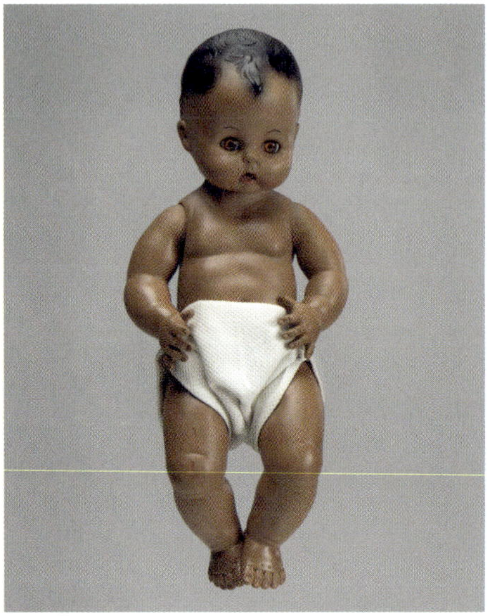

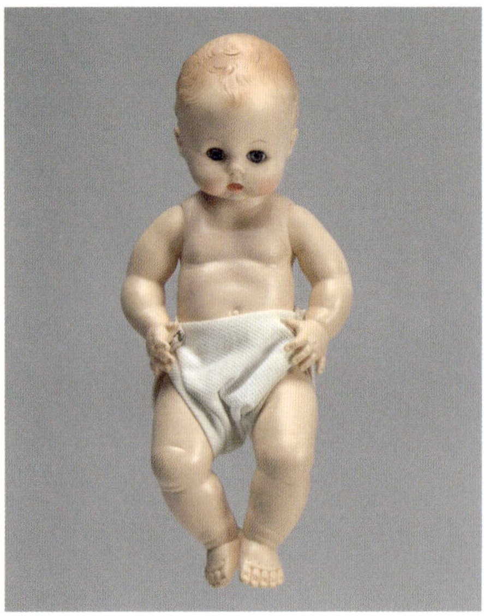

Kenneth Clark and Mamie Clark, a Black husband-and-wife team of psychologists, conducted a series of experiments in Springfield focusing on Black children's self-concept, self-esteem, and self-identification in relation to skin tone, and they also examined the psychological effects of segregation (Byrd et al. 2017). The Clarks' experiment was an offshoot of Mamie's master's degree thesis at Howard University.

The Clarks wanted to understand how segregation, or keeping people separate based on their race, affected African American children (Legal Defense Fund, n.d.). Known colloquially as the Doll Test, this experiment asked children to choose their preference between dolls of two separate races (white and Black) and to associate each doll with positive and negative attributes. Each child tested was Black, and all but one group attended segregated schools (Spector 2024). The dolls were made in identical casts, with their only difference being the color of their skin. The participants were required to classify the dolls in various ways. The instructions included, but were not limited to, the following:

1. Indicate which doll is "colored" or a "Negro."
2. Indicate which doll is "white."
3. Give me the doll you like to play with.
4. Give me the doll that you like best.
5. Identify the good doll.
6. Identify the bad doll.

Finally, the children were asked to identify the doll that looked most like them. Famously, most of the children preferred the white doll to the Black one and attributed positive traits to the doll they later acknowledged did not share their skin tone. The findings of the experiment were used in the *Brown v. Board of Education* case to show that segregation not only hurt Black children's feelings but also contributed to their feelings of inferiority (Blakemore 2018; Legal Defense Fund, n.d.). The Clarks noted that the Black children largely demonstrated a preference for the white dolls over the Black dolls, denoted in observations that the Black dolls were "bad" and even that the white dolls resembled the children more than the Black dolls did, and were more like them overall. The positive traits to which the white dolls were assigned included "nice" and "good," which led the Clarks to conclude that segregation and racial discrimination instilled a sense of inferiority in Black children that led them to deny even a sense of visual association with the Black dolls. A sense of pride in having dolls that accurately represented them had been erased by inherited, racialized stereotypes about perceptions of beauty and goodness.

The Clarks didn't start this study to change laws; they wanted to show other psychologists how race and color affected children's feelings about themselves. But their findings became very important in the fight for Civil Rights, helping to prove that separating people by race was damaging and wrong.

The Doll Test is an early example of the coded ways in which internalized racism, a form of oppression whereby negative stereotypical beliefs concerning individuals from minority races/ethnicities are accepted by those ethnic minorities themselves as truths over time, can be perpetuated through seemingly innocuous objects and artifacts within our lived environments. If we consider, even for an instant, that enslaved people were stripped of their original names in order to elevate and centralize whiteness (and, in this case, ownership of Black bodies by the white ruling elite), and that the cultural erasure of Black Americans' African roots is the result of a legacy of violent disenfranchisement, then we cannot deny the ways that whiteness is reproduced and perpetuated through BIPOC folks' internalized self-representation—which is also mirrored in the Clarks' test.

Although US society in general has made progressive efforts toward diversity at the macro level, children continue to deal with micro-level racial-identity issues on a daily basis. Andrew N. Meltzoff and Walter S. Gilliam (2024) explain that even very young children pick up on hidden social group biases by seeing how adults act. For example, by the age of seven, kids may already believe that Black children feel less pain than white children. These biases aren't taught on purpose; kids learn them when seeing how adults treat different people (Meltzoff and Gilliam 2024).

Microaggressions are small, often unintentional, acts of bias that kids face daily. In schools, this can mean Black preschoolers are more likely to be expelled than white kids, even when their behavior is the same (Meltzoff and Gilliam 2024). Other examples include teachers expecting Black boys to misbehave more, leading to closer monitoring and more discipline. These subtle actions reinforce negative racial stereotypes and cause kids to absorb and repeat these biases (Meltzoff and Gilliam 2024).

This demonstrates the importance of continuing to monitor changing racial attitudes in the context of the social development of Black youth. Experiencing racism can make Black children feel less confident and proud of who they are. However, when parents teach their kids about their culture and history, it helps them feel stronger and more optimistic about their identity. This kind of teaching, known as racial/ethnic socialization (RES), can help children handle unfair treatment better and maintain a high self-esteem (Equity Alliance, n.d.; American Psychological Association Task Force 2008).

RES involves both direct and indirect messages about race. For example, a parent might buy books with Black main characters or discuss news events related to racial issues. These messages help children understand and cope with racism, building resilience and a positive self-image (Neblett et al. 2008). Without these conversations, children might internalize negative stereotypes, leading to psychological difficulties like depression and anxiety (Sellers et al. 2006). Even young children can benefit from RES, as it helps them develop a healthy sense of their racial and ethnic identity, which serves as a buffer against the negative impacts of discrimination (HighReach Learning 2009).

White children can also be affected by discrimination, but in a different way. When they see or take part in racist behaviors, it can make them feel confused or guilty. They might start to think that being white makes them better than others, which is not valid. Parents and teachers teaching white children about the value of diversity and fairness helps them grow up with a healthier sense of who they are and how to treat others respectfully (Equity Alliance, n.d.). Teaching children about the value of diversity and respect helps them understand and appreciate different perspectives, which is crucial for their social and emotional development (HighReach Learning 2009).

As the Clarks' test demonstrates, it is important to study youths' views on skin tone and develop paradigms that attenuate children's negative perceptions of Black skin tone. In 2017, Toni Sturdivant re-created the Clarks' Doll Test. Sturdivant (2001) found similar results: Black girls still showed bias against Black dolls by rarely choosing them or treating them poorly during play. Unlike the Clarks' structured interviews, Sturdivant observed free play with racially diverse dolls, revealing that anti-Black bias persists today. This underscores the need for empowering environments that boost cultural esteem and personal identity among Black children (Sturdivant 2021).

Acknowledging and reclaiming cultural identity, resisting erasure in the face of discrimination and imposed social norms, and embracing social heterogeneity as a strength rather than a deficit are crucial steps toward fostering a more inclusive and just design practice, especially as we consider the subtle ways in which visual representation can unknowingly recapitulate unstated social norms regarding attitudes about beauty and goodness.

References

American Psychological Association Task Force on Resilience and Strength in Black Children and Adolescents. (2008). *Resilience in African American Children and Adolescents: A Vision for Optimal Development*. https://www.apa.org/pi/families/resources/resiliencerpt.pdf

Blakemore, E. (2018, March 27). "How Dolls Helped Win *Brown v. Board of Education*." History.com. Retrieved June 27, 2024, from https://www.history.com/news/brown-v-board-of-education-doll-experiment

Byrd, D., Ceacal, Y. R., Felton, J., Nicholson, C., Lakendra, D. M., McCray, N., and Young, J. (n.d.). "A Modern Doll Study." *Race, Gender & Class* 24, nos. 1–2: 186–202. https://www.jstor.org/stable/26529244

Equity Alliance. (n.d.). "More Than Reading, Writing, and 'Rithmetic: Racial Socialization for Black Children." https://equityalliance.stanford.edu/content/more-reading-writing-and-'rithmetic-racial-socialization-black-children

Legal Defense Fund. (n.d.). "Brown v. Board: The Significance of the 'Doll Test.'" Legal Defense Fund. Retrieved June 27, 2024, from https://www.naacpldf.org/brown-vs-board/significance-doll-test/

Meltzoff, A. N., and Gilliam, W. S. (2024). "Young Children and Implicit Racial Biases." *Dædalus*, Winter.

Neblett, E. W. J., White, R. L., Ford, K. R., Philip, C. L., Nguyên, H. X., and Sellers, R. M. (2008). "Patterns of Racial Socialization and Psychological Adjustment: Can Parental Communications About Race Reduce the Impact of Racial Discrimination?" *Journal of Research on Adolescence* 18, no. 3: 477–515. doi:10.1111/j.1532-7795.2008.00568.x

Sellers, R. M., Copeland-Linder, N., Martin, P. P., and Lewis, R. L. (2006). "Racial Identity Matters: The Relationship Between Racial Discrimination and Psychological Functioning in African American Adolescents." *Journal of Research on Adolescence* 16, no. 2: 187–216. doi: 10.1111/j.1532-7795.2006.00128.x

Spector, C. (2024, May 6). "70 years after *Brown v. Board of Education*, New Research Shows Rise in School Segregation." GSE IT. Retrieved June 27, 2024, from https://ed.stanford.edu/news/70-years-after-brown-v-board-education-new-research-shows-rise-school-segregation

Spofford, T. (2024). *What the Children Told Us: The Untold Story of the Famous Doll Test and the Black Psychologists Who Changed the World*. Sourcebooks.

Sturdivant, T. (2021, March 6). "What I Learned When I Recreated the Famous 'Doll Test' That Looked at How Black Kids See Race." *The Conversation*.

Winkler, E. R. (2009). "Children Are Not Colorblind: How Young Children Learn Race." https://www.academia.edu/3094721/Children_Are_Not_Colorblind_How_Young_Children_Learn_Race

1.9

Understanding the Oppressive Grid

In hindsight and from a sociological view, we now recognize that our identities are constructed. Like a carefully designed font, a wheelchair, or a skyscraper, ideas rely on collective adherence to a specific ideology. As Peter L. Callero argues in *The Myth of Individualism: How Social Forces Shape Our Lives* (2018), just as a language fades without use, social identities can wither without active social engagement.

Social identities run the gamut, from race, ethnicity, gender, and sex to socioeconomic status, age, dis/ability, religion, and national origin. Overall, social identity, while it may appear to be an aspect of individual self-determination, is tied to the aspect of our self-concept that derives from the way we are perceived by society, as well as our membership in specific groups (which do not always arise from our own volition). Many social identities, built and sustained over decades, can be metaphorically compared to fixtures controlled within a design grid.

As a graphic designer, I've learned to define a grid as a system organizing visual elements. However, what if this grid controls not just visual elements but people and communities?

In a recent conversation, the architect Sekou Cooke discussed the "oppressive grid" and its impact on people of color. Originally seen as a neutral tool for organizing space, the traditional architectural grid has historically been used to control marginalized communities, all the while diminishing and neglecting these communities' cultural identities, including their particular set of customs and norms (Cooke, pers. comm.).

Historically, the oppressive grid dehumanizes people, especially people of color, which is evident in such examples as slave-ship packing, slave-quarters layout, and public-space design—all of which seem to treat their inhabitants as objects rather than living, breathing beings with aesthetic and emotional responses to the spaces in which they live, work, interact, and transform. For people of color, it symbolizes a system prioritizing efficiency over well-being, evoking states of being from demoralization to discomfort (Cooke, pers. comm.).

Architecture and urban spaces are not merely physical structures; they encapsulate intricate narratives of race, class, identity, and social dynamics. Dianne Harris and Susan Bickford delve into the profound influence of these elements on how we perceive and interact with our surroundings. Harris's "Seeing the Invisible: Reexamining Race and Vernacular Architecture" (2006) and Bickford's "Constructing Inequality: City Spaces and the Architecture of Citizenship" (2000) unravel the interplay between design, culture, and social constructs, painting a comprehensive picture of the hidden forces that shape our built environments.

Harris opens her discourse with an exploration of the intersection of race, class, and architecture, examining the experiences of the Myers family, a Black family living in Levittown, Pennsylvania, in the mid-twentieth century. Published in *Perspectives in Vernacular Architecture*'s twenty-fifth anniversary issue, Harris's work dissects the intricacies of racial and class identity in the context of suburban living (Harris 2006). Through the lens of Daisy Myers, an emblematic figure navigating the complexities of race and class, Harris brings to light the Myers family's choices when they moved to a predominantly white, middle-class neighborhood in 1957. This bold move sheds light on conscious decisions related to home design that might serve to reinforce or challenge racial stereotypes. The article underscores the profound interconnectedness of race and class, asserting that they are deeply related, influencing and shaping each other's dynamics.

The Myers family was the first Black family to buy a house in Levittown. Because of this, they faced a lot of harassment and even a race riot. In Levittown, being accepted often meant following the standards set by the white community. The Myers family wanted their house to fit in with their white neighbors' houses to avoid negative stereotypes. Daisy felt pressured to keep her house very clean and nicely decorated so that people wouldn't think they were lowering the neighborhood's property values. The Myers knew that how their house looked inside and outside was important in showing their racial and class identity, and they were careful about how they designed and decorated their home to send the right message and appropriately shape how people saw them.

Racial identity often intertwines with social and economic status, leading Harris to advocate for a comprehensive understanding of these intersections to grasp the unique web of social dynamics. Harris argues that in order to understand social dynamics, we need to look at how race and space intersect. She emphasizes the importance of examining how the built environment serves to either give or take away power. Harris highlights the need to study the layout of spaces to see how privilege is distributed, linking social justice to environmental or spatial justice by examining the spaces themselves. She believes that studying housing is crucial to understanding discriminatory practices that come from where people live, which affects their access to services and opportunities. Harris points out that terms like *segregation* and *marginalization* are related to space, so understanding how power works in the built environment is necessary to address issues of privilege and social justice.

By looking at the relationship between space and race, Harris says we can uncover how privilege operates. This can help link social justice with environmental or spatial justice. She argues that the built environment is not neutral but influences social norms and values, manifesting in physical structures, landscapes, and spaces.

Bickford's essay "Constructing Inequality: City Spaces and the Architecture of Citizenship," published in *Political Theory* in 2000, amplifies this exploration by dissecting how urban spaces and architectural designs contribute to social dynamics and the construction of citizenship. Bickford's analogies bring complex concepts into relatable terms. She likens cities to puzzles, wherein the arrangement of diverse pieces determines whether individuals feel that they belong or are excluded from specific areas. This concept highlights the profound relationship between the construction of a city and the construction of a sense of belonging, which Bickford suggests doesn't arise merely from individual choices. The separation between "clean" and "dirty" spaces in cities is an example of how architecture can either foster order and control or inadvertently lead to isolation and an oppressive uniformity. The notion of cities resembling theme parks or shopping malls underscores the risk of homogenization, limiting the authentic vibrancy that defines cities, in service of antiseptic conformity to an unquestioned ideal that usually hails from the dominant culture's sentiments about matters like cleanliness, security, and public gathering (Bickford 2000).

As we examine the many facets of the oppressive grid, the proximity of different groups to one another within urban spaces holds significant implications. This proximity can influence whether individuals reside near similar peers, suggesting an unquestioned desire for homogeneity (usually under the guise of safety or comfort), or embrace diversity for growth, learning, and other opportunities. Again, individual choices are constrained by the foregone conclusion of structural divisions within cities, which can exacerbate separation and indeed make it a preconceived condition of the constructed environment.

Spaces designed with the oppressive grid can make people of color and other marginalized folks feel unwelcome, creating a hostile environment. Often, cities' approaches to urban planning are functional, focusing on what can be done to draw businesses and consumers, and how easily people can navigate the built environment through transportation and other forms of infrastructure. However, the lived experience of people who habitually navigate these spaces is crucial to consider, especially as we think of the persistent social problems of isolation, polarization, and poor mental health that plague so many of us today. Opportunities for inclusivity can be catalyzed through attention to the built environment, as well as awareness of the historical forces (including slavery, gentrification, and any other factors that have shaped the populations of the area, as well as how they interact with one another) that have influenced social norms. Addressing the oppressive grid in justice-oriented ways also requires an in-depth engagement with the people who actually make up the social and cultural fabric of a city, rather than simply designing for the purpose of generating economic wealth and commercial success (or bowing to the desires of the groups that preside over the economic domain), which all too often hinge upon the further marginalization of folks of color and people who make up the lifeblood and culture of a city.

Our colonial legacy supports a historical mindset that continues to prioritize control over adaptation, perpetuating disconnection and environmental injustice. Opportunities for the future should focus on making spaces that are fair and welcoming for everyone. This means listening to and working with all groups, especially those who in the past have been left out, to create areas that reflect their stories and needs. By including different voices in planning and building, we can break down unjust structures and create places where everyone is truly valued and included.

References

Bickford, S. (2000). "Constructing Inequality: City Spaces and the Architecture of Citizenship." *Political Theory* 28, no. 3: 355–76.

Callero, P. L. (2018). *The Myth of Individualism: How Social Forces Shape Our Lives.* Rowman & Littlefield.

Harris, D. (2006). "Seeing the Invisible: Reexamining Race and Vernacular Architecture." *Perspectives in Vernacular Architecture* 13, no. 2: 96–105.

1.10

The Unseen Cage: Henrietta Lacks, Hippolyta, and the Oppression of Space

Our contemporary understanding has gradually evolved to acknowledge the constructed nature of our identities, which resembles a carefully designed grid that shapes our perceptions and interactions.

The grid has long been a tool of organization and control in design, often seen as a Western colonial imposition used to manage assets across a given space. This influence is evident in how we lay out pages for magazines, construct rooms and buildings, and even in how we understand our social identities. Despite these critiques, grids remain a fundamental design tool, employed in various practices to ensure alignment, consistency, and structure. In graphic design, grids play a crucial role. Print design, for instance, relies on grids to organize text and images in newspapers, magazines, brochures, and posters, leading to coherent and visually appealing layouts. Grids also assist in creating consistent branding elements such as logos, business cards, and letterheads. In web design, grids are indispensable for generating responsive designs that adapt to different screen sizes and devices. They ensure that elements like buttons, images, and text are aligned, making the user interface intuitive and easy to navigate. Similarly, in typography, baseline grids align text on a horizontal plane, ensuring consistency in line spacing, while column grids organize text into columns in newspapers and books, enhancing readability.

Architecture also benefits from the structured approach that grids provide. In designing floor plans, grids help in spacing and alignment; in facade design, they organize the placement of windows, doors, and other architectural elements. Product design similarly utilizes grids to ensure that text, images, and other design elements on packaging are aligned and spaced consistently. They are also used in designing control panels, dashboards, and other product interfaces for consistent layout and ease of use. Photography employs grids in various

Statue of Henrietta Lacks by the sculptor Lawrence Bechtel, Roanoke, Virginia. Lacks's cells, known as the HeLa line, have contributed to many advances in medicine.

ways, such as the rule of thirds, which uses a grid-based guideline to compose photographs by dividing the image into nine equal parts, positioning the subject in a more aesthetically pleasing way. Alignment grids in photo-editing software help align and balance elements within a photograph.

If grids have historically been used to organize spaces and cities, it is reasonable to assume that they have, at times, contributed to perpetuating inequality and dehumanization, particularly for people of color. This can be seen in practices like redlining and segregation, where boundaries are drawn in ways that designate specific areas where people or assets can operate within society.

For example, in 1951, Henrietta Lacks, a Black woman diagnosed with cancer in a segregated hospital, was the victim of a socially constructed identity that shaped her treatment and limited her options. The medical industry unethically used her cells (HeLa) for research without her permission, highlighting how marginalized voices are often overlooked and even exploited, even in groundbreaking discoveries (Skloot 2019). Despite contributing to medical breakthroughs, Lacks received no acknowledgment, illustrating the ongoing challenges faced by people of color in the health care system. The constructed identity assigned to Lacks determined the attention she received and the spaces she was able to occupy. This failure by the medical industry to give fair treatment to Lacks reveals the dangers of being in a lower position in the social hierarchy—which is also concretely enacted through the structure of the oppressive grid.

Lacks's experiences are mirrored by those of the fictional character Hippolyta (portrayed by Aunjanue Ellis) in the HBO original series *Lovecraft Country*, an American horror drama developed by Misha Green, based on the 2016 novel by Matt Ruff. The series closely follows the novel, depicting a Black community in Chicago entangled with an ominous occult society while fighting everyday and cosmic-scale racism. Ruff's novel grapples with the legacy of H. P. Lovecraft's influential but racist writing.

The show follows Atticus Freeman, his friend Letitia, and his Uncle George on a road trip across 1950s Jim Crow America to find Atticus's missing father. Along the way, they face both the racist horrors of white America and terrifying monsters similar to those in Lovecraft's stories.

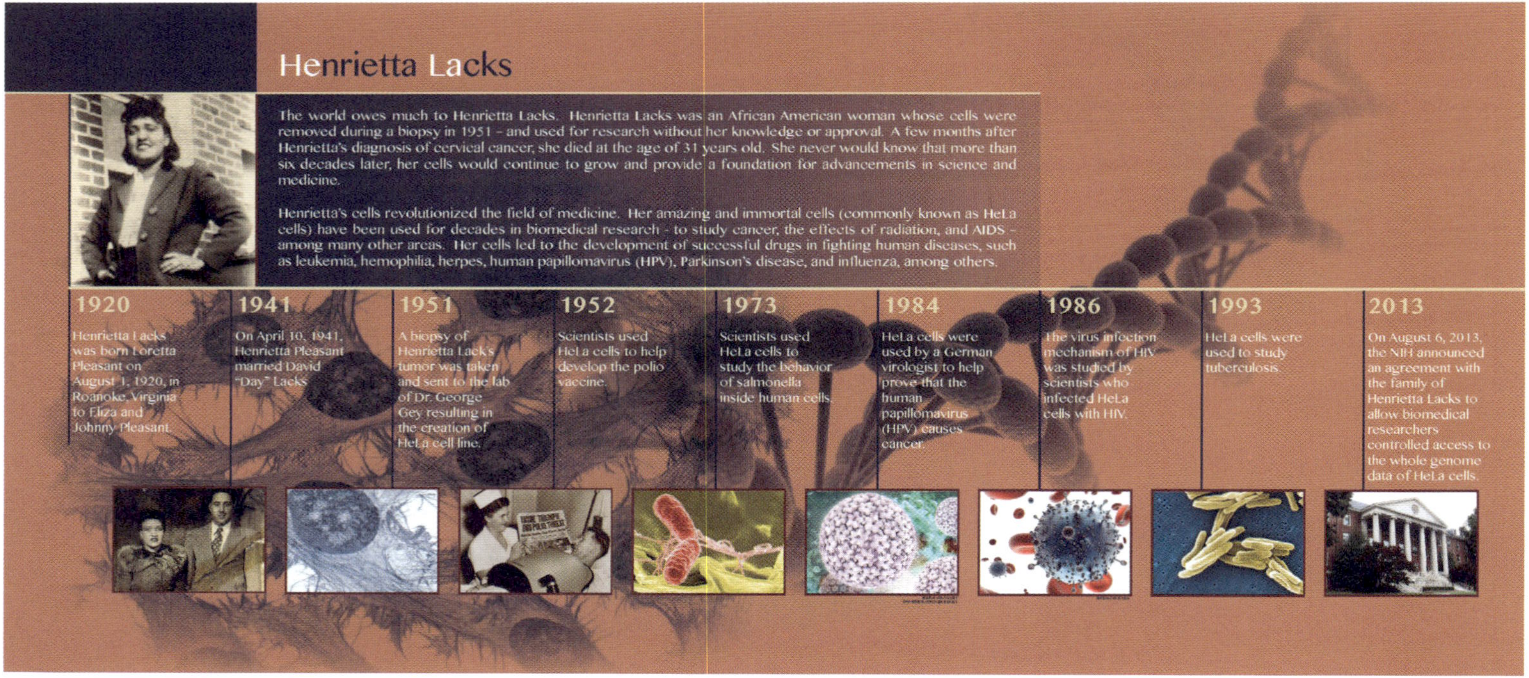

Henrietta Lacks
The world owes much to Henrietta Lacks. Henrietta Lacks was an African American woman whose cells were removed during a biopsy in 1951 - and used for research without her knowledge or approval. A few months after Henrietta's diagnosis of cervical cancer, she died at the age of 31 years old. She never would know that more than six decades later, her cells would continue to grow and provide a foundation for advancements in science and medicine.
Henrietta's cells revolutionized the field of medicine. Her amazing and immortal cells (commonly known as HeLa cells) have been used for decades in biomedical research - to study cancer, the effects of radiation, and AIDS - among many other areas. Her cells led to the development of successful drugs in fighting human diseases, such as leukemia, hemophilia, herpes, human papillomavirus (HPV), Parkinson's disease, and influenza, among others.
1920
Henrietta Lacks was born Loretta Pleasant on August 1, 1920, in Roanoke, Virginia to Eliza and Johnny Pleasant.
1941
On April 10, 1941, Henrietta Pleasant married David "Day" Lacks
1951
A biopsy of Henrietta Lack's tumor was taken and sent to the lab of Dr. George Gey resulting in the creation of HeLa cell line.
1952
Scientists used HeLa cells to help develop the polio vaccine.
1973
Scientists used HeLa cells to study the behavior of salmonella inside human cells.
1984
HeLa cells were used by a German virologist to help prove that the human papillomavirus (HPV) causes cancer.
1986
The virus infection mechanism of HIV was studied by scientists who infected HeLa cells with HIV.
1993
HeLa cells were used to study tuberculosis.
2013
On August 6, 2013, the NIH announced an agreement with the family of Henrietta Lacks to allow biomedical researchers controlled access to the whole genome data of HeLa cells.

Throughout the series, Atticus, a Korean War veteran, searches for his missing father, learns about his deceased mother, and deals with his personal struggles. The show embeds America's racist history in tropes from popular-entertainment genres like pulp fiction and comic books, making racism a central theme in every scene and relationship. Unlike *Watchmen*, a series that touched on race as one theme among many, *Lovecraft Country* deeply integrates racial dynamics into its narrative (Romano 2020). The main characters navigate sundown towns (areas where Black people were intentionally excluded and warned to leave by sundown, or else they'd be subjected to violent retaliation), businesses, and people dedicated to maintaining these racial boundaries, illustrating the pervasive impact of racism.

In episode 7, season 1 of *Lovecraft Country*, Hippolyta shares a personal realization with American-born French entertainer and Civil Rights activist Josephine Baker (portrayed by Carra Patterson). Hippolyta expresses to Josephine that due to her race and gender, she has consistently been asked to shrink herself, echoing the historical struggles of Black bodies. By occupying less space and diminishing her personality, she has been able to make others (particularly white people) comfortable at her own expense. She recounts, "All those years I thought I had everything I ever wanted only to come here and discover that all I ever was was the exact kind of Negro woman white folks wanted me to be. I feel like they just found a smart way to lynch me without me noticing the noose."

Although Hippolyta is a fictional character, the link between Black bodies and space is anything but fictitious. Segregation legislation was used to keep Black and white bodies separated, for example, by redlining delegated Black and white sections of cities. All-white municipalities deployed intimidation and violence to keep minorities out of white communities. Navigating the Jim Crow South was an incredibly challenging experience for African Americans, whether they were traveling by train or car or simply living in that region. The entire social structure was designed to maintain racial segregation and enforce a strict social order, making everyday life a constant battle against oppression. It is little wonder that characters like Hippolyta voice the stark realities of life for Black people during this era, when being seen as palatable to white people was a matter of survival—something that Lacks herself surely also experienced.

opposite:
HeLa timeline

To understand the difficulties experienced by Black residents and travelers, consider the challenges of traveling by train during this era. African American travelers were confined to Jim Crow cars, which were often less comfortable and lacked the amenities available to white passengers. Inside the Jim Crow cars, conductors and white passengers often treated Black travelers with hostility and disrespect, creating a tense and unpleasant environment. The introduction of dining cars, which were meant to improve the travel experience, did not apply to Black customers in the South due to state segregation laws. Even in the North, African American passengers were subjected to segregation, being forced to move to Jim Crow cars without any regard for their dignity. Train stations were oppressive, with segregated waiting rooms already in place before the 1890s; these often lacked basic amenities like heat and food options (Bay 2021).

Traveling by car in the Jim Crow South was equally, if not more, dangerous for African Americans. Discriminatory laws and practices meant that Black travelers routinely were denied essential services like gas, food, restrooms, and lodging. Stopping in unfamiliar places could lead to humiliation, threats, or even violence. To navigate these dangers, African American travelers relied on the *The Negro Travelers' Green Book*, a guidebook listing safe accommodations, restaurants, service stations, and other establishments that served Black patrons. Published from 1936 to 1966 by Victor H. Green, a New Jersey postal worker, the *Green Book* was essential for Black travelers seeking to avoid the dangers of the segregated South. This guide not only increased their safety but also improved their overall travel experience during a time when racial segregation and discrimination were rampant (Smithsonian, n.d.).

During this time, designed artifacts reinforced social hierarchies and dictated where people were allowed to be. Signs designating "White Only" or "Colored Entrance" were common, sometimes replaced by painting one door black and another white to maintain segregation even after the signs were removed. Resistance to desegregation sometimes involved painting out the words *White* or *Colored*, leaving the words still visible but defaced. Today, there is a market for reproducing Jim Crow signage, with many imitations sold as originals at inflated prices. These signs and other "Black memorabilia," such as "mammy"

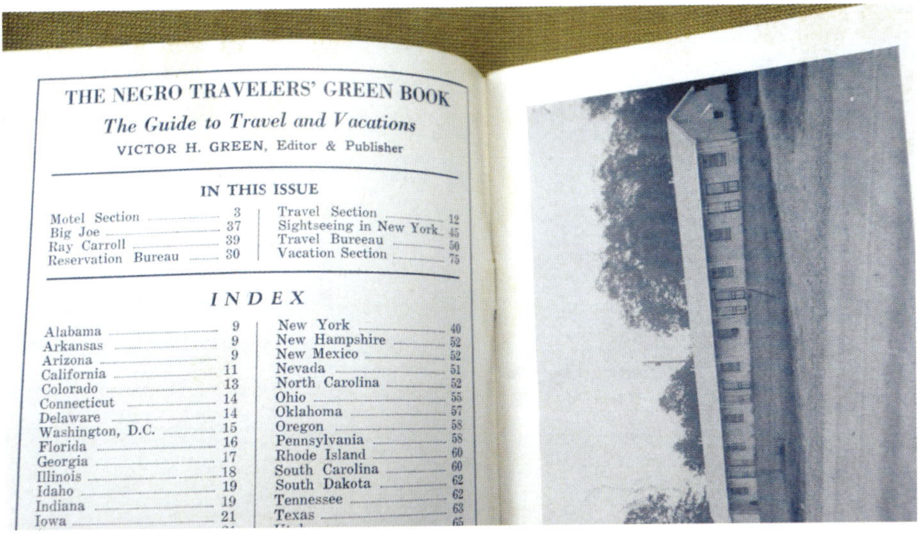

THE NEGRO TRAVELERS' GREEN BOOK

The Guide to Travel and Vacations

VICTOR H. GREEN, Editor & Publisher

IN THIS ISSUE

INDEX

top: A 1955 copy of *The Negro Travelers' Green Book* at the Manuscript, Archives, and Rare Book Library at Emory University, Atlanta, Georgia.; bottom: Three different *Negro Travelers' Green Book* covers used by Negro motorists to know where it was safe and welcoming.

top: *A man drinks from a water cooler labeled "Colored" at a bus terminal in Oklahoma City, Oklahoma. Photograph by Russell Lee.*; bottom: African Americans stand beneath a "Colored Waiting Room" sign at a bus station in Durham, North Carolina. Photograph by Jack Delano.

cookie jars and imitation chains, have become objects of interest for collectors. For some white collectors, these items reflect a nostalgic longing for the Old South. In contrast, for many African American collectors, they serve as a form of "political witnessing," a reminder of the painful past (Cockrell 2011).

Elizabeth Abel's book *Signs of the Times* explores how these signs shaped perception, experience, and representation for almost a century in the Deep South and across the coasts and Midwest. These signs reflected Jim Crow laws controlling Black individuals' use of various spaces and amenities, from drinking fountains and lunch counters to bus stations. The official end of legal segregation with landmark laws in the mid-1960s led to the removal of these signs, marking the end of the Jim Crow system (Cockrell 2011).

Overall, the architecture of cities, the design of train cars, and the presence of segregation signs all worked together to enforce an oppressive social order in the Jim Crow South that entrenched both internalized and externalized forms of oppression—and justified poor treatment of Black people. This order was dangerous to challenge and created a harsh reality for African Americans trying to navigate their daily lives. Hippolyta's words echo this process, whereby anything other than shrinking may have engendered conflict that could end in violence for marginalized people.

Even after segregation was abolished, many institutions, including high schools and colleges, required the National Guard's support to safely permit the entry of Black students into formerly all-white spaces. All of this highlights the enduring impact of historical systems and the ongoing need for social change—especially in thinking of the ways that space is concretely demarcated by restrictive and oppressive ideologies that have real-life impacts on the bodies and well-being of marginalized people (Newby 2020).

As mentioned, although Hippolyta is a fictional character, her story has many parallels throughout history. The oppressive grid is also visible in the ways in which the medical industry failed Henrietta Lacks—which can be attributed to the perception of her assigned identity. Although she was granted more freedom than a slave, she was still required to travel farther because of her race and treated with less regard than her white counterparts. The ways in which Lacks moved through the oppressive grid illuminate the dangers associated with having a lower perceived status in the social hierarchy.

It's important to consider that the social grid can be seen across the globe. A modern parallel can be seen in occupied Palestine. Similarly, recent systems of racial segregation and discrimination, such as apartheid in South Africa, exemplify social-grid structures that influence design approaches and outcomes in their respective spaces. Despite their unique historical and geographic contexts, these systems share common themes of perpetuating inequality and injustice.

In South Africa, apartheid enforced a strict racial hierarchy and segregation in all aspects of life, from housing and education to employment and health care (Zinkel 2019). The government's response to these systems' demise reveals a crucial difference between South Africa and the United States. In South Africa, the Truth and Reconciliation Commission was established in 1995 to address the harm caused by apartheid and to promote national unity. In contrast, the United States did not take similar steps after the end of Jim Crow, leading to lingering racial disparities and unresolved historical grievances (Zinkel 2019).

Jim Crow laws existed in only certain states in the United States, while apartheid was uniformly enforced across South Africa. When apartheid ended, South Africa undertook comprehensive legislative reforms to reverse discriminatory laws. In the United States, the principle of federalism allowed states to retain discriminatory laws despite the Civil Rights Act of 1964. Although Jim Crow laws were not as overtly authoritarian as apartheid, they still imposed severe limitations on Black Americans, hindering their upward mobility and subjecting them to violence and discrimination.

Both systems had damaging effects on Black Americans and nonwhite South Africans, with discrimination persisting even today. But another significant difference lies in population dynamics: Black Americans are a minority in the United States, whereas nonwhite South Africans form the majority in South Africa. This demographic difference influenced the nature and implementation of segregation policies, with apartheid enforcing minority rule over a majority population and Jim Crow laws maintaining white supremacy in regions where whites were the majority (Zinkel 2019).

Over the last half-century, Israel has faced accusations of implementing policies toward Palestinians that amount to apartheid, according to reports by Human Rights Watch and Amnesty International (Zhou 2023). These investigations conclude that the Israeli government engages in systematic oppression and inhumane practices directed at Palestinian communities (Amnesty International 2022). It's also significant that in February 2024, South Africa argued for charges against Israeli apartheid at the United Nations' highest court, the International Court of Justice. The term *apartheid* has been applied to policies in the occupied territories and within Israel's borders, highlighting severe movement restrictions on Palestinians, lack of voting rights in Israeli elections, and a discriminatory legal system favoring Israeli Jewish settlers over Palestinian residents.

The passage of the 2018 "nation-state law" in Israel, prioritizing the rights of Israeli Jewish residents, has been seen as relegating non-Jewish residents to second-class citizenship. Human-rights analyses continue to assert that Israel's treatment of Palestinians aligns with the definition of apartheid under international law (Amnesty International 2022). This assessment is based on the international legal framework rather than direct similarities in policies between South African apartheid and Israeli practices. Reports on Israel's discriminatory practices highlight severe movement restrictions in the Occupied Palestinian Territories (OPT), chronic underinvestment in Palestinian communities in Israel, and the denial of refugees' right to return. These actions are part of a broader system of oppression and domination against Palestinians that is codified in the demarcation of space and the built environment (Zhou 2023).

Following the October 7, 2023, attack by Hamas on Israel, which led to over twelve hundred Israeli casualties, the conflict has escalated, resulting in significant humanitarian consequences for Palestinians. Since the attack, more than fifteen thousand Palestinians, including thousands of children, have been killed due to continued military operations, with many more displaced and facing severe restrictions on movement, food, water, and medical resources (Byman & Holtz 2023). The conflict has also intensified violence in the West Bank, leading to further civilian casualties and displacement. As the crisis unfolds, international calls for ceasefires and humanitarian assistance continue to grow, underscoring the ongoing complexities and urgent humanitarian needs in the region (Snopes 2023).

All three aforementioned systems—Jim Crow laws, apartheid in South Africa, and the oppressive grid as it is currently being deployed in the OPT—have perpetuated inequality and injustice, with long-lasting effects on nonwhite populations. The harmful effects of such policies are evident in the persistent socioeconomic disparities, restricted opportunities, and continued marginalization of nonwhite communities. Confronting these issues requires not only acknowledging past wrongs but also committing to meaningful and sustained efforts to dismantle systemic racism and promote inclusivity and equality.

References

Amnesty International. (2022, February 1). "Israel's Apartheid Against Palestinians: A Cruel System of Domination and a Crime Against Humanity." Amnesty International. Retrieved June 10, 2024, from https://www.amnesty.org/en/latest/news/2022/02/israels-apartheid-against-palestinians-a-cruel-system-of-domination-and-a-crime-against-humanity/

Bay, M. (2021, June 7). "Jim Crow Journeys: An Excerpt from Traveling Black." Southern Spaces. Retrieved June 10, 2024, from https://southernspaces.org/2021/jim-crow-journeys-excerpt-traveling-black/

Byman, D., & Holtz, M. (2023, December 6). "Why Hamas Attacked When It Did." Center for Strategic and International Studies. Retrieved from https://www.csis.org/

Cockrell, C. (2011, February 15). "Jim Crow Signs as Symbols of Subjugation, Trophies of Triumph." *Berkeley News*. Retrieved June 10, 2024, from https://news.berkeley.edu/2011/02/15/jim-crow-signs/

Heazlewood, J. (n.d.). "Combatting Unconscious Bias in Design." UX Collective. Retrieved June 10, 2024, from https://uxdesign.cc/combatting-unconscious-bias-in-design-bff4dfb013c3

Romano, A. (2020, August 15). "HBO's *Lovecraft Country*: A Spoiler-Free Review of the Clever New Series." *Vox*. Retrieved June 10, 2024, from https://www.vox.com/culture/21367860/lovecraft-country-hbo-review-no-spoilers

Skloot, R. (2019). *The Immortal Life of Henrietta Lacks*. Picador Classic.

Smithsonian. (n.d.). "Traveling Through Jim Crow America." National Museum of African American History and Culture. Retrieved June 10, 2024, from https://NMAAHC.si.edu/explore/stories/traveling-through-jim-crow-america

UXtweak. (2023, December 25). "Prototype User Testing—Step-by-Step Guide for 2024." UXtweak blog. Retrieved June 10, 2024, from https://blog.uxtweak.com/prototype-user-testing/

Zhou, L. (2023, October 20). "Is Israel Apartheid? Why Some Human Rights Groups Say Israel Practices Apartheid." *Vox*. Retrieved June 10, 2024, from https://www.vox.com/23924319/israel-palestine-apartheid-meaning-history-debate

Zinkel, B. (2019). "Apartheid and Jim Crow: Drawing Lessons from South Africa's Truth and Reconciliation." *Journal of Dispute Resolution* 1.

Part 2
Practice

2.1

Whose Knowledge Is It? Reclaiming Histories, Narratives, and the Plurality of Knowledge

Lesley-Ann Noel

Designers use storytelling at various stages of the design process: to understand the experience of others, to set the scene for generating ideas, and to create buy-in from clients. *Design Is Storytelling* is the title of a well-known text by Ellen Lupton (2017). This titular statement is true—designers often use personas or representations of users of a product or service to tell a story about that product or service (Lupton 2017). They create these personas in various ways, making representations based on demographic data and qualitative and quantitative research.

The dominant culture in any setting establishes the norm or the standard for everyone. This dominant culture may change according to specific contexts, but it is often the culture of a specific race or ethnicity, religious group, gender, and so on. Storytelling traditions in design are often influenced by dominant cultures and narratives. For instance, the design of public spaces in the United States often prioritizes the needs and perspectives of able-bodied individuals, with little consideration for those with disabilities.

Similarly, the visual aesthetics of many tech products frequently reflect Western ideals, overlooking the preferences and needs of diverse cultural groups. As we tell stories in design, we must acknowledge that these stories are often told from the viewpoint of people from the dominant culture—usually white, often European or American, often male, often middle to upper class.

Designers may be trained to think that if they focus on this group of people, they are serving the average population. However, people holding nondominant social status may experience their identities and statuses being flattened, made invisible, or othered. For example, in fashion design, the standard sizing and fit paradigms are often based on Western body types, which can marginalize those from different ethnic backgrounds. Likewise, architectural designs for public housing may not consider the cultural or communal living practices of immigrant communities, leading to spaces that feel alienating or inadequate. It's also true that those with nondominant status may feel pressured to assimilate into social norms that are often standardized by overt or covert displays from the dominant culture—such as modifying one's accent to be less distinguishable from the dominant group, despite one's place of origin. For instance, in the corporate world, individuals with accents or dialects distinct from the mainstream may feel compelled to alter their speech to avoid being perceived as unprofessional or less competent.

Epistemologies of design are often rooted in the values and assumptions of dominant cultures, particularly those of Euro-Western origin. These epistemologies prioritize specific ways of knowing and being that reflect individualistic, compartmentalized, and hierarchical social structures. For example, the design of homes in many Western societies emphasizes separate rooms for different activities, reflecting a worldview that values privacy, individuality, and control over space. In contrast, traditional homes in many non-Western cultures, such as in India, were often designed with communal living in mind, where spaces were shared and multifunctional, and where the boundaries between indoor and outdoor, private and public, were more fluid.

This Western-centric design epistemology also extends to the objects we use. The design of furniture, like chairs and beds, often follows a specific ergonomic logic that assumes sitting or sleeping at a certain height is the most civilized or advanced way to interact with one's environment. However, in many cultures, including precolonial India, sitting and sleeping closer to the earth were the norm. These practices were deeply connected to local climates, spiritual beliefs, and social practices. Yet, with the infiltration of Western ideas—often underpinned by colonialist notions of primitivism—these traditional practices were devalued or erased, leading to a shift in how people conceive of their homes and the objects within them.

By recognizing that design epistemologies are culturally situated and not universal, we can begin to question and expand what is considered valid knowledge in design. This means valuing and integrating diverse ways of knowing that have been marginalized or overlooked. It also involves critically examining how dominant cultural narratives shape our understanding of what good design is—a crucial step toward promoting a more inclusive and equitable design practice.

How might designers use storytelling techniques throughout the design process to promote greater collaboration and participation by diverse stakeholders? Consciously exploring multiple epistemologies and world-views through alternative storytelling traditions could be a powerful way to develop restorative design practices and to articulate and utilize those that already exist.

References

Lupton, E. (2017). *Design Is Storytelling.* Cooper Hewitt, Smithsonian Design Museum.

2.2

Storytelling as a Tool to Dismantle Harmful Narratives, Empower Marginalized Voices, and Promote Healing and Reconciliation

My elementary school years were split between two schools: Our Lady of Mount Carmel, a Catholic school in the South Bronx, a few miles from the prestigious Fordham University, and P.S. 78X, a public school in the borough's northeast region. My two-year experience at Mount Carmel left a profound impact on me. Much like the children who took part in the Doll Test of the 1940s, I was influenced by the classroom surroundings in ways that I wasn't immediately aware of.

The spaces of Our Lady of Mount Carmel featured walls adorned with images of over a century's worth of white male presidents and stained-glass windows portraying everything white as holy. The method by which history, salvation, and heroism were taught followed a paradigm that not only centered Eurocentric ideals but also celebrated heroes of American imperialism, such as Theodore Roosevelt, William Howard Taft, and Woodrow Wilson. Imperial themes in American history, such as Manifest Destiny, were explored as positive milestones, and students were given a bookmark featuring Warner Sallman's *Head of Christ*, with light eyes and hair.

This sense of imperialist nostalgia, which I explore more explicitly in the essay titled "Unveiling the White Gaze: The Narrative of Whiteness and Colonial Nostalgia," stems from the descendants of colonizers yearning for a romanticized past in which they maintained control and dominance over occupied territories. My teachers presented course material and information that stemmed from a perspective that neglected to take my identity into account, failing to recognize its impact on individuals like me. The content seemed to function as an altar of Eurocentric idolatry, and I found myself revering rather than questioning this altar, which shaped my own self-image and influenced my concept of heroism.

While no instructor or priest seemed to be purposely trying to make me feel inferior, the pervasive symbols of exceptionalism and salvation stirred within me a desire to distance myself from the culture into which I was born. I sought to adopt an identity that wasn't inherently mine. I made numerous attempts to shed my given name, Omari, as it felt so distinct from that of my peers. I temporarily embraced the name Zach, borrowed from the blond protagonist of the 1990s television series *Saved by the Bell.* This character bore a striking resemblance to the light-haired Christ I encountered on my school's bookmarks.

Fortunately, my self-concept evolved in a different direction when my family relocated to a new section of the Bronx, where I began second grade at Public School (P.S.) 78X. My experience at this school was vastly different. The student population was predominantly Black and Afro-Latino. My second-grade instructor, Mrs. Greenwich, was a tall Black woman and my first teacher of color. She wore African garb to class daily. Her attire consisted of a vibrant dashiki, a colorful garment that covers the upper body and is commonly worn in West Africa, paired with sokoto (drawstring pants) and a matching kufi (hat). Complementing this ensemble was her collection of bracelets, necklaces, and earrings made from Krobo Fancy Powder Glass Beads. Her classroom walls were covered in pictures of prominent Black figures like General Toussaint-Louverture, Frederick Douglass, Duke Ellington, Marcus Garvey, Langston Hughes, and Zora Neale Hurston. When kids left the classroom, whether for lunch or recess, we would march from one end of the school to our intended destination singing Negro spirituals and West African warrior chants. These experiences opened my eyes to heroism, martyrdom, and leadership—ideals that had been taught to me while studying at Mount Carmel. However, this time, people who looked like me were performing the actions.

One of the most formative experiences in that class was our daily story time and the way the chosen books paralleled my personal experiences. One of the books Mrs. Greenwich picked was *The Black Snowman* (1989), by Phil Mendez. The story's main character, Jacob Miller, was similar to me—an inner-city boy and older sibling who struggles with both his race and his social class. Jacob helps his little brother, Peewee, make a snowman. However, the snow in their environment is no longer white and freshly fallen. The once-pristine snow, trampled by city residents, has taken on a dark-gray hue. The black snowman they build symbolizes Jacob's belief that his race and socio-economic standing render him inferior to others. However, Peewee finds a fragment of a magical kente, a West African textile that has been worn by African storytellers (also known as griots) for hundreds of years that signifies cultural pride and an illustrious wisdom tradition in the form of philosophy, oral storytelling, and political thought.

The cloth found by Peewee immediately brings to life the snowman, who challenges Jacob's perspective of Black inferiority. Using the magic of the cloth, a powerful and symbolic design element, the snowman continues to expose Jacob to the history of the African continent and ultimately helps him save Peewee from a fire in an abandoned building. Once the two brothers are reunited, the melting snowman implores him to believe in the magic of the kente.

The metaphors of this story continue to resonate with me. Similar to Jacob, I, too, have questioned the value of my identity and, by extension, my value as an individual. Every image I consumed, the stories I read, and the heroes I was introduced to centered on a skin tone I did not share or represented a culture that did not view my ancestors or me in a favorable fashion.

Similar to the snowman, my teacher challenged my perspective regarding both my own value and the value of my people. Mrs. Greenwich had a beautiful mind and a powerful command, and she worked tirelessly to uplift her students. Like the snowman, the magic of heritage strengthened her while she chanted and led the Cadence (a rhythmic call-and-response tradition) as we marched through the school hallways. Similar to the snowman, Mrs. Greenwich skillfully wove tales of resilience and restoration in the face of hardships. Although I didn't know it then, Mrs. Greenwich was *uplifting* her students through her restorative approach to narrative. Like the snowman, she used storytelling for healing and cultural preservation.

This experience vividly illustrates the profound impact of restorative design practice on an individual's sense of self and identity. The journey I underwent, from feeling marginalized and excluded in one educational environment to finding *strength* and validation in another, underscores the transformative potential of embracing diverse counter-narratives to monolithic and incomplete narratives.

In a world where stories have the power to shape perceptions, restorative design practice emerges as a force that can dismantle harmful narratives, empower marginalized voices, and promote healing and reconciliation. By harnessing the power of storytelling and memory, designers and writers can directly promote understanding, empathy, and positive change.

Mrs. Greenwich helped to shape my awareness that storytelling has traditionally been a way for marginalized communities to maintain their traditions and beliefs, as it does not require significant resources or even education for participation. As the Métis artist and filmmaker Judy Iseke (2013) writes, storytelling in Indigenous communities "sustains communities and validates experiences." In many cultures, storytelling also creates opportunities for intergenerational connections, as elders freely share their experiences with younger people.

In my experience, Mrs. Greenwich embodied the role of an elder passing down stories that Black people have preserved for generations, demonstrating their ongoing influence on the diasporic community today. I was no longer merely learning about heroes who bore no resemblance to me and led lives vastly different from my own. The manner in which these stories were shared helped me shape my identity against a backdrop of others who faced similar struggles and triumphed. This understanding allowed me to realize that I did not need to abandon my own identity or culture to embody these positive qualities.

African storytelling involves listening, sharing, laughter, music, rhythm, and a dialogic relationship between the storyteller and the audience. Storytelling traditions focus on community: bringing people together after dinner and after a hard day's work. African oral storytelling entertains, informs, and instructs while passing on traditions, codes, and values that demarcate acceptable behavior (Tuwe 2016). Trickster characters are especially popular in African folktales. Anansi, the trickster spider in West African and Caribbean culture, could be viewed as a master designer. Anansi uses his design ability to solve problems (generally for himself) and to outsmart others. Imagine being a child in the Caribbean, hearing stories that praise how Anansi designs his way out of conundrums, rather than emphasizing that he is just a trickster.

Zora Neale Hurston's storytelling prowess, which I also learned about in Mrs. Greenwich's classroom, was deeply rooted in the rich African American oral storytelling tradition. Drawing from this heritage, she masterfully wove narratives that explored themes of faith, love, family, race, and community, transporting readers into the complex and enchanting world of southern Black communities. Through her stories, not only did Hurston preserve the unique folk idioms of the South, but she also illuminated the challenges and victories of African American communities, contributing to a fortified sense of shared identity.

David Robinson and Kayt Robinson (2005) describe some of the key ways that discussions based in oral storytelling strategies differ from Eurocentric strategies: They are not time-bound, they are controlled by participants, they use ceremony to set the scene, and they create space for all voices to be heard.

Non-Eurocentric traditions use storytelling for aims that could be explored in design practice. Whereas Western designers tend to use storytelling to build empathy and share concepts, other examples suggest that Indigenous storytelling methods might also influence the ideation phase, in a participatory forum in which all members might share their ideas.

The stories shared in my class at an early age deepened my understanding of how storytelling, both written and visual, can amplify marginalized voices. Similarly, my exploration of works by African and African American writers like Richard Wright, Chinua Achebe, and Toni Morrison showcased the power of storytelling in addressing identity, history, and the African American experience.

Today, I view design as a tool with similar potential to foster understanding and create equitable solutions, and I have adopted this approach in my design and research methods. By embracing global storytelling methodologies throughout the design process, designers can gain a deeper understanding of the diverse experiences, traditions, and values of the individuals they serve. The power of storytelling in design cannot be overstated. Storytelling is not merely a tool for creating aesthetically pleasing designs; it is a way to craft solutions and experiences that resonate on a profound level, enhancing their impact and relevance.

Incorporating storytelling methods from various cultures broadens the design landscape, allowing for a more inclusive, authentic, and resonant approach. Designers can learn from the wisdom of these traditions, understanding that storytelling is not limited to inculcating empathy but can profoundly influence ideation, fostering a participatory environment in which every voice is heard and valued—and in which the multiplicity of human experiences helps us to shape our own identities.

References

Iseke, J. (2013). "Indigenous Storytelling as Research." *International Review of Qualitative Research* 6, no. 4: 559–77.

Mendez, P. (1989). *The Black Snowman*. Scholastic.

Robinson, D., and Robinson, K. (2005, January). "Pacific Ways of Talk—Hui and Talanoa." New Zealand Institute for Economic Research.

Tuwe, K. (2016, February). "The African Oral Tradition Paradigm of Storytelling as a Methodological Framework: Employment Experiences for African Communities in New Zealand." African Studies Association of Australasia and the Pacific (AFSAAP) Proceedings of the 38th AFSAAP Conference: 21st Century Tensions and Transformation in Africa, Deakin University, October 28–30, 2015.

2.3

Restorative Storytelling and Exploring Counternarratives

Resistance to dominant narratives can offer protagonists of color a sense of power, agency, and control over their futures. However, dominant accounts of history, as well as dominant visions of the present and future, continue to influence the field of social design. In fact, the field is rife with examples of saviorism and white supremacy in the way issues are framed and stories are told. Designers and design firms are portrayed as heroes and the protagonists of design stories, while people of color, poor people, and those from oppressed identities are often portrayed as recipients of design support who lack agency altogether.

To become more aware of the ways we may inadvertently harm the communities we desire to serve, we must be especially stringent in considering our storytelling methods, which are often based on models we've unconsciously absorbed from the dominant culture. If we aim to promote social justice and antiracist teaching, the social-justice scholar Lee Anne Bell (2020) encourages us to consider four models that are commonly used in stories about race:

1. **Stock stories** are told by dominant groups. They assume a normative position and often validate racist and oppressive agendas while celebrating history and tradition.
2. **Concealed stories** may be unknown to people from the dominant group but live in the communities of people at the margins. Concealed stories are told from the viewpoint of the marginalized, highlighting community strengths over community deficits. Bell proposes deconstructing stock stories by comparing them with concealed stories to gain a more accurate understanding of the larger context.
3. **Resistance stories** show how people have fought oppression and provide needed inspiration to continue liberation-focused work.
4. **Emerging or transforming stories** are created as counternarratives to stock stories, to critique and challenge the status quo, and to create new visions and possibilities for our existing systems and societies.

The emerging or transforming story is a powerful model for the act of restorative storytelling, which enables us to tell stories that center the lives and concerns of those who have been historically marginalized—sometimes even stricken from the historical record altogether. Restorative storytelling also offers us an opportunity as a society to come to terms with the incompleteness of our so-called historical record, and to call into question biases that may contribute to the stereotyping or dehumanization of certain groups. As the old adage goes, history is told by the victors, but what if we were to upend this model altogether? What if, in envisioning new futures, we could retroactively amend the vacant spots that exist in renditions of our past, which often act more as a kind of mythmaking than objective accounts telling us all we need to know?

In addition to recognizing the types of stories we are perpetuating, restorative storytelling requires, first and foremost, that we acknowledge the past. "Acknowledging the past" refers to recognizing and accepting the historical injustices and wrongdoing that have occurred. It involves confronting dark chapters of history, such as past national crimes, harmful policies, and unfair treatment of certain groups.

The act of acknowledging the past is essential for several reasons. First, it paves the way for reconciliation and healing. In her book *Survivor Café: The Legacy of Trauma and the Labyrinth of Memory* (2017), Elizabeth Rosner talks about a special event she refers to as a "Survivor Café." At these gatherings, Holocaust survivors and their families, along with those impacted by other forms of historical trauma, come together to share their stories and memories. Rosner uses the term "Survivor Café" not only to describe specific events but also as a metaphorical space for collective remembrance and intergenerational healing. These gatherings provide a valuable space where people can work through difficult experiences and share stories that help build understanding and empathy between generations. By coming together in this way, individuals can find connection and strength, creating a bridge between the past and present that supports both personal and collective healing. This helps connect different generations, so younger people can learn about what happened during the Holocaust directly from those who lived through it. Rosner mixes her own family's stories with ideas from science, therapy, history, and philosophy to help readers understand trauma in many different ways.

Survivor Cafés are important because they help people heal and find peace. They provide a safe space in which survivors and their families can talk about their experiences, which helps them feel less alone and more supported. These events also teach people about the Holocaust and other terrible events in history, helping everyone understand how important it is to remember and learn from these events to prevent them from happening again. By sharing these stories, Survivor Cafés keep the memories of the Holocaust alive and build stronger communities.

These gatherings also help with reconciliation by recognizing the pain and suffering people went through, and by bringing different communities together. They encourage people to grow and become stronger by hearing stories of survival and resilience. Survivor Cafés also inspire people to stand up for what is right and work toward a better world.

David Temin and Adam Dahl (2017) characterize the vital process wherein a society recognizes historical atrocities and works to understand their current impact. As they write, by acknowledging historical injustices, societies can create spaces for dialogue, understanding, and empathy among different groups. This allows for a collective reckoning that includes more perspectives and experiences than were previously afforded by the historical record. Although the process of collective reckoning can be painful and uncomfortable and is not without its fair share of voluble detractors (open any newspaper or turn to any TV commentator, and you're likely to encounter someone bemoaning the teaching of critical race theory or anything else that challenges historical accounts and social mores associated with the dominant culture), it is a necessary growing pain. It allows us to move beyond oppressive systems and into uncharted territory that we all ideally have a hand in shaping. By leaning into our growth edges and recognizing our blind spots, we can choose to transform our own ignorance (after all, we don't know what we don't know) into learning that fosters mutual understanding and positive change.

In addition, by confronting and learning from past injustices, societies can strive to avoid repeating similar injustices in the future. This leads to greater political responsibility as societies become more aware of the impact of their actions and decisions on various communities (Temin and Dahl 2017).

In Germany, social responsibility meant that everyone, especially the younger generation, took it upon themselves to learn about and understand the wrongs of the past. After World War II, Germany faced its past by holding events like the Adolf Eichmann trial, which was televised worldwide (Dalton-Bradford 2022). This trial highlighted not only the crimes of Eichmann, a German Austrian official in the Nazi Party, but also the widespread antisemitism that had existed for generations. This led to a major change in how people in Germany thought about their history. Members of the younger generation, who were called "Hitler's children," began to ask tough questions and demand the truth about what happened during the Nazi era. This was a big step toward healing because it allowed the nation to confront its dark past openly and honestly, and to assume responsibility for future generations. By remembering the past and teaching it in schools, Germany built a society that values human rights and recognizes the importance of facing history, no matter how difficult.

When societies acknowledge diverse perspectives, they gain a more comprehensive understanding of the past. Involving and acknowledging often unheard or unacknowledged perspectives and voices when remembering historical events can foster understanding among communities, strengthening social cohesion and collective action for positive change. One tool for achieving this understanding is the commemoration—an event or practice that honors and remembers important historical events, individuals, or narratives. In societies with a colonial history, commemorations can foster reconciliation and promote a path forward.

The Truth and Reconciliation Commission (TRC) in South Africa was created to help the country heal from the painful history of apartheid, a time when people were treated unfairly because of their skin color (Tutu 2024). The TRC allowed many people, including victims, perpetrators, and other citizens, to share their stories. This helped to contribute to a more complete picture of what really happened during apartheid. By bringing together different perspectives, the TRC helped South Africa remember its past more comprehensively. Victims could talk about their experiences and pain; those who caused harm could explain their actions and sometimes even apologize. Bystanders added their own memories, making the story even richer. Hearing from everyone helped create a fuller, more honest picture of history. This collective remembering was crucial for the country's healing. The TRC's work ensured that the injustices of apartheid were acknowledged, laying the groundwork for reconciliation and a more united society.

Of course, apologies are also necessary in redressing historical injustices. Although some might argue that they were not the ones who perpetuated harm that may have occurred generations ago, many of us continue to receive the benefits of other people's wrongdoing (e.g., the generational wealth among white people that was one of the repercussions of colonization and the slave trade). An apology is a symbolic act that expresses remorse and recognition of the harm caused to individuals, as well as communities. According to Temin and Dahl (2017), responding to historical injustices goes beyond assigning blame; it involves confronting the ongoing ramifications of past inequalities, power dynamics, and dominance. Apologies offer a sense of validation and closure to those communities that have been wronged, contributing to healing and reconciliation. Moreover, apologies are essential for building trust and repairing relationships between groups.

Overall, by understanding the politics of memory, societies can navigate contemporary challenges related to historical injustices more effectively, ensuring that the past is not forgotten or repeated. This is an essential lesson for people in the field of social design, who can strive to understand community context and explore counter-arguments of resistance to come into better alignment with those they aim to serve.

The expressive arts, such as dance, music, theater, and design, can be significant agents in shaping how people remember historical events and envision possible futures. According to the performance scholar John S. Gentile (2011), the arts uniquely help people remember events differently by presenting alternative angles and exposing underlying hierarchies and injustices. They become vital acts of resistance to cultural hegemony; for example, the Japanese dance form Butoh was developed in the late 1950s as a reaction against Western imperialism.

The arts can challenge dominant historical narratives and highlight marginalized voices in an overtly political way that can be a necessary form of protest. Systems of dominance and subordination can be deftly dismantled, and new possibilities can be birthed into existence on a stage or a canvas. Like designers, artists make real what was once only hypothetical.

Artists can also harness word power, according to Gentile (2011), to contribute to the formation of a collective memory that allows communities to make sense of past, present, and future. Gentile specifically refers to the griots of Mali, Africa, whose remarkable skill with words enables them to evoke a panoply of emotions in their listeners. Griots act as performers, genealogists, historians, spokespeople, and leaders in their communities—working to keep the cultural identity of their society alive through both preservation and transformation. As storytellers, they pass down Mali's history, myths, and traditions through symbolic language and music, using instruments like the balafon, kora, and ngoni. By sharing multiple versions of stories, they preserve the collective memory while adapting to changing times. Though there is a tension between modernizing and preserving traditional ways, griots continue to honor the heroic past and keep their culture alive.

Overall, social designers can learn a great deal from methods of restorative storytelling that span cultural contexts and disciplines. If we are unaware of the dominant models of storytelling, it's likely that we'll continue to unwittingly perpetuate harm. The act of restorative storytelling in the arts and other sectors of our society is an act of acknowledging the past and also moving toward models of social justice that enable us to tell new stories in novel ways.

References

Bell, L. A. (2020). *Storytelling for Social Justice: Connecting Narrative and the Arts in Antiracist Teaching*. Routledge.

Dalton-Bradford, M. (2022). "From Stumbling Blocks to Stepping Stones: What America Can Learn from Germany about Reconciliation." *BYU Studies Quarterly* 61, no. 1.

Gentile, J. S. (2011). "Storytelling and Myth: Reimagining the Hero's Journey in Contemporary Culture." *Journal of Mythological Studies* 7, no. 2: 45–62.

Rosner, E. (2017). *Survivor Café: The Legacy of Trauma and the Labyrinth of Memory*. Catapult.

Temin, D. M., and Dahl, A. (2017, July). "Narrating Historical Injustice: Political Responsibility and the Politics of Memory." *International Political Science Review* 70, no. 4.

Tutu, D. (2024, April 14). "Truth and Reconciliation Commission, South Africa." Britannica. Retrieved June 12, 2024, from https://www.britannica.com/topic/Truth-and-Reconciliation-Commission-South-Africa

2.4

Strategies for Restorative Storytelling

Lesley-Ann Noel

Our intersectional identities affect how storytelling and narratives feed into how we work as designers. If you are from a dominant group, you may be enacting your internalized dominance in your design work through the way you interpret narratives. Internalized dominance occurs when we assume that we are superior to the people with whom we are working. This may manifest through how we construct project aims and the way we describe and judge clients' social practices, how they dress, what they eat, how they talk, and more.

When we tell stories through a lens of internalized dominance, the people we are telling stories about will always be victims or disadvantaged. They will lack agency. They will need to build certain capacities or character traits. Their characters will be flattened and one-dimensional.

If you are part of a group that is objectified or portrayed through damaging narratives, these portrayals can reinforce or ignite your own internalized oppression. This occurs when members of the oppressed group turn the strategies used by the oppressors against themselves. Absorbed prejudice is essentially achieved when the oppressed group believes the narrative that is presented by the oppressors.

Storytelling is an element of restorative approaches. People from outside the dominant design culture can draw on the storytelling traditions of their own groups and cultures to recontextualize design and create new cultures and stories in design, and to use these storytelling methods and traditions during different parts of the design process. People from both dominant and nondominant groups can keep in mind the importance of empowering narratives in the restorative process.

Here are some questions to help shape a restorative approach to storytelling in design.

For everyone:

1. Who is the hero of the story?
2. Who is portrayed as strong? Who is portrayed as weak? Who needs help?
3. How does the story change when we tell it from a different point of view?
4. Have we created rich portrayals of key people in the story? Or are they flattened and one-dimensional?
5. Has the context in which the story takes place been richly explored and described?

6. How might storytelling techniques improve the design process?
7. How might storytelling techniques improve the design experience?
8. As a person who may hold oppressed identities, which of your stories are not told? What is your perspective on the issue at hand?

For students:
1. Examine the storytelling traditions of your own culture.
2. What is the role of storytelling in your family?
3. When telling stories about others, whose point of view are you privileging?

For educators:
Educators can be important in interrupting one-dimensional stories and including restorative storytelling approaches in their classes. In teaching about the Bauhaus Design Academy, for example, a professor could introduce a more critical understanding of the social context that created the Bauhaus rather than focus on the details of the objects that were designed there. The essay "Bauhaus Already Lives Here and Why the World Still Doesn't Know It" (Serumaga-Musisi 2016) is a useful resource, as it reminds us that the context that created the Bauhaus does, in fact, exist in other places. In this article, the Ugandan architect Namata Serumaga-Musisi informs readers that Africa is not the "dark continent" it has been construed as; indeed, it provides a rich space for creative experimentation and expression, just as Weimar, Dessau, or Berlin provided for the Bauhaus. This understanding that a context that can lead to experimental design education can exist in many different places could be a small step toward expanding student perceptions of who makes and can make design.

For design practitioners:
A restorative approach in storytelling requires:
1. **Asset-based framing:** When designing a new playground, consider the great things the community already has, like friendly neighbors and lots of kids who love to play, instead of only what it lacks.
2. **A therapeutic approach to storytelling that necessitates a critical analysis of traditional narratives:** For instance, instead of perpetuating the

stereotype of lazy teenagers, we can showcase examples of teens who initiate community projects, thereby presenting a more balanced and inclusive narrative.

3. **Multiple points of view, including less-examined ones:** When designing a new school, ask a variety of stakeholders, such as the lunch staff and janitors, for their ideas, not just the teachers and principal, to get a complete picture of what everyone needs.
4. **Examination of power in storytelling:** In a project to make a park safer, look at who usually makes the decisions, such as city officials, and also include ideas from kids and families who use the park every day.
5. **Examination of the portrayal of various characters in the story:** This practice promotes more nuanced and empathetic storytelling. For instance, when telling the story of a family getting a new house, it's important to depict them as people with diverse interests, talents, and hobbies rather than just as people in need of help.
6. **Examination of the emotional responses the storyteller wants to evoke in the reader:** When sharing the story of a neighborhood cleanup, try to make people feel inspired and proud of their community instead of feeling sorry for it.

References

Serumaga-Musisi, N. (2016). "Bauhaus Already Lives Here and Why the World Still Doesn't Know It." Chimurenga. Retrieved August 27, 2024, from http://chimurengachronic.co.za/bauhaus-already-lives-here-and-why-the-world-still-doesnt-know-it/

2.5

Restoring Through Curiosity and Care

Cassini Nazir

Gaining empathy for users has long been considered a central task in design. In the early 1980s, the British design researcher Nigel Cross (1982) listed empathy as one of the values that distinguished the design field from other more-established cultures of the sciences and humanities. Many design practitioners closely adhere to this notion without being able to adequately explain empathy.

A number of studies have demonstrated the following about empathy:

- We easily confuse and conflate empathy, sympathy, and compassion. The differences between these capacities are critically important.
- Empathic resonance in the brain is highly biased. We find it difficult to empathize with people who are unlike us.
- We feel empathy only for humans and some animals—not for objects, spaces, places, or our planet.

Designers build products, services, and systems for humans (and others). To which of the nouns in the previous sentence—products, services, systems, humans—can we extend empathy? The British philosopher Gregory Currie (2011) argues: only humans. He notes: "We think of empathy as an intimate, feeling-based understanding of another's inner life. We do not think of it as a way of understanding inanimate objects."

Empathy, while necessary in design, has specific limitations. My colleague and I (Nazir and Lin 2023) identified sixteen limitations of empathy as applied to design (see table 1). These limitations are categorized across four areas: limitations that apply to the individual (or self), limitations we have regarding people who are similar to us, limitations regarding those who are dissimilar to us, and empathy at the scale of society. The four categories allude to the Australian philosopher Peter Singer's (1981) notion of an expanding circle of moral concern that begins with our own family or tribe, expanding to include larger groups, nations, all humans, and even nonhuman animals. These sixteen limitations indicate that empathy is primarily directed toward humans and that it weakens as it is redirected from those similar to us to those dissimilar to us.

Table 1. Sixteen limitations of empathy

Empathy toward self	1.1	Empathy is often confused with other emotions.
	1.2	Empathy sometimes has negative consequences.
	1.3	Empathy opens us up to manipulation.
	1.4	We are unreliable narrators of our experiences.
	1.5	We can fall into the empathy trap.
	1.6	Empathy can provide an illusion of understanding.
Empathy toward similars	2.1	We spotlight empathy on whom we choose.
	2.2	We snapshot people in time.
	2.3	Empathic reasoning is biased.
Empathy toward dissimilars	3.1	Empathy can promote side-taking.
	3.2	We can filter our empathy through others.
	3.3	Empathy for dissimilars is limited by imagination.
	3.4	Neurotypical and neurodivergent empathy are expressed differently.
Empathy in society	4.1	Western empathy is primarily human centered.
	4.2	Empathy can fuel division in society.
	4.3	Empathy is culturally embedded.

If we can empathize only with humans and only in limited ways, perhaps designers could benefit from an assemblage of emotive capacities beyond just empathy. Curiosity and care are two emotive capacities that are necessary to restorative design and that can help address the problems of bias that are inherent in empathy.

Curiosity can be a powerful way to unsettle certainties and explore new ways of looking, feeling, and doing. The bioethicist Jodi Halpern (2001) states that "genuine curiosity and openness to learning something new" is the "most important pathway to empathy." The English word *curiosity* is linguistically rooted in the notion of care. It traces its origin to the Latin word *cūra*, which has several meanings, including care, concern, and cure. This relationship of curiosity to care transcends linguistics. Becoming genuinely curious about others is one way that we can lend care to others. Curiosity can reinforce care. Greater curiosity about a person can often lead to greater care about that subject. Care is an attentive conscientiousness—for that which we choose to build, as well as those with whom we build—that undergirds restorative design.

Coaxing curiosity is challenging. What are ways that designers might create moments of curiosity? Built on the psychologist Robert Plutchik's model of emotions, the Inviting Curiosity framework (Nazir and Wang 2022) is a tool by which designers may begin to fashion experiences that enable moments of curiosity, exploration, or play that can lead to greater care.

Curiosity starts with an invitation (see page 122). Some object, system, experience, or notion extends an invitation for us to be curious. Invitations adopt a variety of common approaches that can elicit a spectrum of emotions. But the invitation must be interesting, and we must be interested. Trust is also needed; otherwise, curiosity evaporates.

Most invitations require us to act or respond in some way. We don't always perceive invitations, and they can be accepted, rejected, or ignored. Some invitations may not be acted upon, like a wrapped gift that has been accepted but never unwrapped.

If accepted and acted upon, there is then an inflection point at which the necessary emotion of surprise begins to be felt. Surprise requires us to confront our notions and reevaluate our thinking. The inflection point marks the beginning of curiosity being meaningfully engaged and satisfyingly rewarded. This reward may be informational, sensory, or experiential—or a combination of all three. In some cases, the response may also be the reward. Inviting curiosity can serve as a catalyst for embedding curiosity and care into the design process.

Paul Rodgers and Craig Bremner (2017) identify care as an important part of the concept of the design discipline: "Care refers to designing with the macro and micro social, technological, economic, environmental and political effects of design decision-making well in mind."

Curiosity and care are important to restorative design and building sustainable futures. It is common to conceptualize the future in a position external to the body. Western narratives conceptualize the future as being in front of us. In other cultures, the future is at our backs—behind

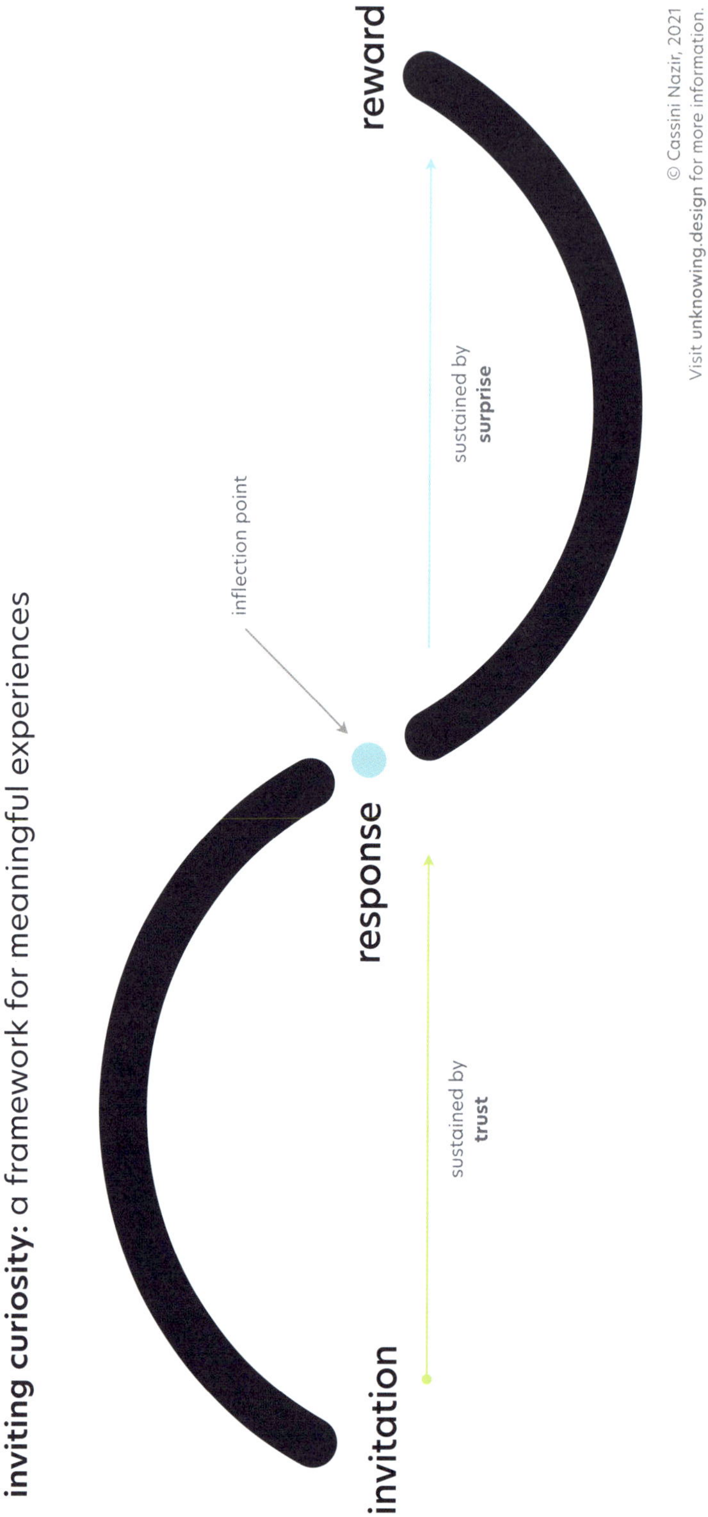
inviting curiosity: a framework for meaningful experiences
invitation
sustained by
trust
response
inflection point
sustained by
surprise
reward
© Cassini Nazir, 2021
Visit unknowing.design for more information.

us—with the past in front, clearly visible. The Māori proverb *Kia whakatōmuri te haere whakamua* translates to "I walk backward into the future with my eyes fixed on my past" (Rameka 2016). The Māori conceptualization bears higher fidelity to our collective experience: If the future is behind us, we cannot see it, and therefore, we must carefully tread into it. This implies that the past is inherent in the future. Curiosity and care can help us to see additional frames of our past and give us courage to move forward along the uneven ground of the future.

References

Cross, N. (1982). "Designerly Ways of Knowing." *Design Studies* 3, no. 4: 221–27. https://doi.org/10.1016/0142-694x(82)90040-0

Currie, G. (2011). "Empathy for Objects." In *Empathy: Philosophical and Psychological Perspectives*, edited by Amy Coplan and Peter Goldie, 82–95. Oxford University Press.

Halpern, J. (2001). *From Detached Concern to Empathy*. Oxford University Press.

Nazir, C., and Wang, J. (2022, February). "Designing Curiosity: A Beginner's Guide." *User Experience Professionals Association Magazine*. https://uxpamagazine.org/designing-curiosity-a-beginners-guide

Nazir, C., and Lin, M. (2023). "Beyond Empathy: How Curiosity Promotes Greater Care." *Connectivity and Creativity in Times of Conflict*. https://doi.org/10.26530/9789401496476-115

Rameka, L. (2016). "*Kia Whakatōmuri Te Haere Whakamua*: 'I Walk Backwards into the Future with My Eyes Fixed on My Past.'" *Contemporary Issues in Early Childhood* 17, no. 4: 387–98. https://doi.org/10.1177/1463949116677923

Rodgers, P. A., and Bremner, C. (2017). "The Concept of the Design Discipline." *Dialectic* 1, no. 1. https://doi.org/10.3998/dialectic.14932326.0001.104

Singer, P. (1981). *The Expanding Circle*. Oxford University Press.

Wakkary, R. (2021). *Things We Could Design for More Than Human-Centered Worlds*. MIT Press.

opposite: Inviting Curiosity framework

2.6

Combating Erasure and Building Trust, Cooperation, and Understanding Among Marginalized Groups

We must come to terms with the ongoing legacies of colonialism as we enter the process of restorative design, which helps us to understand where we are and how we got here. Taking stock of the reality on the ground must then extend to our solutions in the present. The inclusion of marginalized voices is paramount when it comes to fostering innovation and offering restitution for the violence and appropriation of resources (cultural and material) that have continued to bear bitter fruit in the postcolonial era.

Despite the strides we have made toward greater liberation in the twentieth century and beyond, colonialism's impact on Western capitalism shapes our present-day economies, influencing social structures and persistent inequalities. Embracing marginalized communities' perspectives is key to fostering innovative solutions that challenge oppressive systems and help us to locate meaning and beauty outside the dominant paradigms and worldviews that have influenced our very notions of "civilization." Thus, restorative design requires us to confront the detrimental effects of maintaining the status quo for the sake of comfort.

The Black feminist scholar bell hooks (1990) advocates for a revolutionary feminist ideology that challenges the oppressive systems of capitalism and patriarchy, which have led to the erasure of marginalized people. She highlights the unique experiences of Black women, shaped by historical factors like slavery, capitalism, patriarchy, and racism. According to hooks, in order to achieve true liberation, feminism must confront the cultural hegemony imposed by capitalist patriarchy and strive for material and concrete change, not just abstract reform.

In the essays "Eating the Other: Desire and Resistance" (1992) and "Representing Whiteness in the Black Imagination" (1992), hooks delves into the dynamics of racial and cultural interactions, highlighting the commodification of "otherized" populations and the need for a shift in perspective to foster genuine understanding. hooks addresses the concept of commodity culture, wherein white individuals seek encounters with nonwhite individuals as a form of fetishism and self-transformation. This desire for engagement with the "other" is driven by a romanticized longing for the perceived intensity and pleasure associated with different racial and cultural experiences. However, hooks emphasizes that this commodification perpetuates imbalanced power dynamics, erases the specificity of the other, and reinforces systems of racial domination.

To counteract these oppressive tendencies, hooks advocates resistance as a way to challenge white cultural imperialism, capitalism, and ongoing racist domination. Genuine resistance can be a tool for decolonization and a way to challenge oppressive power dynamics. Further, hooks calls for a shift in perspective and understanding of the experiences of the other, urging readers to deconstruct negative perceptions and restore suppressed knowledge to foster empathy and understanding among diverse communities.

As hooks and others allude to in their work, so much of the work of restoration requires addressing our own perspectives, which have been skewed by oppression. In her book *Sister Citizen: Shame, Stereotypes, and Black Women in America* (2013), Melissa Harris-Perry references a post–World War II cognitive psychology research study on field dependence. *Field dependence* refers to how a person's perception is influenced by the surrounding environment, making it harder to distinguish details from the background. The study investigated how people locate their vertical alignment within a space. Subjects were placed in a crooked chair in a crooked room and were then asked to align themselves vertically. To the researchers' surprise, some subjects could be tilted as much as 35 degrees while assuming they were still aligned vertically. In contrast, others could get themselves upright, regardless of how crooked the room was.

Harris-Perry suggests that when confronting issues of race, African American women have been placed in a metaphorical crooked room where they contend with systemic biases and obstacles. Expanding on this notion, I argue that colonialism and its cultural practices have tilted the room for all of us, irrespective of race. To restore equilibrium, in addition to listening to the voices of the marginalized and building trust where it has been broken, we must embrace cultural pluralism, which entails understanding different cultures on *their* terms rather than comparing them to our own as the default standard. By adopting this approach, we can begin restoring the room to its rightful position and fostering a more inclusive and just design practice.

We can honor cultural pluralism in our design in a number of ways. Empowering historically excluded communities is essential to countering colonialism. Anticolonial actions should prioritize the involvement of marginalized communities in decisions about their land, communities, and neighborhoods. Their desires, goals, and aspirations must be considered and consulted during design and development. Treating these communities as equals rather than perpetuating power imbalances based on race, class, gender, or place of birth is crucial for challenging and dismantling existing power structures.

In "Establishing Social Conditions of Trust and Cooperation" (2003), hooks provides a model for designers, as she highlights the critical role of trust and cooperation in postconflict stabilization and reconstruction efforts that help restore peace and rebuild communities that have been affected by war and other atrocities. This involves creating safety, fixing damaged buildings and roads, promoting fair government, helping the economy recover, and encouraging people to trust and work together again. hooks identifies trust as a foundational element for social stability and cooperation as essential for facilitating collaboration among previously warring parties. Rebuilding trust is crucial for creating an environment in which communities and factions can work together, heal past wounds, and engage in cooperative efforts for mutual benefit.

By resisting external imposition and embracing context-specific approaches, postconflict societies can develop trust-building mechanisms that cater to their unique circumstances. Additionally, media and peace education, as emphasized in "Establishing Social Conditions," can play significant roles in challenging fixed viewpoints and promoting understanding among a plurality of groups. While trust building is essential, it must entail the willingness to withstand bumps in the road and the courage to address the wounds of the past—which, in many cases, persist in the present. Restorative practices that acknowledge historical pain and foster understanding are crucial in this transformative journey.

It is important to recognize and acknowledge the significant challenges that arise when attempting to gain trust and access to marginalized communities, particularly if we are outsiders studying their cultures. These communities have valid reasons to be cautious, due to historical and systemic factors that have led to distrust and apprehension; after all, they have directly experienced not just erasure but the alienation that arises from being the designated "other"—the blank canvas upon which those in positions of power have historically projected their own fears, desires, and assumptions.

Building trust requires time, patience, and genuine efforts to establish meaningful relationships that do not unwittingly perpetuate colonial thinking and power differentials. It is important to approach this process with humility and adaptability, acknowledging that mistakes and failures may occur before success is achieved.

References

Harris-Perry, M. (2013). *Sister Citizen: Shame, Stereotypes, and Black Women in America*. Yale University Press.

hooks, b. (1990). *Yearning: Race, Gender, and Cultural Politics*. South End Press.

hooks, b. (1992). "Eating the Other: Desire and Resistance." In *Black Looks: Race and Representation*, 21–39. South End Press.

hooks, b. (1992). "Representing Whiteness in the Black Imagination." In *Black Looks: Race and Representation*, 165–78. South End Press.

hooks, b. (2003). "Establishing Social Conditions of Trust and Cooperation." In *Teaching Community: A Pedagogy of Hope*, 29–42. Routledge.

2.7

Positionality: Acknowledging Yourself

Lesley-Ann Noel

Your positionality is determined by a combination of many factors that have created your identity. These can include your race, your gender, the social context in which you were brought up, and a multitude of complexities that all combine to create who you are as an individual. Qualitative researchers learn about the importance of writing a positionality statement when they start and later share their research. A positionality statement helps them reflect on who they are, because they are, in fact, the starting point in their own research.

As argued by the Swedish doctor and researcher Kirsti Malterud in her paper "Qualitative Research: Standards, Challenges, and Guidelines" (2001):

> A researcher's background and position will affect what they choose to investigate, the angle of investigation, the methods judged most adequate for this purpose, the findings considered most appropriate, and the framing and communication of conclusions. (483–84)

A positionality statement is applicable not only to scientific researchers but to anyone who is embarking on any kind of restorative design or justice process. Your statement should address who you are, how you see the world, your relationship with project participants, and the solution you are hoping to achieve. Such a statement can uncover both strengths and biases and clarify how the identities of the people helming a project intersect with the topic itself, as well as the identities of other participants and stakeholders. A positionality statement also sheds light on how the topic at hand might be represented, as well as opportunities for addressing blind spots and growth edges and for creating greater collaboration with users from marginalized spaces. After all, in design, we often craft solutions for others, so our awareness should not be limited to our own positions but should also include the positions of those for whom we are designing.

In *Designing for Diversity: Gender, Race, and Ethnicity in the Architectural Profession* (2001), the American architecture professor Kathryn H. Anthony argues that the creators of built environments have often neglected the needs of women; public restrooms in theaters, stadiums, and airports are quick examples. Anthony highlights the speed with which men can use the restroom compared with their female counterparts. Between 1880 and 1960, this discrepancy was not considered by architects and their clients, or by building-code officials. Even if male and female bathrooms provided an equal number of stalls, blind spots and gaps in understanding related to the needs of a broad user base failed to provide equitable access, resulting in longer bathroom wait times for non-male-identifying visitors.

Societies in the United States and elsewhere might send us messages that we all occupy the same globalized space, since we all listen to the same pop music and use the same social-media platforms. However, as designers, researchers, and educators, slowing down to understand who we are, how we (and our identities) show up in this work, and how our positions may differ from those of others is always a best practice.

The spaces in which design takes shape can send the unconscious (or overt) message that one must fit in. For example: In California, I took part in a meeting with four people at a design studio. We were speaking about differences and leaning into each of our positionalities as individuals within our work teams. One colleague interrupted the conversation and said, "Hang on, but we're all American!" in an attempt to get everyone on the same page. The colleague was diverting the speaker from seeing and acknowledging differences, and toward finding similarities. However, not all the participants were American. We were not all white. We were not all male. We were not all straight. We did not all speak English as a first language. We probably did not share the same ability status. Even the colleague who made that statement was not American. The everyday trauma of American life may have made them forget their non-Americanness or nonwhiteness at the time. Even though there were no white American men on the work team, this colleague acted as if we were all the same because of the messages they had received about the importance of conformity and fitting in.

Yet differences do not have to be divisive. We do not have to fear them. We can see our differences and use them to gain a deeper understanding of an issue or context. We do not have to give in to mass-media messages about sameness and erase our identities in the process of reaching some kind of consensus or unity. If the individuals at that meeting had been brave enough to acknowledge who they really were and to see themselves clearly, they could have done better work as they brought their complete selves to the collaboration and co-creation process—and they could have gained a deeper understanding of the problem at hand from many different points of view. A restorative design process opens space for us to bring these multiple identities into perspective.

In a society that often expects our conformity, we can pause to intentionally reflect on our identities and positionalities, as well as how these show up in our work as designers. Most people experience some level of both privilege and oppression, and many of us hold both historically excluded and included identities. This historical exclusion and inclusion may change according to where we are.

For example, I am a Black woman from Trinidad and Tobago in the Caribbean. In my country, my historically included identities might be that I am from Trinidad, not Tobago. I was born and grew up in the north, near (and sometimes in) the capital city. I am middle class. When I relocated to Brazil for college, I gained a different historically included identity because I spoke English. However, being Black gave a new dimension to my historically excluded identities. Later, in migrating to the United States, I went from being upper middle class to a situational, temporary state of poverty due to my status as a student. My non-Americanness was another new, excluded identity.

Not all our identities are visible. Some are invisible but still significant, and we may feel pressured to hide some of our identities. For example, some might hide their gender identity and others might hide their ethnic origin if they blend in with the dominant group.

These examples demonstrate that we can all identify with inclusion and exclusion. As designers working with and for others, we can reflect on other people's experiences through the lenses of historical inclusion and exclusion and learn to empathize with these positions. Being able to see and appreciate our own varied identities clearly, as well as those that our colleagues, clients, and intended users choose to share with us, helps us recognize that we are not designing for large, monolithic groups—in fact, we are designing for individuals with specific characteristics. Recognizing this may help us better understand the multiplicity of perspectives that we should take into consideration as we design for varied audiences.

As the first step of the restorative process, meet yourself where you are and reflect on who you are, with the help of these questions:

1. Reflect on specific elements of your identity, such as your:
   - Race
   - Gender
   - Age
   - Ability status
   - Native language
   - Class as a child versus class today
   - Education level
   - Job/title
2. If you were to describe yourself to another person, which of the above descriptors would you automatically include, and which would you exclude? Why might you include or exclude them? These identity markers could reveal some of your biases. Being aware of these tendencies could help you mitigate such biases.
3. What are your historically included and historically excluded identities? By identifying both where you have experienced privilege and where you have experienced marginalization or oppression, you can begin to understand the complexity of other people around you. This can give you an entry point to conversations about inclusion and exclusion with others as you seek to understand their perspectives.
4. What do you know about your racial and ethnic background and the experiences of other people within your group? Your racial and ethnic background is much richer than what is described in the media. Spend some time understanding who you are. Explore where your name came from and where your people may have come from. Research the lives and experiences of people with a similar heritage if your story has been lost within your own family.

   My own last name, Noel, is French, and my father's parents were from Grenada, where people spoke French and French patois. Noel, which means Christmas, is probably a name that was given to an enslaved person. We have speculated that it was because the plantation or its owners may have been called Noel, or the original Noel arrived at Christmastime.

It is a very common name in Grenada. One of my relatives traced our history all the way back to the Congo.

5. What elements of your own identity do you feel pressured to hide? Why? Understanding why you might feel this pressure could support you as you move beyond the trauma of the pressure to fit in. Are you hiding these identities for the perceived comfort of others? To escape judgment? To advance socially? What would be the real consequences of not hiding these identities?

   First, understand and encounter yourself, then seek to understand others and encounter them with openness and love. How can you support others on their own identity development journeys?

References

Anthony, K. H. (2001). *Designing for Diversity: Gender, Race, and Ethnicity in the Architectural Profession*. University of Illinois Press.

Malterud, K. (2001). "Qualitative Research: Standards, Challenges, and Guidelines." *Qualitative Research* 358, no. 928: 483–84.

2.8

Eurocentrism and the Disconnect in Design Education: Fostering Diversity and Inclusion

Omari Souza and Lesley-Ann Noel

The conversation about inclusivity in design is not a new one, and it has been percolating in the academy and beyond for decades. In a 1999 article on design education, the British design professor Teal Triggs (1999) highlighted the significance of publishing the work of emerging researchers to develop new design narratives. Almost thirty years later, in an op-ed published January 2, 2017, the design journalist Margaret Andersen highlighted the importance of seeking inspiration and insights from programs across the globe that embrace diversity and inclusion in their approach to design education. Andersen emphasized the need for American design programs to learn from the perspectives and approaches of their international counterparts in order to foster a more inclusive and diverse educational community for students.

It helps to exercise a conscious awareness of whose stories we've told and ignored in design education, which can unwittingly affect design students who have internalized messages about "good" versus "bad" design. For example, when Lesley-Ann taught design in Trinidad, it frustrated her that the students who considered themselves at the top of the design class would often erase all the "Trinidadian-ness" from their work to do work that they considered "designerly" enough.

The dominant narrative about "good" design is that it is modern, male, European or American, and expresses wealth or affluence. Traditionally, it focuses more on objects and artifacts than on process or on possibilities for other modes of practice. Students who constantly receive messages in their industrial design and graphic design classes that the work they produce must follow a specific type of aesthetic will erase their own identities and knowledge as they try to meet this more homogenized standard.

In design histories, we have told stories about design from Europe and North America, not about design from Latin America, the Caribbean, Asia, and Africa. We have told stories about white people and not stories about design by people of color. We have told stories about design for the rich and not design for the masses. Until recently, examples of grassroots design, co-design, and bottom-up design were not often shared without some anthropological curiosity. When design stories are told that include people of color, people who are not rich, or people who are from Africa, the Caribbean, Latin America, and Asia, these people are often othered. The stories are not told from their own point of view, either; rather, they are presented from an outside perspective.

When Lesley-Ann grew up in Trinidad, she never experienced being the "only one," as many Black and Brown people in the United States have experienced. As a child, she was never perceived as a threat to others just because of the color of her skin. She wasn't at the top of her class in high school, but she was close enough. She grew up with the confidence to assert herself and occupy a variety of spaces. And as an undergraduate student in Brazil, her foreignness and English-language ability trumped the color of her skin. So, even though she was one of very few Black students in her program, she never suffered for that. She was popular with other students and with professors. People were curious about her and her background. She didn't really notice how design and design history courses—even the Brazilian design history course—ignored or erased people like her.

As a child, Omari's time at Our Lady of Mount Carmel, a Catholic school in the South Bronx, exposed him to a curriculum steeped in Eurocentric narratives. The lack of diversity in the images and stories presented left him questioning his own worth and identity, as the historical figures and heroes he learned about did not reflect his background. This initial experience of feeling disconnected from his educational content underscored the need for diverse representation. However, a transformative shift occurred when his family relocated and he began attending P.S. 78X, a public school with a predominantly Black and Afro-Latino student body. Under the guidance of his second-grade teacher, Mrs. Greenwich, who introduced him to role models and stories that mirrored his experiences, Omari was able to more fully embrace his cultural identity. This newfound connection to his heritage through education was pivotal in shaping his self-understanding and highlighted the critical need for inclusive narratives in both design and education.

The dichotomy of exploring his culture versus navigating its acceptance in design classrooms became a challenge Omari would grapple with during his college years. Attending a small private art college in Cleveland, Omari was one of the first people of color many of his classmates had seen outside of television. The lack of familiarity with

Black culture was stark; for example, his roommate could not differentiate between DMX, the rapper, and Malcolm X, the Civil Rights leader. This ignorance was accompanied by a notable lack of curiosity about Black culture, which made it difficult for Omari to engage with non-Eurocentric subject matter in his design work. As a result, he found himself having to limit his classroom explorations to what was acceptable within a Eurocentric framework while pursuing his explorations in non-Eurocentric visual cultural independently. This experience underscores the challenge of navigating and integrating one's marginalized cultural identity in environments that lack appreciation or understanding of diverse perspectives.

It is imperative that we reshape the narrative in design education. As designers, our traditional focus is often on creating for individuals different from ourselves. If we exclusively design based on shallow assumptions about the identities and needs of others, we risk perpetuating stereotypes and unintentionally creating barriers to meaningful experiences. Even as designers of color, we must be intentional about breaking away from the limited, Eurocentric perspective that has dominated the field for too long. Design should not be synonymous with a singular, standardized aesthetic; instead, it should embrace the richness of global diversity and representation. It is only when we genuinely decentralize the design aesthetic, inviting practitioners from all backgrounds to participate as their whole and authentic selves, that we can unlock the field's full potential. By doing so, we not only expand the horizons of design but also dismantle the harmful stereotypes and biases that persist in broader society.

Fostering a comprehensive conversation about design requires recognizing and embracing diverse voices and perspectives. Universities are tasked with the responsibility to create a more inclusive and well-rounded learning experience for students by prioritizing diversity and decolonizing design education.

In the United Kingdom, integrating research degrees in art and design has fostered a broader appetite for an approach that includes interdisciplinary studies and engages with decolonization. The United States can and should consider adopting a transdisciplinary approach to design education that acknowledges and incorporates Indigenous design history. Certainly, the lack of diversity in design curricula and the dominance of Eurocentric perspectives in American higher education are deterrents to such an approach. However, First Nations designers like Sadie Red Wing and Neebin Southall are strong advocates for the inclusion of Indigenous design and the promotion of visual sovereignty. Red Wing emphasizes the importance of using specific cultural visual languages instead of perpetuating generalized "pan-Indian" motifs. Unfortunately, many tribal colleges in the United States lack comprehensive design programs, limiting opportunities for Native American students.

Design programs in other parts of the world are also addressing the need for a more inclusive approach. Initiatives in Australia, Zimbabwe, and South Africa focus on Indigenous principles, rediscovering suppressed visual languages and advocating for Indigenous African design systems. Design historians and professors worldwide are curating exhibitions, developing curricula, and promoting cross-cultural experiences to decolonize design education.

Let us recognize that the excellence of a design hinges not on its resemblance to the traditions of a specific identity or location but on its capacity to reflect and serve the diverse needs and experiences of our interconnected world. This transformative shift in perspective holds the power to foster inclusivity, innovation, and genuine representation in the realm of design education, which will have massive impacts on students who do not see their own cultures and identities reflected in the classroom.

References

Andersen, M. (2017, January 2). "Design Education Must Embrace Global Diversity." *Design Week*.

Triggs, T. (1999). "A Critical Reflection of Design Education in the 1990s." *Design Issues* 15, no. 3: 15–25.

2.9

Design Tools for Engagement: With, Not For

In the field of UX design, personas are a commonly used tool. The UX designer or principal investigator will combine user interviews, surveys, case studies, and a variety of other research methods to craft a persona, which is a user profile that is intended to place the designer in the shoes of users. However, without the thoughtful incorporation of co-design (participatory design that involves all stakeholders), personas center the expertise of the designer and prioritize collected insights over the lived experience of the user—an approach that is anti-restorative.

As a professor, I've often used dating profiles to illustrate the difference between personas and co-design. Many dating companies ask singles to complete a survey and to provide a series of headshots or lifestyle images. Once the user has matched, some providers encourage a first call (or mutual interview) before the first date.

During these initial steps, each party attains only a surface-level understanding of their prospective partner. Neither at this stage can confidently identify the long-term goals, cultural values, or ideological center of their potential. This detailed degree of knowledge requires a vulnerability that is earned only over time. Dating profiles are comparable to personas, while the process of dating, with the extended interaction it involves, is more like the act of co-design.

We have an opportunity to identify new roles and skills for designers if we choose to move away from uncontested personas that privilege the so-called expert, and to move toward co-design.

First, we can acknowledge that everyone designs. It's an innate human ability. People in communities use design with or without designers, even when they do not call it design. For example, when people organize a space by arranging the furniture to make it more functional or pleasing, they engage in interior design. Choosing colors for clothing, home decor, or websites based on preference or mood involves design principles, even if they don't realize it. Setting up workspaces to improve productivity and comfort is also a form of design. Gardening and landscaping, which involve deciding where to plant flowers or trees based on sunlight and aesthetics, are types of design, too. Organizing events, arranging items in a kitchen for efficiency, and even cooking and presenting food all involve design principles, as do digital content creation, fashion choices, and travel planning. In these examples, people make design decisions based on their preferences and needs, even if they don't formally recognize these activities as design.

When designers recognize this existing capacity before co-designing even begins, they embrace humility and collaboration. At the same time, this process can send a designer into a kind of existential crisis—especially if they think, *So, what am I doing if people are already designing?*

As designers, we have been taught to see ourselves as the experts. Those of us in service design may have had different aspirations, but many of us in industrial and graphic design wanted people to remember our names because of the chairs, posters, or fonts we created.

Some designers today are being educated in a different way, focusing instead on social benefits and transformational processes. They are attempting to create more participatory processes that are compatible with activism, social justice, and collective wellness. And the good news is that the field of social design is booming.

Social design is, in its broadest sense, the use of design to address and ultimately solve social problems (Janzer and Weinstein 2014). These issues may include poverty, homelessness, climate change, overpopulation, immigration stresses, racial discrimination, gender inequality, access to health care, and more. The field of social design has created new opportunities for designers to engage with communities—often, communities that are underserved and routinely ignored by designers.

In social design, designers are no longer experts, but rather co-designers and facilitators. Sometimes we amplify other people's work rather than creating something for them. Sometimes we are activists, organizers, logistics planners, listeners, and counselors. In these versatile roles, we must ensure that there is space for others to participate, perhaps by doing things they may never have previously considered doing.

Acquiring additional skills becomes essential when taking on multiple roles within community-engaged social design practice. We must learn to observe, listen, respect, negotiate power dynamics, and provide support. In this process, co-design aims to shift power and democratize design by fostering collaboration and active participation.

Creating communities is a fundamental aspect of this practice. As Henri Nouwen (2018), a Jesuit priest, suggests, "Caring together is the basis of community life." A community can be defined as a group of people who are connected around a shared experience. It can be geographic, organized around where the individuals live or work, and it also can be based on a shared identity, like race or gender.

Identifying shared concerns and interests allows communities of like-minded individuals to form, but we must be especially intentional about *how* we form. In her work on teaching community, bell hooks (2003) emphasizes the need to challenge and dismantle socialization that perpetuates domination and conformity. Critical pedagogues advocate for "desocialization," which involves unlearning ingrained oppressive practices. Such approaches can ensure that instead of perpetuating systems of oppression, communities serve as nourishing spaces of support, especially when engaging in challenging work and resisting racism, patriarchy, and other potentially harmful systems that may undermine essential efforts to harness the gifts of all stakeholders.

Designers can take a variety of approaches to community-level design: design *for*, design *with*, and design *by* the community. In the first example, a designer might address issues on behalf of the community, based on conducting research and proposing solutions. In the second, a designer could emphasize collaboration and participation, working alongside the community in a restorative approach. In the third, community members cluster together as a collective, helming the design process under the premise that everyone involved is bringing their expertise to the table, regardless of whether they hold the title of "designer." This final approach is the most radical and restorative when it comes to community design. In design by, the designer can play a supporting role in the design process.

Co-design principles (which largely center on the idea of design with) include sharing power and building relationships through participatory means. Building trust and relationships is crucial, and the process often requires slowing down and creating the right environment for collaboration, involving elements like food, drink, music, dance, and storytelling. As an aspect of co-design, participatory design involves end users in the design process,

Design Steps	Nonrestorative	Restorative
Research	1.1 Designer-led research without community involvement 1.2 Focus on quantitative data only	1.1 Conducting surveys, focus groups, and community meetings involving community members
Problem Definition and Framing	2.1 Framing problems based solely on designer's perspective 2.2 Ignoring historical and cultural context	2.1 Understanding the historical and cultural context 2.2 Framing problems considering socio-economic dynamics
Engagement and Outreach	3.1 Sporadic or one-time engagement 3.2 Minimal feedback collection	3.1 Regular engagement with community members for input and feedback
Ideation	4.1 Designer-driven ideation 4.2 Minimal community input	4.1 Encouraging collaborative decision-making with community members
Co-Creation and Collaboration	5.1 Limited or no community participation in the design process	5.1Workshops and charrettes with community input foster shared ownership of solutions.
Prototyping	6.1 Developing prototypes without community input	6.1 Developing prototypes without community input
Design Iteration and Feedback	7.1 Limited iterations based on internal feedback 7.2 Ignoring community feedback	7.1 Implementing iterative design cycles Regularly seeking and incorporating feedback from the community
Capacity-Building and Education	8.1 No effort to educate or empower community members	8.1 Training empowers residents to engage in design process.
Testing	9.1 Testing solutions without community involvement	9.1 Pilot solutions and assess effectiveness with community input.
Implementation and Monitoring	10.1 Implementing solutions without ongoing community engagement 10.2 No monitoring	10.1 Develop solutions with community input; monitor and adjust based on feedback.
Sustainability and Long-Term Engagement	11.1 Short-term focus 11.2 Lack of plans for sustained community involvement	11.1 Ensure sustainable designs and ongoing community involvement.
Evaluation and Reflection	12.1 Limited or no evaluation involving the community	12.1 Evaluating outcomes and impact with community input 12.2 Reflecting on the process and identifying lessons learned in collaboration with the community

This chart is influenced by restorative design principles, which emphasize the importance of community engagement, shared ownership, and iterative collaboration throughout the design process. It contrasts traditional, nonrestorative approaches that center the designer's expertise with restorative methods that involve community members at every stage. The framework can be used to guide designers in adopting more inclusive, participatory practices that prioritize the needs, experiences, and voices of the communities they serve, ultimately fostering more equitable and sustainable design outcomes.

aiming to create products and services that better meet community members' needs and expectations by leveraging their knowledge and experiences. Both co-design and participatory design bring the beneficiaries of the design process closer to or into the process, granting the community more agency.

A Spectrum of Restorative Approaches to Community Design

Bringing restorative design methods into community practice can create new modes of practice. Several theorists have questioned design's focus on solving problems and the creation of artifacts, products, and services. In community work, and through a worldview that celebrates interdependence and relationality, new design questions can emerge and design methods with wildly different aims (such as the creation of new societies) can be employed. In this process, co-design can occur at the community level, free of a corporate agenda. This application of design is focused not merely on generating more goods but on constructing spaces that reflect more human, egalitarian, and collaborative values that are intentionally inclusive and mindful of all the voices that can be given a rightful seat at the table.

References

hooks, b. (2003). *Teaching Community: A Pedagogy of Hope*. Routledge.

Janzer, C., and Weinstein, L. (2014). "Social Design and Neocolonialism." *Design and Culture* 6, no. 3: 327–43. Retrieved August 27, 2024, from https://doi.org/10.2752/175470814X14079468624169

Nouwen, H. J. M. (2018). *Community and Growth: Our Pilgrimage Together*. Image Books.

2.10

Branding America: Expanding the Lens Beyond Eurocentrism

Nike, personification of victory, driving a four-horse chariot. Terracotta bell krater used for wine, Classical 5th century BC, Greek Attic, 40 cm.

A brand is much more than a name or a logo. As competition creates infinite choices, companies strive to connect emotionally with consumers, aiming to become irreplaceable and to create lifelong relationships (Wheeler 2013). A strong brand stands out in a densely crowded marketplace, fostering love, trust, and a sense of superiority among its followers. How a brand is perceived significantly affects its success, regardless of whether it is a startup, nonprofit, or product. Brands communicate through signs that consumers can interact with, generating feelings of authenticity, patriotism, and community. Although they may be artificially generated (through the power of suggestion and repetition), these connections are construed as meaningful, as they help people relate to each other and the brand itself.

Consider Nike, initially known as Blue Ribbon Sports, which has evolved into a multinational corporation known for its footwear and apparel (Frisch 2009). The name Nike, chosen by an employee named Jeff Johnson, pays homage to the Greek goddess of victory, symbolizing the desire to win. The iconic Nike swoosh represents her speed and power. By pairing the swoosh with athletes like Michael Jordan, Mia Hamm, Roger Federer, Serena Williams, and

Tiger Woods, Nike connects its products with champions. This association makes Nike apparel the choice of champions, promoting the idea that buying into the brand is the first step to becoming a champion.

This phenomenon exemplifies what the Frankfurt school calls *pseudo-individuality*, wherein culture industries create the illusion of individuality while selling a homogeneous experience. Branding is a powerful force that extends beyond products and services, embedding itself deeply within social hierarchies and cultural identities. The concept of branding can be dissected to reveal how it influences perceptions of value and status within a society, often perpetuating existing social hierarchies and creating new forms of inclusion and exclusion—in sectors as far-ranging as national identity.

Artists like Kara Walker have highlighted such themes in their work. Walker's installations, such as her sugar sculptures in the old Domino Sugar Factory, directly confront the legacy of slavery and the commodification of Black bodies (Forster 2014). The use of sugar, a product historically linked to slave labor, as a medium for her art underscores the deep connections between branding, consumer culture, and social hierarchies. Walker's work forces viewers to confront the uncomfortable truths about how historical injustices continue to shape contemporary branding and identity.

The concept of branding as a marker of social status is further explored by artists like Hank Willis Thomas. In his series *Branded*, Thomas draws connections between modern product branding and historical practices of branding livestock and enslaved people. This comparison forces us to consider how branding functions as a form of social stratification (Mora 2020).

In the past, enslaved people were branded to signify ownership, a dehumanizing practice that reduced human beings to property. In contemporary society, voluntary branding through consumer choices signifies social mobility or status. Individuals lower in the social hierarchy may use branded products to signal their allegiance to higher-status groups, as they seek recognition and acceptance.

The American flag, with its specific color palette—blue for vigilance, perseverance, and justice; red for hardiness and valor; and white for purity and innocence—serves as a powerful brand symbol for the United States (USA.gov

2023). These colors and their associated values create a unified national identity yet also expose underlying social hierarchies. For example, the concept of brand architecture can be applied to the nation itself. The United States is the parent brand, with states acting as subsidiaries, each with its own identity yet contributing to the overall brand. Territories like Puerto Rico can be seen as products or services, often marginalized within the larger national narrative.

National tragedies often serve as a lens through which the complex hierarchy and dynamics of brand perception can be observed. The way these events are handled, by both the nation and the media, reveals much about the underlying social structures and the value placed on different "subsidiaries" and "products" within the nation.

On September 11, 2001, the United States experienced a catastrophic terrorist attack that forever changed the national landscape. The immediate response from the federal government, led by then-President George W. Bush, was to launch the War on Terror, targeting those responsible for the attacks. This decisive action was aimed at protecting the nation's brand and reassuring its subsidiaries—states and cities—of their safety and unity.

New York City, the site of the World Trade Center attacks, received an outpouring of support and solidarity from across the nation. This display of unity was crucial in maintaining a cohesive national identity and demonstrating resilience in the face of adversity. However, despite the national focus on unity and resilience, the first responders—firefighters, police officers, and medical personnel—who played a crucial role in managing the immediate aftermath of the attacks were often overlooked in the long term. Many suffered from cancer, respiratory illnesses, and other health issues due to the toxic dust and debris at Ground Zero (Centers for Disease Control and Prevention, n.d.). While initially hailed as heroes, these individuals faced significant challenges in receiving necessary medical care and support. Media coverage initially highlighted their heroism, but over time, the narrative shifted toward the broader geopolitical ramifications, often sidelining the ongoing struggles of the first responders.

In contrast, the response to Hurricane Katrina in August 2005 highlighted significant disparities in how different regions and populations were valued within the national hierarchy. The hurricane devastated parts of the Gulf Coast, particularly New Orleans, leading to catastrophic flooding, significant loss of life, and widespread destruction. The federal response to Hurricane Katrina was widely criticized for its lack of urgency and efficiency, exposing deep racial and socioeconomic fissures (Walsh 2015). Unlike the solidarity that was witnessed after 9/11, the response to Katrina revealed significant neglect and prejudice, particularly toward the predominantly Black residents of New Orleans.

Media coverage of Hurricane Katrina was starkly different from that of 9/11. Black residents seeking food and supplies were often labeled looters (NBC News 2005), while white residents were described as "finding" food (Jones 2005). This biased portrayal reinforced harmful stereotypes and underscored the racial inequities in the nation's response. Images of Black residents waving the American flag were particularly poignant. These individuals, stranded and desperate, used the flag to signal their citizenship and plead for the same recognition and aid as other Americans (Harris-Perry 2011). This act of waving the flag symbolized their assertion of belonging to the nation, despite evident neglect.

The long-term impact on New Orleans residents, particularly the Black community, has been profound. Many have struggled to rebuild their lives and homes, as they've continued to face systemic barriers and ongoing discrimination. The racial and socioeconomic disparities exposed by Hurricane Katrina continue to resonate, underscoring the need for a more inclusive and equitable national identity rather than a superficial "brand" that signals solidarity without actually offering it. National tragedies illuminate the complexities of brand perception and the inherent inequalities within the nation. By analyzing these events, we gain insight into the value placed on different regions and populations, calling for a reevaluation of national identity and aiming for a more inclusive and equitable representation of all constituents.

Cultural representation and inclusivity are crucial concepts in understanding how brands, media, and society at large depict and integrate various cultural identities (Storr 2018). The narratives and symbols we encounter daily shape our perceptions of different cultures and influence social norms and values.

Cinqué, The Chief of the Amistad Captives. Painting by Nathaniel Jocelyn (1796–1881), dated 1839.

Historically, representation has often been skewed toward Eurocentric ideals, marginalizing other cultural identities. This imbalance is evident in various aspects of media, from the portrayal of characters in films and TV shows to the selection of models in advertising campaigns (Shohat and Stam 2014). For instance, until very recently, Disney princesses had long epitomized Eurocentric beauty standards, with characters predominantly featuring fair skin, slim figures, and European facial features. This limited representation can have profound effects on how young and impressionable viewers perceive beauty and worth.

Cultural representation in media is crucial because it shapes our perceptions of the world and our understanding of different people. Unfortunately, media sometimes portray racial and ethnic groups in ways that reinforce harmful stereotypes. For instance, in children's cartoons, villains often have darker skin tones and exaggerated ethnic features. This can perpetuate the false notion that having darker skin or different features is inherently negative. Such portrayals can imply that being white is inherently good and being nonwhite is bad, which is deeply damaging.

One historical example of the struggle for positive cultural representation is the story of the *Amistad* slave revolt in 1839. Joseph Cinqué, the leader of this revolt, was captured and taken on a ship called the *Amistad*. He led a successful rebellion against his captors, and abolitionists used images of Cinqué to support their cause (Pinder 2002). Abolitionists aimed to demonstrate that Africans were not savages but human beings deserving of freedom. They commissioned a painting of Cinqué by the artist Nathaniel Jocelyn to achieve this. Robert Purvis, a wealthy African American abolitionist from Philadelphia, requested the painting, which depicted Cinqué in a dignified manner, akin to a hero from ancient Greece or Rome, to ensure that he was represented as a noble, wise leader.

The painting was created with good intentions, but it conformed to artistic styles familiar to Western audiences at the time. By presenting Cinqué as resembling Western philosophers and Christian icons, abolitionists hoped people would recognize the humanity of the *Amistad* captives. Some even referred to Cinqué as a "Roman African" due to his depiction (Pinder 2002). However, this approach had limitations; while the painting helped people view Cinqué and the *Amistad* captives as human, it also suggested that their worth was contingent on their resemblance to white, Western ideals. In some regards, the toga placed on Cinqué in the image had a function similar to Black New Orleans residents' waving of the American flag in hopes of rescue—a plea for the same recognition and aid as other Americans.

There was little to no interest in sharing aspects of the *Amistad* captives' culture, which was viewed as inferior or inconsequential. This raises questions about how the captives would have represented themselves if permitted. Even if they chose to utilize Western elements in their representation, how would they have challenged perceptions of themselves? How would they have posed? What symbols or icons would they have used to depict who they truly were?

Despite these complexities in representation, the image of Joseph Cinqué became a powerful symbol in the fight against slavery. It helped many to recognize the injustice of slavery and to simultaneously behold the strength and dignity of those who resisted it. This image remains an important icon in the history of the antislavery movement.

The story of Joseph Cinqué and the *Amistad* revolt underscores the historical struggle for positive representations of African Americans in art and culture. It sets the stage for understanding the contemporary efforts of artists like Kehinde Wiley and Faith Ringgold, who have worked to challenge and subvert the white gaze in their art. By reclaiming artistic spaces and redefining narratives surrounding Black identity, both Wiley and Ringgold offer powerful counternarratives that confront historical and ongoing misrepresentations, celebrating the dignity, resilience, and rich cultural heritage of African Americans.

Wiley, a contemporary American artist, is renowned for his striking portraits in celebration of Black identity. Born in Los Angeles in 1977, Wiley merges classical European portraiture with modern African American culture. His large-scale paintings are known for their vibrant colors, ornate patterns, and detailed realism. These elements help Wiley challenge historical norms and present a bold counternarrative to traditional depictions of power and nobility in Western art (Cadet 2023).

Wiley's art is significant because it portrays Black men and women in poses and settings traditionally reserved for white subjects of power and privilege. Kehinde Wiley's art puts Black people at the center, celebrating them in bold poses and modern clothing that doesn't follow European styles or aim to make white viewers comfortable. Unlike Nathaniel Jocelyn's painting of Cinqué, which dressed him like a Western hero to appeal to a white audience, Wiley's approach lets Black subjects be powerful on their own terms. Wiley challenges the typical art tradition that often ignores or sidelines Black people, showing them with dignity and strength instead. By drawing inspiration from old European paintings, Wiley places his modern subjects in heroic and noble stances. This act of reclaiming space for Black people in art asserts their dignity and worth where they have historically been excluded (Moss 2019).

One of the most important aspects of Wiley's work is how it challenges the white gaze. Historically, art has often marginalized or made Black individuals invisible. Wiley disrupts this practice by placing Black figures at the center of his compositions, depicting them with grandeur and respect typically reserved for white aristocracy. This elevates his subjects and forces viewers to reconsider their perceptions of race and beauty (King 2023).

Wiley's work also critiques systemic racism and state-sanctioned violence against Black people. His series, *An Archaeology of Silence*, reflects on the deaths of Black individuals due to police brutality, drawing parallels between contemporary issues and historical martyrdom. By depicting lifeless Black bodies with reverence and resilience, Wiley underscores the ongoing struggle against oppression and the importance of valuing Black lives (Cadet 2023).

While Wiley paints Black people in ways that challenge old ideas about who can be a hero in art, Ringgold uses quilts and storytelling to show Black experiences that demand respect and understanding. Ringgold, born in Harlem in 1930, was a revolutionary artist whose works include painting, quilting, sculpture, performance art, and children's literature. Her art addresses issues of race, gender, and social justice. Influenced by the Harlem Renaissance and the Civil Rights Movement, Ringgold's early work, like the *American People* series, reflects the racial tensions of the time. For instance, *Die* (1967) depicts graphic scenes of street violence, highlighting social issues often ignored by mainstream media (Guggenheim, n.d.; NPR 2024).

Ringgold's style evolved to include quilting, a medium rich in African American history. Her first quilt, *Echoes of Harlem* (1980), created with her mother, marked the start of her story quilts. These quilts blend visual art and narrative, allowing Ringgold to publish her unedited words and stories. For example, *Who's Afraid of Aunt Jemima?* (1983) challenges the stereotypical representation of African American women by transforming the Aunt Jemima figure into a powerful, business-savvy character (Ringgold, n.d.; VoCA 2021).

Ringgold's quilts consistently challenge the white gaze by presenting African American experiences that demand recognition and respect. By addressing themes of identity and resistance through a medium associated with women's domestic labor, she reclaims space for African American stories and histories. This subversion of traditional connotations of quilting highlights the broader critique of social injustice, making her a pivotal figure in the Black Arts Movement (Artsy Editorial 2016; VoCA 2021).

To make design more inclusive and move it beyond Eurocentric ideas, design firms, companies, and practitioners need to incorporate individuals from a variety of cultural backgrounds into their teams, particularly when creating artifacts, services, or experiences intended for a multicultural audience. If designers are uncertain about whom to contact, especially when on a nondiverse team and not in charge of hiring, working with community leaders and cultural organizations can offer valuable insights. This collaboration enables brands to understand and represent diverse cultures more accurately, thereby connecting with a broader audience and making everyone feel valued and included.

Additionally, brands must strive to break away from harmful stereotypes and portray diverse characters in positive and authentic roles, reflecting their true identities rather than offering mere caricatures or distortions. Designers must move beyond clichéd depictions and instead tell stories that highlight the strength, creativity, and everyday lives of people from different backgrounds. This approach fosters a more balanced and fair representation of the world, allowing everyone to see themselves reflected positively in the media they consume.

References

Artsy Editorial. (2016). "The Enduring Power of Faith Ringgold's Art." *Artsy*. Retrieved from https://www.artsy.net/article/artsy-editorial-why-faith-ringgold-matters

Cadet, A. (2023, February 23). "Kehinde Wiley's Reclamation of Black Lives." Fine Arts Museums of San Francisco. Retrieved from https://www.famsf.org/stories/kehinde-wiley-reclamation-black-lives

Centers for Disease Control and Prevention. (n.d.). "Health Risks Associated with 9/11 and the WTC Disaster: Lessons Learned." World Trade Center Health Program. Retrieved June 22, 2024, from https://www.cdc.gov/wtc/training/healthRisks/911_Health_Risks.pdf

Forster, I. (2014, May 23). "The Making of Kara Walker's *Sugar Sphinx*." *Art21 Magazine*. Retrieved June 22, 2024, from https://magazine.art21.org/2014/05/23/the-making-of-kara-walkers-sugar-sphinx/

Frisch, A. (2009). *The Story of Nike*. The Creative Company.

Guggenheim. (n.d.). Faith Ringgold. Retrieved from https://www.guggenheim.org/artwork/artist/faith-ringgold

Harris-Perry, M. V. (2011). *Sister Citizen: Shame, Stereotypes, and Black Women in America*. Yale University Press.

Jones, V. (2005, September 1). "Black People 'Loot' Food . . . White People 'Find' Food." *HuffPost*. Retrieved June 22, 2024, from https://www.huffpost.com/entry/black-people-loot-food-wh_b_6614

King, E. (2023). "Kehinde Wiley: Redefining Portraiture Through Symbolism and Subversion." My Art Broker. Retrieved from https://www.myartbroker.com/artist-kehinde-wiley/articles/kehinde-wiley-redefining-portraiture-symbolism-subversion

Mora, M. (2020, June 25). "Hank Willis Thomas: Branding Black Identity." *Musée Magazine*. Retrieved June 22, 2024, from https://museemagazine.com/features/2020/6/24/hank-willis-thomas-branding-black-identity

Moss, M. (2019, December 8). "Highlighting Black Artists: Kehinde Wiley." Contemporary Racism. Retrieved from https://contemporaryracism.org/27607/highlighting-black-artists-kehinde-wiley

NBC News. (2005, August 30). "Looters Take Advantage of New Orleans Mess." NBC News. Retrieved June 22, 2024, from https://www.nbcnews.com/id/wbna9131493

NPR. (2014, April 13). "Faith Ringgold, Quilt and Visual Artist, Dies at 93." *Morning Edition*. Retrieved from https://www.npr.org/2024/04/13/685930840/faith-ringgold-quilt-and-visual-artist-dies-at-93

Pinder, K. N., ed. (2002). *Race-ing Art History: Critical Readings in Race and Art History*. Routledge.

Ringgold, F. (n.d.). Faith Ringgold website. Retrieved from https://www.faithringgold.com

Shohat, E., and Stam, R. (2014). *Unthinking Eurocentrism: Multiculturalism and the Media*. Routledge.

Storr, W. (2018). *Selfie: How We Became So Self-Obsessed and What It's Doing to Us*. Harry N. Abrams.

USA.gov. (2023, December 29). "The American Flag and Other National Symbols." USA.gov. Retrieved June 22, 2024, from https://www.usa.gov/flag

VoCA. (2021, February 26). "An Exploration of the Work of Faith Ringgold." VoCA Network. Retrieved from https://voca.network/blog/2021/02/26/an-exploration-of-the-work-of-faith-ringgold/

Walsh, K. T. (2015, August 28). "Hurricane Katrina Was the Beginning of the End for George W. Bush." USNews.com. Retrieved June 22, 2024, from https://www.usnews.com/news/the-report/articles/2015/08/28/hurricane-katrina-was-the-beginning-of-the-end-for-george-w-bush

Wheeler, A. (2013). *Designing Brand Identity: An Essential Guide for the Whole Branding Team*. Wiley.

2.11

Africatown: A Space of Liberation and Generational Transformation

Cudjoe Kazoola Lewis (born Oluale Kossola), whose story was told by Zora Neale Hurston in *Barracoon: The Story of the Last "Black Cargo,"* was one of the last known survivors of the transatlantic slave trade. He was captured in West Africa and brought to the United States aboard the illegal slave ship *Clotilda* in 1860. The *Clotilda* smuggled 110 African captives into the United States, despite the transatlantic slave trade being outlawed.

In 1866, after gaining freedom, Lewis and other survivors of the *Clotilda* established the community of Africatown near Mobile, Alabama (Cetta et al. 2023). Africatown was one of the few communities in the United States founded and governed by formerly enslaved Africans. Altogether, Africatown stands as a testament to resilience, community, and the pursuit of freedom. Its founders sought to live independently and evade white supervision; the community became a safe haven for Black individuals and a place to preserve their African traditions and heritage (Keyes 2019). In the aftermath of the Civil War and emancipation, Africatown welcomed individuals from diverse ethnic backgrounds, creating a close-knit community spanning approximately fifty acres. An additional seven-acre section, situated two miles west, further expanded the reach of this unique enclave forged in the crucible of enslavement (Waters and Latham 2023). Today, Africatown still exists as a residential community, though it faces challenges related to preservation and environmental concerns, as efforts continue to honor and maintain its rich cultural heritage.

Africatown's founding was rooted in the desire to live free from the white gaze, allowing residents to forge their own destinies. This act of establishing a community was a deliberate effort to deconstruct the oppressive grid system that had historically constrained marginalized communities. Africatown demonstrates a different way of living, in opposition to the oppressive grid, which attempts to control and erase people's identities and agency.

The *Clotilda* was the last known ship to bring enslaved Africans to the United States. To keep it a secret, its crew had purposely sunk and hidden it in the Mobile River, as the slave trade had already been made illegal. When the ship was finally discovered in 2019,

Africatown Boulevard, the main road into Africatown. Africatown was founded by slaves from the slave ship *Clotilda*. Mobile, Alabama, March 5, 2021.

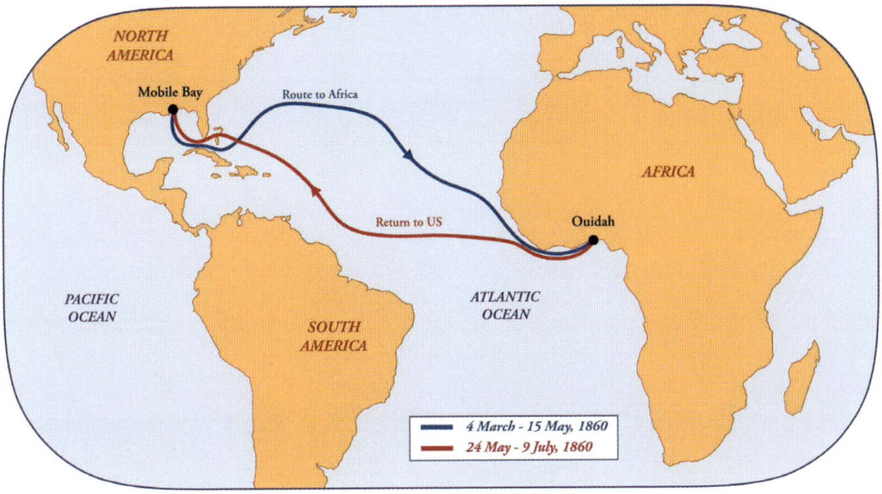

Map showing the journey of the *Clotilda* slave ship.

it proved the stories that had been told by the Africatown community for many years and brought this important part of history back into the light (Keyes 2019). The Africatown community worked hard to preserve that story and make sure it was remembered.

Over time, Africatown has evolved, with significant efforts made to honor its history and culture through intentional design and development. This includes the creation of educational and cultural spaces that tell the community's full story.

As we have explored, design can be understood as the thoughtful creation of spaces and experiences that add meaning to life. Africatown's modern design, which includes monuments, memorials, educational centers, and cultural landmarks, has been carefully developed to tell the story of the community's origins and its ongoing legacy. The Africatown Cemetery and the Cudjo Lewis House are historical sites that honor the founders and their families. In addition, the Africatown Heritage House and the Africatown Museum educate visitors about the community's rich history and cultural significance (Greene, n.d.).

The Africatown Cultural Mile connects these significant sites, creating a unified narrative about Africatown's past and present (Keyes 2019). The design process for these developments included descendants of Africatown's original residents, ensuring that the stories and heritage

National Museum of African American History and Culture, National Mall, Washington DC

of the community have been accurately and respectfully represented. Initiatives such as recording oral histories from current Africatown residents help to preserve and deepen the community's narrative. Through these efforts, Africatown's design not only honors its past but also ensures that its history, culture, and stories continue to be shared with future generations. By preserving African culture and traditions, Africatown demonstrates the enduring power of marginalized communities to stand against unfair treatment, inspiring others to make positive change even when faced with significant challenges.

In parallel, the architects David Adjaye and Francis Kéré are celebrated for their work in preserving and celebrating African heritage while empowering marginalized communities through innovative design. Adjaye's Smithsonian National Museum of African American History and Culture in Washington, DC, and Kéré's community-centric projects, like the Gando Primary School in Burkina Faso, reflect a deep commitment to cultural preservation, sustainability, and social empowerment. Though not directly influenced by Africatown, the work of each resonates with its spirit, challenging traditional architectural norms and embodying resilience, cultural continuity, and community strength.

The angular metal architecture of the National Museum of African American History and Culture contrasts with the Washington Monument at night.

Providing space for marginalized communities to exist and thrive is not merely an act of physical liberation; it is a profound restoration of humanity. Africatown's enduring legacy and the work of architects like Adjaye and Kéré reveal the transformative power of creating spaces that honor and preserve cultural identity. These efforts not only challenge oppressive systems but also offer a blueprint for a future where cultural heritage is celebrated and communities are empowered to shape their own destinies.

Africatown was created by people who overcame great hardships to make a safe and independent place for themselves. Likewise, Adjaye and Kéré design buildings that honor African heritage and help communities thrive. Their work, like the story of Africatown, demonstrates the power of standing up against unfairness and keeping cultural traditions alive. As we explore the achievements of these architects, we see how they, like Africatown, create spaces that celebrate history and inspire strength and pride.

In the heart of Washington, DC, the Smithsonian National Museum of African American History and Culture (NMAAHC) stands as a testament to resilience and cultural pride. Designed by Adjaye, this monumental structure embodies more than just architectural innovation—it is a beacon of African American heritage deeply embedded in its every facet (Smithsonian, n.d.; McKnight 2017).

Adjaye's journey as an architect is a tale of cultural integration and narrative-driven design. He was born in Ghana and raised across several countries, experiences that instilled in him a profound appreciation for global cultures. His architectural firm, Adjaye Associates, founded in 2000, has since become synonymous with designs that bridge the gap between cultural heritage and contemporary aesthetics.

The NMAAHC, completed in 2016, is perhaps Adjaye's most celebrated work. Its design is a deliberate homage to African and African American history, from the three-tiered Yoruban-inspired structure to the intricate bronze-colored lattice that envelops the building—a nod to the skilled ironwork of enslaved African Americans in the southern United States (McKnight 2017; Wainwright 2018).

Walking through the museum is akin to embarking on a journey through time and identity. The lower floors delve into the dark chapters of slavery and segregation, grounding visitors in the harsh realities faced by African Americans throughout history. As one ascends, the narrative shifts, celebrating the achievements and contributions of African Americans to art, science, and culture (Wainwright 2018).

Adjaye's approach extends beyond architectural aesthetics; it embodies a philosophy of cultural preservation and representation. By integrating symbols and narratives of African American heritage into the very fabric of the NMAAHC, he challenges Eurocentric architectural norms that have historically marginalized diverse cultural identities (Smithsonian, n.d.; McKnight 2017).

Across the Atlantic, in the West African nation of Burkina Faso, another architect's journey unfolds—a narrative of sustainability, community empowerment, and cultural continuity. Kéré, born and raised in Gando, a village without basic infrastructure, understands the transformative power of architecture in uplifting communities (Pritzker Architecture Prize 2024).

Kéré's architectural practice, Kéré Architecture, founded in Berlin, Germany, exemplifies his commitment to sustainable and community-driven design. His projects, like the Gando Primary School, are not just buildings but catalysts for change. Built using local materials and traditional building techniques, such as clay and wood, these structures not only blend seamlessly into the landscape but also serve as symbols of cultural pride and resilience (Kéré Architecture 2024; "Francis Kéré," n.d.).

The design of the Benin National Assembly reflects Kéré's deep reverence for African culture. Inspired by the palaver tree—a traditional symbol of community discourse and decision-making in West African societies—the building's architecture fosters natural ventilation and communal spaces, honoring cultural heritage while addressing practical needs (Kéré Architecture 2024; "Francis Kéré," n.d.).

Kéré's innovative approach lies in his ability to adapt traditional techniques to modern engineering standards, demonstrating that sustainable architecture can be both culturally relevant and globally impactful (Pritzker Architecture Prize 2024; *ArchDaily* 2024).

The philosophies of Adjaye and Kéré resonate deeply with Africatown. Like Adjaye's and Kéré's architectural endeavors, Africatown stands as a testament to resilience against historical oppression and cultural erasure

The architect Francis Kéré during second day of Web Summit 2021, Lisbon, Portugal, November 2, 2021

(Africatown Heritage House, n.d.). Similarly, Adjaye and Kéré combat cultural erasure through their work. Adjaye's NMAAHC and Kéré's community-centric projects empower marginalized communities by preserving and celebrating cultural heritage through the constructed space (Smithsonian, n.d.; Kéré Architecture 2024).

The oppressive grid, akin to a restrictive framework, has historically confined marginalized communities, dictating their spaces, mobility to navigate both within and beyond these spaces, and economic and other opportunities. Africatown, as a deliberate act of building outside this grid, signifies a powerful counternarrative. By establishing safe spaces beyond the control of the grid, the community demonstrated the possibility of living freely and thriving despite historical constraints. Similarly, Adjaye and Kéré use their designs to build more than just structures; they tell stories, preserve history, and empower communities. Their innovative methods challenge traditional architecture, celebrate cultural diversity, and encourage a deeper understanding of our shared human experience. Through their work, they reflect the original spirit of Africatown—a community devoted to resilience, cultural preservation, and empowerment, despite all challenges.

References

Adjaye Associates. (n.d.). "Who We Are." Retrieved August 24, 2024, from https://www.adjaye.com/who-we-are/

Africatown Heritage House. (n.d.). Welcome to Africatown. Retrieved August 24, 2024, from https://africatown.org/

Cetta, D. S., Brennan, K., and Cooper, A. (2023, November 19). "Descendants of Alabama Slave Owner Say They're 'Figuring Out Next Steps' to Make Amends." CBS News. Retrieved June 22, 2024, from https://www.cbsnews.com/news/clotilda-meaher-descendants-talk-reconciliation-africatown-60-minutes/

Florian, Maria-Cristina. ArchDaily. (2024). "A Look at the Last 8 Editions of the Serpentine Pavilion." Retrieved August 24, 2024, from https://www.archdaily.com/976381/a-look-at-the-last-5-editions-of-the-serpentine-pavilion?ad_campaign=normal-tag

"Francis Kéré. Faculty Profile." (n.d.). Retrieved from https://www.architecture.yale.edu/faculty/858-francis-kere

Kemp-Rotan, R. (n.d.). "Sites of Interpretation | The Africatown International Design Idea Competition." The Architectural League of NY. Retrieved June 22, 2024, from https://archleague.org/article/africatown-sites-of-interpretation/

Kéré Architecture. (2024). "About Kéré Architecture." Retrieved June 22, 2024, from https://www.kerearchitecture.com

Keyes, A. (2019, May 22). "The 'Clotilda,' the Last Known Slave Ship to Arrive in the U.S., Is Found." *Smithsonian Magazine*. Retrieved June 22, 2024, from https://www.smithsonianmag.com/smithsonian-institution/clotilda-last-known-slave-ship-arrive-us-found-180972177/

McKnight, J. (2017, February 20). "David Adjaye's African American Museum photographed by Brad Feinknopf." Dezeen. Retrieved June 22, 2024, from https://www.dezeen.com/2017/02/20/david-adjaye-smithsonian-national-museum-african-american-history-culture-new-photography/amp/

Pritzker Architecture Prize. (2024). "Diébédo Francis Kéré—Laureate." Retrieved June 22, 2024, from https://www.pritzkerprize.com/laureates/diebedo-francis-kere#laureate-page-2421

Smithsonian. (n.d.). "African American Life, History, and Culture Explored in Washington D.C." Retrieved from https://NMAAHC.si.edu/about/building

Wainwright, O. (2018, January 25). "Already Iconic: David Adjaye's Black History Museum Wins Design of the Year." *The Guardian*. Retrieved June 22, 2024, from https://amp.theguardian.com/artanddesign/2018/jan/25/david-adjaye-black-history-museum-wins-design-of-the-year-NMAAHC

Waters, C., and Latham, I. (2022). *African Town*. G. P. Putnam's Sons Books for Young Readers.

2.12

Hip-Hop Architecture: Transforming Spaces Through Culture and Innovation

The architect Sekou Cooke's enlightening presentation at the third State of Black Design conference on March 6, 2022, marked a pivotal moment in the dynamic intersection of design, culture, and creativity. At the heart of Cooke's discourse was the revolutionary concept of hip-hop architecture, showcased in his eponymous book.

Hip-hop architecture emerges as a transformative force that fuses the principles of hip-hop culture with architectural design. Originating in the 1990s, it gained momentum in 2014 by emphasizing innovative methods reminiscent of DJs remixing tracks. This interdisciplinary approach encompasses consciousness, society, culture, identity, technicality, and artistry, fostering a multifaceted perspective on design. Hip-hop architecture, with its community-centric approach, blends consciousness, society, culture, identity, technical skill, and artistry. It aims to redefine architecture by uplifting cultures that are often overlooked, challenging traditional norms, and promoting fairness. The goal is to create a more just society by involving the community in the design process, questioning outdated spatial rules, and reflecting the unique aesthetics, values, and beliefs of the people it serves. As a movement, it rejects notions of equality and universality, aiming to elevate the ideas, cultures, and practices of marginalized peoples to prominence previously reserved for Western ways of thinking (Cooke 2021). Cooke's hip-hop architecture imagines a world designed by the many instead of the few, advocating for a less constrained and more inclusive approach to architectural design.

Hip-hop architecture creates innovative spaces inspired by hip-hop principles such as borrowing ideas, layering elements, repeating patterns, creating rhythm, and improvising. It offers diverse perspectives on design by addressing community needs and expressing community members' identities. Examples include:

- Transforming abandoned buildings into public housing (Hip-Hop Housing)
- Installing DJ booths beneath sidewalk grates (Hip-Hop Sidewalk)
- Designing temporary living spaces suspended below elevated train tracks (Hip-Hop Under and Over)

Each design uses dense collages inspired by hip-hop's core principles to create immersive environments that capture the essence of hip-hop culture. These projects embody the creative spirit of hip-hop pioneers, moving beyond nostalgic views to celebrate their authentic roots and offer a fresh approach to architectural design.

Hip-hop architecture tackles social issues by redefining architecture to elevate marginalized cultures. It seeks to engage directly with communities, breaking away from traditional spatial norms and reflecting the unique aesthetics, values, and philosophies of the people it serves (Cooke 2021). Emphasizing authenticity and relevance, it encourages cooperation, provides education, and honors community values. Overall, hip-hop architecture strives to increase representation within the architectural field, addressing issues of race, gender, and socioeconomic class.

Comparing this approach to traditional architectural practice reveals stark differences: While contemporary design adheres to standardization, hip-hop architecture disrupts norms, encouraging experimentation with form, function, and materials. The pivotal role of DJ culture in shaping hip-hop architecture is evident, with DJs pioneering the hacking and repurposing of technology, pushing its limits to create new art forms and adopting unconventional tools and techniques. Much like a DJ remixes and manipulates sounds, hip-hop architecture remixes and uses physical forms, resulting in dynamic and engaging spaces.

In 2021, Cooke's 3D Turntables project involved manipulating 3D printers to challenge traditional boundaries by likening hip-hop DJs to pioneers of phonographic technology, paralleling their innovations with architecture's adaptation of fabrication tools. Students who participated in the project experimented with laser cutters, 3D printers, and CNC mills. This exploration echoed early hip-hop DJs' quest to innovate (Cooke 2021).

The project also prompted students to rethink 3D printing norms by asking questions like "What if we minimize instead of maximize software-defined support structures?" and "Can we laser cut a nonflat surface?" By bridging the gap between human creativity and digital precision, the project embraced errors as opportunities, drawing insights from DJ culture to inspire architectural analysis. Cooke's initiative not only reimagined technology's potential but also fostered technological advancement, reflecting the inventive spirit of hip-hop culture within architectural practice.

Transitioning from hip-hop architecture's innovative approach, which blends culture and design to promote inclusivity, Dianne Harris's and Susan Bickford's essays offer insights into how architecture shapes identity and community. Harris examines how invisible structures of privilege influence urban design, while Bickford explores how city planning can foster or hinder social cohesion and equity. Together, their work emphasizes the importance of design practices that address racial and social inequalities in shaping our built environments.

In "Seeing the Invisible: Reexamining Race and Vernacular Architecture" (2007), Harris explores how certain phenomena, like white privilege, can be "invisible" because they're so common that people don't notice them. She references scholars who have studied how whiteness is seen as commonplace and affects how buildings and neighborhoods are designed. These designs can demonstrate who's welcome and who's not, influencing how individuals see themselves and others in society.

Harris's argument underscores how race influences architecture. This understanding not only shapes the use of constructed spaces but also empowers individuals to create environments where everyone feels a sense of belonging. This understanding can transform seemingly ordinary structures like gas stations, grocery stores, and houses into symbols that reflect socially imposed ideas about race and class (Harris 2007). For instance, the post–World War II suburban neighborhoods, designed to exclude nonwhite residents, significantly influenced where people could live and how they were perceived.

Some may think it's more important to talk about power than diversity because power decides who gets what in our society. They say learning about different cultures isn't enough to change unfair systems (Harris 2007). Harris reveals how race and class are connected, especially in cities where people might not have equal access to amenities like good schools or safe places to live—all because of their race. By studying how buildings and neighborhoods are constructed, architects can understand these issues and work toward making spaces more accessible for everyone. Harris's essay serves as a powerful reminder that race is not just about skin color—it's also about the planning of buildings and neighborhoods, and the power dynamics that shape these spaces.

In "Constructing Inequality: City Spaces and the Architecture of Citizenship" (2000), Bickford also delves into the profound influence of city spaces on a sense of belonging that shapes people's feelings of community.

Cities are like puzzles because they're made up of different pieces—neighborhoods, buildings, and streets—that fit together to form a whole. These pieces affect where people live, work, and attend school, influencing how they see themselves as part of the community (Bickford 2000). When cities are designed, the placement of schools or police stations can affect different groups of people in various ways. For example, when these services were built in Black neighborhoods, other ethnic groups didn't benefit from them. This occurred because of segregation, as laws and practices kept different racial groups apart. This made meeting and sharing resources harder for people from different backgrounds.

Bickford (2000) also talks about "zoning out," which occurs when people ignore or don't think about the lives of others who are different from them. This deliberate ignorance can lead to misunderstandings and make it harder for people to work together. It's like seeing only one piece of the puzzle without understanding how it fits into the bigger picture. This can reinforce stereotypes and keep inequalities in place, making it challenging for everyone to feel they belong in their city.

When a city's identity is less distinct, it signifies a blend of diverse people and communities coexisting. This can occur when different areas intersect or when a single city encompasses multiple smaller communities. The presence of clear boundaries and shared spaces plays a pivotal role in fostering a sense of unity among these diverse communities. Conversely, blurred lines can lead to disagreements on the city's identity and hinder community cohesion.

Hip-hop architecture revolutionizes the concept of shared space by delving into the nuances of Blackness within design, decoding the cultural practices of the African diaspora. It also challenges and disrupts conventional architectural paradigms by integrating elements rooted in hip-hop culture, offering a distinctive design perspective. The inherently interdisciplinary nature of hip-hop architecture acknowledges architecture as more than just buildings.

In exploring hip-hop architecture alongside the insights of Harris and Bickford, a unified theme emerges: Architecture profoundly influences social dynamics by either reinforcing or challenging inequalities based on race and class. While hip-hop architecture innovates through cultural integration, Harris and Bickford highlight how urban planning can perpetuate or mitigate these disparities. Together, their perspectives underscore the ways in which architecture can reshape our understanding of the constructed space as a catalyst for social change and unity.

References

Bickford, S. (2000). "Constructing Inequality: City Spaces and the Architecture of Citizenship." *Political Theory* 28, no. 3: 355–76.

Cooke, S. (2021). *Hip-Hop Architecture*. Bloomsbury Academic.

Harris, D. (2007). "Seeing the Invisible: Reexamining Race and Vernacular Architecture." *Perspectives in Vernacular Architecture* 13, no. 2: 96–105.

2.13

Afrofuturism as a Design Strategy

Shamika Klassen
and Omari Souza

All design is speculative. According to the political scientist Herbert Simon (1996):

> To design is to devise courses of action aimed at changing existing situations into preferred ones. Once we're designing something, we are thinking about the future use and of future contexts. Everything that we design is about the future, right, because we are imagining for use in the future. (111)

Speculative design goes further than the typical design future and moves beyond the normally anticipated future frame. Anthony Dunne and Fiona Raby, the authors of *Speculative Everything* (2013), say that typical design looks at small issues, while speculative design, which is a particular area in design and research, broadens the scope to tackle the biggest issues in society, particularly what are called *wicked problems*. The design theorists Horst Rittel and Melvin Webber (1973) developed the term *wicked problems* to encapsulate issues in planning and social policy that are complex, challenging, difficult to articulate with clarity, and constrained by the real world, unlike *tame problems*, such as those found in mathematics.

The results of speculative design are not always objects that are functional or useful. Rather, speculative designers create objects that force us to think about problems differently. However, speculative design and future-focused methods can also exclude the dreams and interests of people who are already excluded in the present and actual reality. For example, critical and speculative approaches to design, like a large swath of the science fiction genre, have been criticized for focusing on white male perspectives (Jakobsone 2017).

Representations of the future in science fiction often fail to depict the futures of people of color and other underrepresented minorities as central, heroic, rich, or deep. Individuals in these communities are rarely the protagonists of futuristic science fiction stories. The genre generally focuses on male worlds, created by male authors (Salvaggio 1984). Some science fiction actually replicates the oppression and discrimination of today (Lustila 2011). According to the author, illustrator, and professor John Jennings, the future of Black people in America is supposed to be tied to the slave ship, the plantation, and the grave. One exception is the kingdom of Wakanda in the *Black*

Panther comics and films, which offers the alternative future of an uncolonized, unconquered African nation (Reese 2018). New genres of science fiction, such as Black speculative fiction (Burnett 2015), radical science fiction (Imarisha and Brown 2015), and visionary fiction (Imarisha 2016), among others, have emerged to challenge the nondiverse futures of science fiction and to tackle social-justice themes such as racism, sexism, and other oppressions, as well as to offer collective visioning of new worlds and futures.

Afrofuturism, an evolving concept expressed through a Black cultural lens that reinterprets and reclaims the past, present, and future of Blackness, can be found in the work of everyone from science fiction authors like Octavia Butler to the cosmic jazz of Sun Ra. It is also much more than an artistic genre. Afrofuturism is a way to conceive of the future and of alternate realities through a Black cultural lens. Afrofuturism charts a history of liberated Black futures. The author Ytasha L. Womack (2013) views Afrofuturism as a method of self-liberation and a way to imagine oneself in a future from which one is generally excluded.

Within Womack's work, MacArthur Fellow Kerry James Marshall articulates the importance of Black people contemplating the future and their place in it. Marshall posits, "It comes down to, do we really imagine ourselves to be in the future? And if we imagine ourselves into the future, how are we going to be when we get there?"

Marshall goes on to ask, "Can we be agents of the future or will we be objects of the future, like we were objects of commerce when Black folks were brought to the New World?" He insists that Black people must be "in front of the developing of the material realities that shape the future," because those who will influence the future aren't the ones who design the next high-tech phone but the ones "who determine whether we'll be using phones in the first place" (quoted in Womack 2013). Inserting ourselves and our imaginings into the destiny of how our future world is designed gives us the opportunity to empower ourselves and to craft narratives that make space for our predilections as to how society unfolds.

Afrofuturism can be viewed as a tool for people who are wrestling with hopelessness or factors that limit them, creating opportunities for them to use imagination to transform their circumstances (Jackson 2014). Embracing agency and influence within our imagination as individuals and a collective of the Black diaspora when it comes to crafting the future imbues those who engage with Afrofuturism with hope.

Womack (2013) highlights that "all people can find inspiration or practical use for Afrofuturism to both transform their world and break free of their own set of limitations." Current design approaches are limited in their flagrant absence of the influence of marginalized communities' voices and experiences. A design practice and strategy utilizing an approach like Afrofuturism could drastically improve the experience of communities affected by the outcomes of the process.

Woodrow W. Winchester III (2018) outlines how Afrofuturism can respond to key shortcomings in human-centered design (HCD). He leans on an expanded definition of Afrofuturism from the artist Sanford Biggers. Biggers understands Afrofuturism to be "a way of recontextualizing and assessing history and imagining the future of the peoples of the African Diaspora via science, science fiction, technology, sound, architecture, the visual and culinary arts, and other more nimble and interpretive modes of research and understanding" (quoted in Winchester 2018). Equipped with this interpretation as a lens for design, Winchester applies it to critique HCD for its biases (intentional or not), privileges, and power, which prevent its practitioners from solving design dilemmas in a holistic way.

When HCD produces designs with a narrow perspective about users and their contexts of use, not only is the process of design exploration constrained, but the technological solutions of the present and future omit marginalized people's needs and considerations; this has profound negative implications. With technology design, in particular, inclusivity is paramount. Winchester (2018) warns that without a set of "appropriate processes, countermeasures, and advocacy," designers may construct technologies that simply replicate social biases and stereotypes. Winchester turns his critique to critical and speculative-design approaches like science fiction prototypes that do not often center disenfranchised voices in the way Afrofuturism does. By anchoring design narratives in marginalized experiences, Afrofuturistic approaches garner more empathetic design engagement and strive for universal betterment facilitated through and by technology.

Also in 2018, Winchester, Jameela Al-Jaroodi, and Rika Wright Carlsen published a piece for the American Society for Engineering Education on how Afrofuturism could improve engineering design. While establishing a working definition of Afrofuturism for the paper's positions, the authors again use Biggers's perspective on Afrofuturism as a tool beyond a visual aesthetic and consider it an epistemology—a theory of knowledge that determines how we construct reality (Winchester et al. 2018).

Many of the aforementioned conclusions about design and how an Afrofuturistic design lens can be beneficial are made here, but with an emphasis on engineering culture, which, according to Winchester, is resistant to dealing with issues of power, race, gender, sexuality, etc. Winchester's next publication in 2019 reiterates that designers of technology have a narrow view of users and context, which can be remedied with Afrofuturism as a framework to see marginalized voices, needs, and experiences as a viable and positive starting point, as well as a foundation for innovation. By designing for the margins, one covers the needs of the majority, as well. Expounding upon his earlier points, Winchester (2019) positions Afrofuturism as a design lens that encourages design from the future, instead of being based on present-day understandings; he says that Afrofuturism offers a way to bring biases, along with the means to challenge and address them, to the surface.

Of course, Winchester is not the only voice at the intersection of design and Afrofuturism. To develop an Afrofuturistic design hermeneutic, we can consider examples of how designers/researchers employ this lens in their work to reveal possibilities of praxis. One inspirational instance of applied Afrofuturistic design is a research study involving marginalized young people (ages eighteen to twenty-four) futuring in remote speculative co-design workshops on the South Side of Chicago as a mechanism for envisioning both utopian and dystopian futures (Harrington and Dillahunt 2021).

Christina Harrington and Tawana R. Dillahunt are human-computer interaction (HCI) researchers, as well as designers who led the study. They were inspired by how Afrofuturism engenders design decisions that include and positively influence the design futures of minoritized populations. The background of their research design is anchored in the aforementioned insights from Winchester—namely, that Afrofuturism fosters empathy when engaging in design practices that unapologetically center the marginalized Black voice in the design narrative as a vehicle for improving everyone's experiences with technology.

Through the co-design workshops, a workbook, and a design probe (prompts to elicit self-reflection in the context of the workshop) from the popular science fiction anthology television series *Black Mirror*, which focuses on technology and dystopian possibilities for the present and future, three themes emerged. The participants' analysis of the utopian and dystopian futures included "addressing social conditions in Chicago, returning to normal social behaviors (post-pandemic), and speculative technologies as metaphors of existing oppression" (Harrington and Dillahunt 2021).

Overall, Harrington and Dillahunt found Afrofuturism to be a valid way to facilitate speculative design and imagine tech futures that center Black and Brown histories, cultures, and realities. For this project, futuring grounded in Afrofuturistic probes was imagined from the perspective and experiences of oppressed people. For the broader HCI community, Harrington and Dillahunt recommend that sociocultural dimensions be considered when conceptualizing future technologies—and that Afrofuturism can be a crucial mechanism for doing so.

Another example of a research/design project undergirded by Afrofuturism is the eight-week-long Remixing Wakanda project led by Michael B. Dando, Nathan Holbert, and Isabel Correa in 2019. It is described as an experience that brought together "youth of color, artists, designers, educators, and researchers to construct a new vision for a culturally relevant and sustaining Science, Technology, Engineering, Art, and Mathematics (STEAM)-centered learning and making framework situated in an Afrofuturist design aesthetic" (Dando et al. 2019).

Project leaders intentionally practiced placemaking in the space where workshops occurred, by displaying Black comics, literature, art, music, and so on. Participants experienced a series of activities, including creating their own medallions and engaging with ancient aesthetics and practices from a number of African communities. By combining Afrofuturism with critical design, the researchers deftly sidestepped design practices that narrowly focus on privileged white male experiences by centering those of the young Black participants.

In Omari's role as a professor, he places a strong emphasis on amplifying the voices of marginalized authors in the realm of speculative fiction. Notable figures such as Octavia Butler, known for works like *Parable of the Sower*, are crucial elements in broadening students' perspectives beyond their own lived experiences. Given the challenges of encouraging students to engage with communities outside their immediate surroundings, especially on design campuses that often lack diversity, there is a risk of students designing exclusively for the groups they are familiar with. This limitation may result in solutions that either neglect or worsen problems faced by minority groups not within their direct sphere of interaction.

To address this, it's important to incorporate influential works of Afrofuturism and speculative futuring into the curriculum, assigning students the task of creating a positionality matrix for each significant character in the assigned books. Through participating in Remixing Wakanda, students delve into the experiential challenges faced by these characters, offering a nuanced understanding of issues that might be unfamiliar to them. The objective is to encourage students to explore how these experiential challenges contribute to the overarching conflicts within the stories. Once these issues have been identified, students are prompted to analyze their varied impacts on each character and, subsequently, propose design solutions aimed at ethically addressing the identified problems. This approach aims to expand students' knowledge of diverse experiential obstacles, fostering a more innovative and inclusive approach to their design solutions.

As Dando and his colleagues (2019) put it, "Critical Afrofuturist Design is not a response to Whiteness, but rather a centering of Black, African, and Indigenous histories, cultures, art forms, philosophies and technologies with a socio-political aim of resistance and survival." The decision to introduce young Black people to opportunities to design and engage with Afrofuturistic probes and expose them to STEAM learning and making is an important strategy that typifies the insights of designers and scholars who have directly worked with and considered the far-reaching implications of Afrofuturism.

References

Dando, M. B., Holbert, N., and Correa, I. (2019). *Remixing Wakanda: Critical Afrofuturist Design and STEAM Education*. Proceedings of the 2019 ACM Conference on Interaction Design and Children, 697–700. Retrieved August 27, 2024, from https://doi.org/10.1145/3311927.3325325

Dunne, A., and Raby, F. (2013). *Speculative Everything: Design, Fiction, and Social Dreaming*. MIT Press.

Harrington, C., and Dillahunt, T. R. (2021). *Futuring with Marginalized Youth: Co-Designing Afrofuturist Technofutures*. Proceedings of the 2021 ACM Conference on Computer Supported Cooperative Work and Social Computing, 1–22. Retrieved August 27, 2024, from https://doi.org/10.1145/3462204.3481761

Imarisha, W. (2016). "Visionary Fiction and Organizing." In *Octavia's Brood: Science Fiction Stories from Social Justice Movements*, edited by W. Imarisha and A. M. Brown, 3–7. AK Press.

Imarisha, W., and Brown, A. M., eds. (2016). *Octavia's Brood: Science Fiction Stories from Social Justice Movements*. AK Press.

Jackson, S. (2014). "Afrofuturism as Critical Imagining: The Digital Divide, Technology, and the Re-Making of a Movement." *Journal of Science and Technology* 23, no. 2: 41–53. Retrieved August 27, 2024, from https://doi.org/10.5324/eip.v23i2.2858

Jakobsone, I. (2017). "Critical Speculative Design: A Critical Design Perspective on Design Fiction." Proceedings of the 2017 ACM Conference on Creativity and Cognition, 317–20. Retrieved August 27, 2024, from https://doi.org/10.1145/3059454.3073707

Lustila, D. (2011). "The Reproduction of Oppression in Science Fiction." *Science Fiction Studies* 38, no. 2: 246–61. Retrieved August 27, 2024, from https://doi.org/10.1353/sfs.2011.0071

Reese, A. (2018). "Wakanda Forever: The Black Panther's Identity." *Critical Studies in Media Communication* 35, no. 1: 1–4. Retrieved August 27, 2024, from https://doi.org/10.1080/15295036.2017.1419966

Rittel, H. W. J., and Webber, M. M. (1973). "Dilemmas in a General Theory of Planning." *Policy Sciences* 4, no. 2: 155–69. Retrieved August 27, 2024, from https://doi.org/10.1007/BF01405730

Salvaggio, R. (1984). *The Problem of Woman as Hero in the Work of Four Contemporary Women Writers*. Greenwood Press.

Simon, H. A. (1996). *The Sciences of the Artificial*, 3rd ed. MIT Press.

Winchester, W. W., III. (2018). "Afrofuturism as a Design Lens for Inclusive HCI." Proceedings of the 2018 ACM Conference Companion Publication on Computer Supported Cooperative Work and Social Computing, 99–102. Retrieved August 27, 2024, from https://doi.org/10.1145/3272973.3274052

Winchester, W. W., III. (2019). "Afrofuturism as a Design Lens for Inclusive HCI." *Interactions* 26, no. 4: 10–11. Retrieved August 27, 2024, from https://doi.org/10.1145/3323160

Winchester, W. W., III, Al-Jaroodi, J., and Carlsen, R. W. (2018). "Afrofuturism: Reimagining Human-Centered Design Possibilities." Proceedings of the 2018 ASEE Annual Conference & Exposition. Retrieved August 27, 2024, from https://peer.asee.org/29812

Womack, Y. L. (2013). *Afrofuturism: The World of Black Sci-Fi and Fantasy Culture*. Chicago Review Press.

2.14

Transforming for Workspace and Academic Safety

Kaleena Sales and Zariah Cameron

The phrase *with not for* is often used to refer to designers co-creating with the disabled or any marginalized community. That same mantra should be applied to Black design employees and teammates: Companies should be asking them what they need and how their experiences could be improved—then companies must follow through on what they learn.

At the height of 2020, particularly after the murders of George Floyd and Breonna Taylor, we witnessed an influx of companies and self-proclaimed "allies" flocking to "support" their Black employees and the Black community as a whole by throwing money at systemic injustice, in hopes of mitigating any backlash or avoiding being deemed racist. Companies and individuals placed empty promises and Band-Aids on a perpetual generational issue that requires intense surgery to repair the damage, rather than establishing actionable long-lasting change in a place that would have an actual impact on the community.

Once the hype from the events of 2020 calmed down—though the injustices never have—companies and self-proclaimed allies were no longer critical of the vastly white-dominated public. Diversity, equity, and inclusivity (DEI) initiatives and "promise commitment" statements to do better for the Black community were quickly forgotten. In fact, things have worsened: Those 2020 DEI promises fell to the wayside, Black communities continue to suffer, and Black employees still aren't receiving the pay, promotion, and support they were promised and deserve. In some cases, they are receiving less than they did in 2020. Companies broadcasting dedication to inclusion to their community and customers while neglecting and failing their employees' well-being are cultivating a space for performative inclusion and equity to exist and thrive.

Companies have begun pushing out external efforts by pouring money into creating an inclusive brand presence in their communities and designing products to create a more inclusive experience for customers. However, these same companies are exhausting and overworking their Black employees to bring about these experiences or quieting Black employees' voices as if they weren't a part of the target audience they're solving for. We have to understand that a devoted commitment to our communities is just one step, and the tip of the iceberg when it comes to cultivating an equitable space. It's just as essential to be committed to internal inequities, within the company structure itself. Both have to coexist to create an optimal experience that is equitable.

For example: Utilizing the lingo, language, and culture of the Black community in marketing or design campaigns but scrutinizing that expression of their culture in the office, and deeming it "unprofessional," is the exact definition of performativity. If employees don't feel safe showing up in the workplace, why would they feel safe enough to show up inclusively in design innovations, when they believe that they're just going to be shut down anyway? It's about designing a better and more equitable experience not simply for our customers but also for employees. Otherwise, they'll merely become "the forgotten."

How do we create a safe space for employees? We have to begin by considering what a safe space is. A safe space is a place or environment in which a person or category of people can feel confident that they will not be exposed to discrimination, criticism, harassment, or any other emotional or physical harm. This includes ensuring not only the physical but also the psychological safety of an individual.

The very foundation of trust and belonging starts with creating a place where psychological safety can thrive. At the peak of 2020, Black design hires were recruited simply because of the lack thereof and the need to fulfill diversity quotas. Even if they began with good intentions, many companies didn't devote the resources necessary to sustain the livelihood of these Black design hires entering white-dominated spaces.

When companies lack a clear direction or clue of how to support their Black hires, who have essentially been malnourished from the start, these hires reap the consequences of poor leadership and a complete disregard of true care and compassion for Black people.

A 2022 report by the US Surgeon General on "workplace well-being" underscores the importance of fostering a safe and supportive environment for all employees, with particular emphasis on ensuring protections for those from racial or ethnic groups that have historically faced discrimination. This includes implementing policies that actively promote inclusivity, address bias, and create an atmosphere where all individuals, especially those from marginalized backgrounds, feel secure, valued, and empowered to thrive.

People cannot perform well at work if they feel physically or psychologically unsafe. When workers feel psychologically safe, they speak up without the risk of being punished, retaliated against, or humiliated, and without fear of these risks (US Surgeon General 2022).

A LinkedIn post by Jonathan Ashong-Lamptey (n.d.) explained it best:

> Someone in my team said something insightful and upsetting. They said companies treat "underrepresented" employees like dishcloths. Here's why: they grab them when they need to clean up a mess; they put them back when things are good enough; they don't think about them when they are out of sight; they throw them away when they have no more use; they don't spend a lot of money on them.

Belonging has become the hot new topic that everyone loves talking about but never actually puts into practice. Companies and leadership have to understand that if your goal is to build trust and belonging among your teams and with you as a leader, you must first design a space where psychological safety can thrive.

Inclusion (included), Learner (safe to learn), Contributor (safe to contribute), and Challenger (safe to challenge the status quo) safety are the four key stages of psychological safety; facilitating hires' progress through these stages should be prioritized in the employee life cycle.

- **Inclusion Safety:** Black design employees feel safe enough to express their culture—AAVE (African American Vernacular English), etc.—in work spaces without being ridiculed or questioned or placed in the new design campaign to make a product appear more relatable to customers.
- **Learner Safety:** An incoming designer can thrive and find room to stretch and grow without the worry or fear that often accompanies unfamiliarity. It's about alleviating that fear and creating a protective environment that allows new hires to adapt at their own pace. Companies and managers, in particular, need to ensure there is ample space for growth and question asking without fear of reprimand. Design departments are frequently called upon to resolve complex challenges, yet often remain

undervalued. Expecting them to shoulder responsibilities above their rank without the proper guidance, support, or buffer for mistakes can lead to burnout. To support your employees' growth, consider investing in their professional development by funding relevant conferences and workshops. By doing so, you encourage Black employees to bring renewed energy, insights, and skills into their roles.

- **Contributor Safety:** More experienced staff are mindful not to denigrate a young Black designer's capability to perform well in a job or to operate in the role that they were hired—and fully qualified—to perform. Often with Black women—especially in leadership positions and particularly if they are young—coworkers may deem them inadequate or dismiss their ideas as invalid or less important. This can lead Black women to think that they cannot perform the job they were brought in to do.
- **Challenger Safety:** A designer feels encouraged to advocate and push for a new design concept or experience that may deviate from the process that's always existed. They can propose ideas or challenging thought processes that are different from everyone's mindset in a healthy way without repercussion or ridicule. We often get attached to one process or one way of doing things, especially if those voices that dominate the decision-making are majority white. Just because a Black woman is being assertive and stern doesn't mean she's being aggressive; don't dim her light simply because you were offended by the facts being conveyed or because you felt that she came across as "too defensive" or "too harsh."

Safety is creating an environment of protection that allows employees breathing room and space to be themselves, perform well, and achieve greatly. Don't negate someone's lived or traumatic experience just because it wasn't yours. Their lived experience always adds value and holds weight. In addition, if there are racist people within the company disrupting the safe and equitable culture a company is claiming to have, they should be fired. Strong performance doesn't excuse anyone who is creating a toxic environment for Black employees. And it's not always the blatant racist to look out for—it also could be the liberal white woman who questions why we should be discussing or including race in our work, or the white man who gets his work done but often offers pushback on accessibility or other equity design–centered topics that make him uncomfortable because he may be required to change the way he works and thinks. People throughout the company may be aware of their behaviors and habits, but no one will dare let them go, claiming that "giving them a talk" is sufficient.

Company culture is an ideology that is felt throughout, by both internal and external people viewing the company. Just because you have a strong culture through your brand and external partnerships doesn't mean you have a strong culture among your employees. The care and dedication you give to your customers should be extended equally to your employees, who often get lost in the shuffle.

The center of an all-around healthy culture—if not the company as a whole—is the design department, and design leadership needs to remain vigilant in cultivating a healthy environment. This myth that culture can be cultivated only inside the walls of the office is a fallacy when it has been amply demonstrated in recent years that teams and companies that operate remotely can maintain a healthy culture. It's about how much effort you are willing to put into your team or company, no matter where individuals are located. It can be safer for Black employees to work remotely, to reduce the racial aggressions and trauma that are often heightened through face-to-face contact in the office. At the end of the day, in-office perks aren't going to increase employees' presence in the office if they don't feel safe. Allow for balance and flexibility for employees. Allow in-person attendance to be voluntary, instead of employees feeling forced and obligated to come into the office.

The *we're like family* mantra has been used to invoke a safe, welcoming, laid-back corporate culture. This phrase, which blurs the lines between professional and personal, may have been created with good intentions, but it has often been abused, with negative psychological effects on employees. It may lead employees to emotionally attach themselves to a company and to promise it an undying loyalty that's not often reciprocated. If a culture and company are "burning," management frequently expects Black people, especially Black women, to put out the fire. In a "family" workplace culture, we'll feel obligated to stay committed to the company and fix the issues. Often, we'll be placed in leadership positions when a department or organization is already in shambles; we're then responsible for cleaning up a mess that wasn't our fault, and we're blamed if and when the organization fails, as if we started the mess. This type of behavior can lead to a drop in employee productivity and performance, and to burnout. Then, an employee's dedication is often rewarded by negative evaluations from Human Resources and managers, which lead to that employee being let go.

Again, design departments are often treated as the saviors of everyone's mess, without being truly recognized or valued for all the hard work and tireless hours they put in. It's important to remember that there is no such thing as a design emergency. The work can always wait—and, if it's such an emergency, don't leave it until the last minute to give designers the brief/deliverable.

Finally, it's imperative to establish a mentorship program within your department. Ensure that new hires, especially recent grads or entry-level designers, are paired with more experienced colleagues who will help them adjust to the work environment. The mentor can serve as a guiding anchor who may be able to dedicate more time and attention than the hire's manager is able to. Aligning a Black designer with another Black or person of color design employee who is a rank or two above them can add an extra layer of comfort, relatability, and safety by allowing them to gain knowledge and expertise from someone who has been in their shoes and who can equip them with the strategic tools to perform well and advance.

For employees of color: It can be difficult to find mentors who look like you at companies that are predominantly white—especially in design departments, which seem to have more Black employees at the entry level and fewer in design leadership or at any high rank. When you're the "only one," it can be that much more challenging to find someone to help you to navigate the space and to discover a sense of purpose and grounding. Even if you're unable to have a mentor or even a manager who looks like you and can understand how to help you in your role, find people in other parts of the company who are willing to be your sponsor and champion, who can advocate for you in rooms that you may not have access to.

References

Ashong-Lamptey, J. (n.d.). Post discussing treatment of underrepresented employees as dishcloths. LinkedIn.

US Surgeon General. (2022). *The U.S. Surgeon General's Framework for Workplace Mental Health and Well-Being*. US Department of Health and Human Services.

2.15

Artist Profile: Marryam Moma—Embracing Resilience over Trauma

A collage portrait of James Baldwin titled *Here are your flowers*, by Marryam Moma. Baldwin was an American writer, essayist, and social critic known for his powerful exploration of race, sexuality, and identity in America. His works, including *Go Tell It on the Mountain* and *The Fire Next Time*, challenged prevailing social norms and became central to the Civil Rights movement.

Marryam Moma is a contemporary visual artist specializing in analog collage embodying a spirit of artistic freedom and expression. In my conversation with Moma, we explored her artistic journey, her motivations, the influence of her cultural background, and the challenges she continues to face in a space often dominated by a Eurocentric gaze.

Moma's cultural background as a Tanzanian-Nigerian American profoundly influences her work. Having grown up in a close-knit family with a strong emphasis on joy, travel, rest, family, and sisterhood, she infuses these elements into her art. Her work is a testament to the reimagined future she envisions for Black bodies, celebrating the essence of Black familyhood and culture.

Artist Marryam Moma

Because Moma grew up in predominantly Black spaces where race was not the central focus of her life, it was only when she transitioned to predominantly white spaces in the United States that she became acutely aware of the broader racial dynamics shaping American society.

It is essential to clarify that individuals of Black descent raised in predominantly white environments do not inevitably adopt victim mentalities or necessarily feel oppressed within these settings. However, a unique positional difference exists for those who haven't previously experienced being part of an "out-group" or who haven't had to navigate policies imposed by such a group.

As a thought experiment, consider the experiences of women who have encountered catcalling or microaggressions from men; imagine the countless conversations these women may have had with friends and family about navigating spaces with men. Contemplate the discussions these women are exposed to from men about women. Then, picture introducing a woman who has never had this exposure to a scenario in which misogynistic attitudes toward women prevail, as they do in the so-called manosphere, an assortment of websites and online forums centered on hypermasculinity and virulent hatred of women and feminism.

In Moma's artistic realm, women are free to be themselves and express their thoughts without fearing disapproval from men or concerns about their safety in the presence of men. Moma possesses the ability to share her stories about femininity and race without the burden of conforming to cultural expectations or the triggers of the so-called in-group.

Be Do Have,
by Marryam Moma.
Collage.

Moma's artistic odyssey began at Temple University's Tyler School of Art, where she studied architecture. With a bachelor's degree in architecture, she serendipitously discovered her true passion. Collage ceased to be a mere creative outlet; it became a means of brainstorming and visualizing architectural ideas, a cornerstone of her artistic expression.

Sacred Ground, by Marryam Moma. Hand-cut collage. This intricate piece weaves together fragments of identity, culture, and spirituality, reflecting the sacredness of ancestral connections and the resilience of the human spirit.

Her architectural background deeply informs her approach to collage, allowing her to construct intricate, layered compositions that not only convey powerful narratives but also call conventional design practices into question. By integrating elements of architecture with her visual art, Moma redefines space within the two-dimensional plane, creating works that are not just visually compelling but also conceptually rich. Her designs act as a bridge between art and architecture, demonstrating the potential of design as a tool for cultural and social change.

Moma's art reflects her personal experiences and explores often-uncharted territories in the art world. It delves into themes such as generational wealth, financial literacy, sisterhood, and the passing of knowledge across generations. What sets Moma's work apart is her unyielding commitment to uplifting and empowering Black bodies, especially the Black female body. In a world often overshadowed by divisiveness, her art creates a space in which Black women can be vulnerable, soft, revered, and valued. It doesn't merely celebrate Black joy; it provides a platform for Black women to find empowerment within themselves.

One of Moma's most iconic pieces, *I Am Her*, a self-portrait from 2018, encapsulates the essence of her artistry. This regal yet quietly powerful depiction of a Black woman challenges the conventional consumption and exploitation of Blackness, often seen through the white gaze, in art. It invites viewers to confront the gaze of Black subjects directly and without prejudice, revealing the dignity and strength inherent in Black stories.

top: Marryam Moma's home studio

bottom: Marryam Moma hand-cutting collage pieces

Moma's art isn't merely a visual spectacle; it serves as a platform for conversations that extend beyond the canvas. Her *Austere Imaginary* series, created during her third trimester of pregnancy, addresses Black maternal-health issues. By celebrating the Black pregnant body openly and beautifully, Moma aims to break the stigma and secrecy surrounding the joyous process of maternity and motherhood. She also highlights her personal journey with uterine fibroids, shedding light on a prevalent issue within Black communities.

Notably, Moma consciously avoids focusing on Black trauma, opting to create a space for joy, celebration, and empowerment. This deliberate choice signifies her commitment to changing the narrative surrounding Black life and experiences. She describes the challenges she faces in the art world, where there is often pressure to cater to a European gaze. Her refusal to focus on Black trauma can lead to exclusion or rejection from certain spaces. The fetishization of Black pain in art sometimes causes her work's message of empowerment and positivity to be disregarded.

The concept of Black trauma porn has gained significant attention in recent years, as it touches upon the portrayal and commercialization of Black pain, particularly in media. The term, as discussed by Tina Charisma (n.d.) in her essay "Trauma Porn and the Commercialization of Black Pain," describes a troubling phenomenon whereby narratives and visuals of Black people enduring racism, racial bias, and suffering are repeatedly shown, often for profit.

Black trauma porn can be found in the portrayal of unfortunate and scary events that Black people undergo in movies, TV shows, and social media. It often focuses on incidents in which individuals are harmed due to the color of their skin and is characterized by its repetitive nature. The term *porn* is used to emphasize the commodification and exploitation of Black pain for attention and profit. It is essential to understand that the term is meant not to trivialize the suffering of Black individuals but to highlight the problematic nature of these portrayals.

Charisma's essay suggests that there are individuals who view Black trauma porn as a necessary evil. They believe that these stories serve a crucial purpose in educating the public about the realities of racism, racial bias, and the unjust treatment that Black people have historically endured. These narratives could be seen as antiracist because they shed light on issues that have often been swept under the rug, providing a platform for Black voices to share their experiences and advocate for change. However, despite the intention of raising awareness, watching Black trauma porn can damage viewers. When these narratives are repeatedly presented, they can lead to desensitization, such that individuals become less moved by the emotional impact of these stories because they are shown too often. Moreover, continuous exposure to such traumatic content can lead to emotional distress, mental-health issues, and vicarious trauma, particularly for Black individuals who may identify with the victims. Trauma porn also has the potential to normalize Black suffering, reinforcing harmful stereotypes and perpetuating systemic racism.

While it is vital to address the realities of racism and racial bias, it is equally important to diversify narratives about Black people. Black trauma porn can overshadow

Prodigy I Am, by Marryam Moma. Collage portrait of Stevie Wonder, a legendary American musician, singer, and songwriter renowned for his contributions to soul, R&B, and pop music, with hits like "Superstition" and "Isn't She Lovely"; he is known for his innovative use of synthesizers and his impact on music history.

stories of Black joy, excellence, and cultural richness. There is a wealth of positive and inspiring stories to tell—tales of Black achievement, happiness, and cultural heritage. Such narratives explore the complexity of Black identity beyond suffering and, as evidenced in Moma's work, can be equally enlightening and essential. These stories can emphasize love, family, friendship, and personal growth within the Black community, creating a more balanced and accurate representation.

Moma emphasizes her commitment to focusing on what she can control and aims to create art that inspires and empowers her audience. Our conversation also delved into her recent series *Iconoclast*, which highlights individuals who have influenced her work. This series celebrates Black excellence and aims to bridge cultural divides and promote reconciliation. She explains her choice of such subjects as

James's Legacy, by Marryam Moma. Collage portrait of James Baldwin.

Mahalia Jackson, Fela Kuti, André Leon Talley, Nikki Giovanni, and young activists fighting for gun control, emphasizing their significant contributions to their respective fields and communities.

Creating room for narratives that transcend overemphasis on the suffering of the Black community can serve as a protective shield for those with marginalized identities. In a similar vein, these expanded stories can offer a deeper understanding of diverse experiences to individuals outside this cultural context. This restorative approach does not promote the erasure of the painful chapters in our history, which should be acknowledged. However, as designers and artists, we must advocate for the establishment of a space in which we can authentically express all other facets of our existence, unencumbered by Eurocentric norms and interruptions.

Queen Mother, by Marryam Moma. Hand-cut collage.

Moma's journey as a visual artist is a testament to how artistic expression can specifically reshape existing narratives and challenge social norms. Her contribution to design, particularly in the realm of visual storytelling, is profound; her art is a testament to the beauty, strength, and resilience of Black bodies and a call for a more inclusive and celebratory portrayal of Black life (especially the lives of Black women) in art. Her focus on joy, empowerment, and positive stories, avoiding the depiction of trauma and pain often seen in media, contributes to a media landscape that educates, inspires, and uplifts without exploiting the pain of Black people, thus promoting healing and understanding.

References

Charisma, T. (n.d.). "Trauma Porn and the Commercialisation of Black Pain." *TMRW* Magazine. Retrieved June 12, 2024, from https://www.tmrwmagazine.com/features/opinion/trauma-porn-and-the-commercialisation-of-black-pain

Part 3
Case Studies

3.1 Case Study: Escaping Erasure

Lauren Williams

Designers: Jisoo Han, Naveen Hattis, Qinglin Jin, Samuel Jones, Austin Prouty, Candice Navi, Yize Wang, Aren Willias, and Shu Chin Yeh

Valencia, California, 2020

Workshop facilitator Lauren Williams

As we've explored throughout this collection of essays, designers with oppressed identities are tasked with unlearning the many years of cultural erasure they have experienced. As society excludes various groups of people on the basis of factors such as race, gender, sexual orientation, and ability, we are pressured to conform, ignoring our cultural identity or social ideals. This erasure occurs not only in our social interactions; our very legacies can be altered and misappropriated once we are no longer here. The restorative act of protecting our languages and names goes hand in hand with guarding the memory of who we are and what we stand for.

On February 4, 1968, thirty-nine-year-old Martin Luther King Jr. delivered one of his final sermons. In a lecture titled "The Drum Major Instinct" (1968), King described to the congregation of Ebenezer Baptist Church in Atlanta, Georgia, the human desire to be spotlighted. He detailed how the desire for greatness can be channeled as a tool for generosity and moral excellence. King concluded by specifying that in death, he did not want to be recalled for his Nobel Peace Prize or his copious

Convening on the heels of Martin Luther King Jr. Day, this three-day workshop with nine CalArts students in the graduate graphic design program explored how we remember, memorialize, and euphemize Dr. King. Best remembered for the sound bites of his sermons on peace and equality—less so for his radical views on labor, war, imperialism, and class solidarity—the multidimensionality of Dr. King's memory is erased when we flatten his legacy posthumously.

awards but for his dedication to others. Now known as the face of American nonviolent protests (even though during his lifetime he was viewed by the FBI as America's "most dangerous Negro"), King was assassinated sixty-three days after this lecture, at the Lorraine Motel in Memphis, Tennessee.

Almost fifty years later, in a 2018 Super Bowl commercial, King's sermon of selfless action was repurposed by Dodge Ram to sell motor vehicles and to bolster the Fiat Chrysler subsidiary's "built to serve" tagline. Just as the Nike symbol communicates victory, King's image now symbolizes the fight for racial equality—a battle that cost him his life. The sixty-second commercial brought no awareness to King's struggle, made no mention of current issues of inequality, and barely featured diversity in its shots. The appropriation of King's voice was purely cosmetic and lacked substance; ironically, Dodge used a message of selflessness for self-promotion.

This is just one of many examples of a private entity misappropriating a protest against profiteering. By remembering King more for sound bites from his sermons on peace and equality than for his radical views on labor, war, imperialism, and class solidarity, we erase his multidimensionality and flatten his legacy to promote corporate ideologies of consumerism and individual purchase power—which couldn't be further from the aims of the Civil Rights Movement.

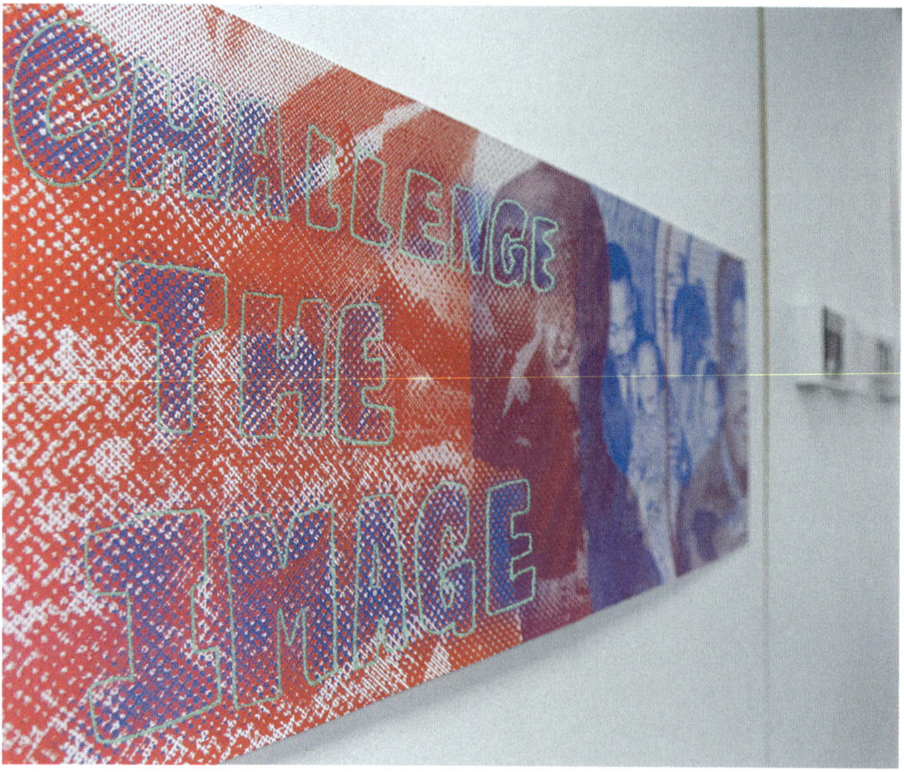

Participants tried to expose the contradictions between King's anticapitalist position and the ways in which his voice and words are used to advance capitalist ends today.

In 2020, the designer, organizer, researcher, and educator Lauren Williams attempted to evoke a more genuine memory of Martin Luther King Jr. through a three-day workshop at CalArts in Santa Clarita, California, in which nine students constructed an escape room. An escape room traditionally functions as a game during which a team of players uncover clues, solve puzzles, and accomplish tasks in a limited amount of time. This workshop encouraged the students to use space, form, and materials to call attention to and critique the flattening of King's legacy.

In one phase of the workshop, participants exposed the contradictions between King's anticapitalist position and how his voice was used in the 2018 Dodge Ram Super Bowl commercial (Williams, n.d.). The installation projected the ad over the entirety of King's sermon. Highlighted phrases from the Dodge ad were directly contrasted with anticapitalist phrases that categorically contradicted them, illustrating the absurdity of using King's voice in the ad. The piece used restorative practices of reflection and unpacking of the ways in which we remember King, as well as how he's been forgotten. The directed options, puzzle sequencing, and spatial elements throughout the room were designed to craft dialogue about what we understand or question about King and his legacy:

> How we remember histories—and the people whose actions shaped the course of history—also shapes our futures. How could the act of imagining, constructing, and realizing the room and the puzzles within it initiate and sustain conversations that wouldn't otherwise happen? (Williams, n.d.)

The escape room puzzles were designed to provoke thought and conversation about fairness and justice across all races, with a particular focus on challenging how history often sanitizes or euphemizes radical positions like Dr. King's in ways that dilute their true legacies. One puzzle had players match halves of letters and pictures to show that King's message is still important today. Another puzzle had players solve five riddles to decode a video and find hidden text behind a screen. This text came from one of King's speeches but had been used in the Dodge Ram ad in a way that went against King's original message. The puzzles were meant to make people think about how King's words are sometimes misused and to encourage critical thinking about history and social issues. Williams's intent was to provoke restorative discussions through the act of designing and as an effect of the experience of that design. In collaboration with her students, she reflected on the ways in which King is both remembered and forgotten. Paralleling these discussions, she and her students also explored the ways in which escape rooms function to conceal and reveal, and examined how they might define the consequences of entrapment and escape in the game they would build together.

Williams wanted to make the point that racial equity, justice, and so on have not yet been achieved, in spite of the discourse around postraciality and the idea that we've "moved past" racism since King's assassination. To achieve this, Williams and the CalArts students created a puzzle that paired halves of letters with images of iconic figures, both past and present. For example, Muhammad Ali with his Black Power fist raised was matched with Serena Williams in the same powerful pose.

At the end of the escape room experience, participants used phrases they had collected around the room to complete the poem "A Dead Man's Dream," written by Carl Wendell Hines Jr. in 1965.

The students who took part in the escape room event wanted to ensure that their design choices demonstrated what they'd learned about Martin Luther King Jr. from his actual intended words and teachings. They wanted to point out how King's image and words are sometimes misused for the purpose of making money, which can oversimplify his legacy. By creating puzzles that showed the contradictions in how King's message is portrayed, they hoped to start conversations about the commercialization of his ideals and highlight the importance of design in continuing the fight for racial equality and justice.

References

Hines, C.W. (n.d.). "A Dead Man's Dream." Carl Wendell Hines Jr. Poem du Jour. Retrieved June 20, 2024, from https://www.poemdujour.com/deadmanHines.html

King, M. L. (1968). "Drum Major Instinct—A Speech by Dr. Martin Luther King, Jr. [abridged]." Bethlehem Farm. Retrieved June 20, 2024, from https://bethlehemfarm.net/wp-content/uploads/2013/02/DrumMajorInstinct.pdf

Participants tried to expose the contradictions between King's anticapitalist position and the ways in which his voice and words are used to advance capitalist ends today.

3.2 Case Study: Nonhierarchical Engagement with Communities—Anti-Racist Design Community Pop-Up

Team: Christopher Rudd, Azra Sungu, Julian Walker, Mithila Kedambadi, Monica Villazon

Photographer: Daniel Chichester

Partners: BirriaTaTaTacos, Blocks Together, Friistyle Chicago, Love All, Norman Teague Design Studios

Chicago, Illinois, 2021

Two individuals holding the W.F.B.M. (White Fragility Bullshit Meter), a tool designed to navigate the discomfort often experienced by white peers when engaging in conversations about racial issues. This tool shifts the emotional labor from people of color to the meter itself.

During the spring of 2021, using design and creative placemaking, our team brought together diverse people, experiences, perspectives, and expertise to intervene and disrupt racist social structures that were being amplified by the pandemic. The article "Mapping the Disparities That Bred an Unequal Pandemic" (2021), by Jeremy Deaton and Gloria Oladipo, reveals how racial segregation in Chicago acted like a preexisting condition, amplifying the impact of COVID-19 on Black neighborhoods.

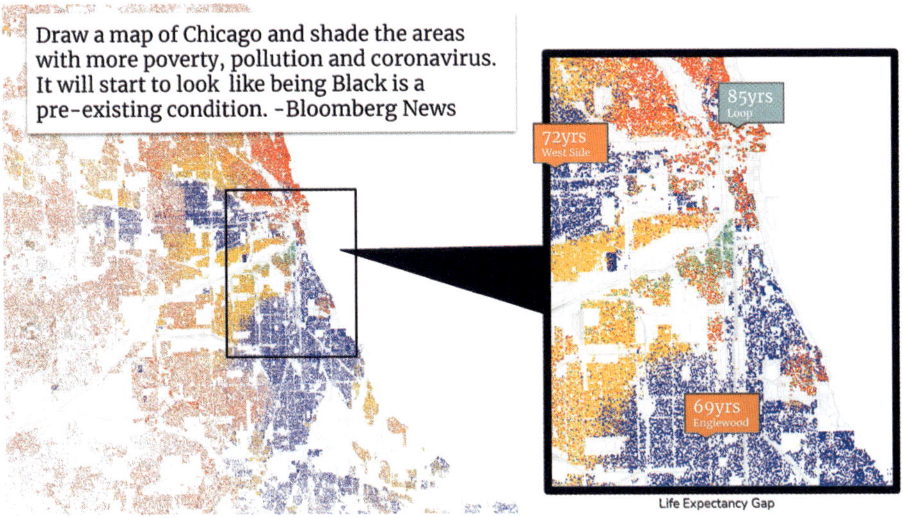

A map illustrating racial segregation in Chicago, with each dot representing a different racial group: blue for Black residents, orange for Hispanic residents, and red for white residents. The box on the right highlights the life-expectancy gap between different racial groups, which can vary by decades and occur within distances as small as two miles.

Despite these areas having the highest death rates and lowest vaccine access, the rollout strategy—dependent on online sign-ups—ignored the broadband deserts prevalent in these communities. The disparity between vaccine distribution and the pandemic's devastating toll on Black and Brown communities starkly highlights the systemic inequities exacerbating health crises (Deaton et al. 2020). We collaborated with nonprofit organizations and small-business owners to bring Chicago residents together to co-design new antiracist infrastructures, led by Christopher Rudd. Rudd, who secured the grant from the Chicago Community Trust for the Healing Illinois initiative—a racial-healing project of the Illinois Department of Human Services and the Field Foundation of Illinois—believes that antiracism is about action rather than mere discussion. He worked alongside students Azra Sungu, Julian Walker, Mithila Kedambadi, and Monica Villazon from a class he taught.

In the aftermath of the summer of reckoning in 2020, as COVID-19 devastated the world, the disproportionate impact on Black, Brown, Indigenous, and immigrant communities took center stage. Healing Illinois was aimed at sparking conversations about racism across the state.

Chicago is distinctly separated by zones. The zoomed-in version on the right of the above map shows that in the Loop in the downtown area (represented by red, where residents are primarily white), people typically live to be about eighty-five years old. If you go just six miles west to the blue dots, your life expectancy decreases by thirteen years; if you go south to the other side of the blue dots, your life expectancy is reduced by almost

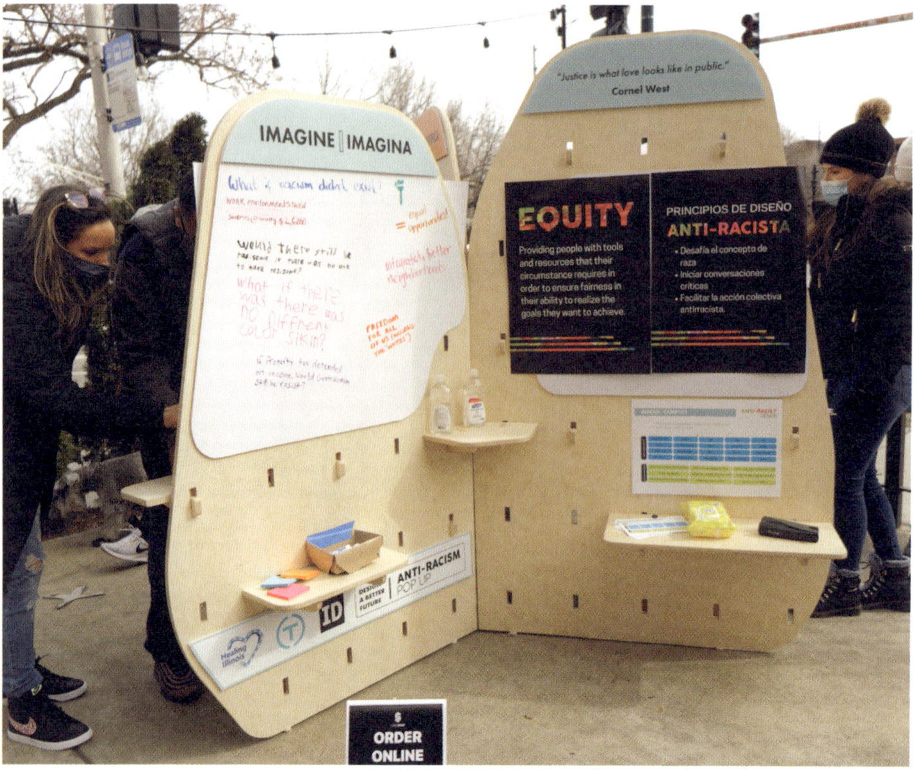

top: The Anti-Racist Design Community Pop-Up, a Chicago-based initiative, utilized design and creative placemaking to engage diverse communities in co-creating antiracist infrastructures and policies. It also supported local minority-owned businesses affected by the COVID-19 pandemic. The image shows the pop-up structure, designed by Norman Teague.; bottom: Christopher Rudd, Azra Sungu, and Julian Walker at the pop-up station.

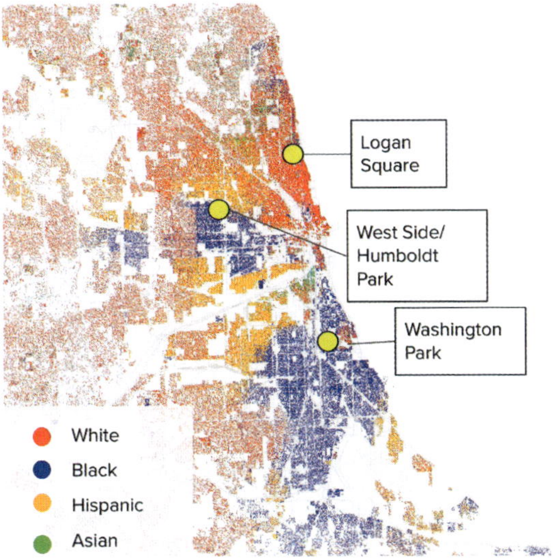

A demographic map of Chicago highlighting population concentrations by race: Blue dots represent Black residents, orange dots indicate Hispanic residents, and red dots show white residents. This visualization underscores the city's racial segregation.

Design as Integrator

twenty. You can probably guess who resides in the blue-dot areas of the map. The South and West Sides are primarily Black communities—they've been that way almost since Black folks moved to Chicago during the Great Migration of Black people throughout the twentieth century.

Racism has severe consequences for Black Chicagoans. COVID-19 has hit Black and Brown communities around the nation extremely hard—affecting employment, mental health, and education. Chicago has not been spared. Black Chicagoans make up 30 percent of the city's population yet represent 60 percent of COVID fatalities. Latinx Chicagoans make up 29 percent of the city's population yet have accounted for 45 percent of the city's reported COVID-19 cases and 31 percent of deaths. These disproportionate outcomes highlight historical racial inequities in the city that need to be identified and redesigned to ensure prosperity for all Chicagoans.

Through design and creative placemaking, we can bring together individuals with diverse experiences, perspectives, and expertise to intervene and disrupt unequal educational outcomes caused by racism and amplified by the pandemic. The question our project asked was: Can design be a force for integration, even in a city as segregated as Chicago?

We chose three neighborhoods for the pop-ups. Washington Park is primarily Black, but it's close to areas where we were able to invite other populations to participate. Logan Square is primarily white now, but it's a historically Latinx community that's going through gentrification. There's a diverse assortment of people in the area, but the different groups don't connect with one another. And then there's the West Side and Humboldt

Park. As the map shows, Humboldt Park is all blue, representing Black residents, but just next to it is an all-orange, primarily Puerto Rican, neighborhood, and there's a lot of tension between them.

The local culinary community adapted and developed innovative ways to serve its customers in the difficult conditions created by COVID-19. The restrictions created in response to the pandemic have caused enormous strain for this group of entrepreneurs, especially Black and Brown ones. The Institute of Design (ID) collaborated with local minority-owned restaurants, food trucks, and nonprofits for the antiracist design-studio pop-ups. ID provided gift cards for participants in the studio to patronize local business, and we used local businesses' brands to attract participants and their COVID-19 plan to ensure the safety of participants at the studio.

The pop-ups use a variety of creative frameworks to help participants create equitable infrastructures. This is a political series of activities, and we use the pop-ups to encourage participants to reflect on personal experiences with racism before designing actionable solutions. The sequence of activities takes participants on a cognitive journey that starts with Identify: grounding in the present. The Identify section is the anchor for participants' experience. It situates their interactions in personal lived experience by asking them to recall an instance in which they were affected by racism. This exercise helps participants surface a chain of key components contributing to the main racist barriers and biases that affect them.

Next, in Imagine, they are propelled into a new future where racism does not exist. Imagine asks participants to think about a future in which they could accomplish their goals in the same environment they identified in the previous section. This helps participants to reflect upon an ideal, equitable future situation or society. They do so by noting their feelings and the reasons behind these emotions. To enable this new equitable future, participants reflect on personal experiences with racism and imagine a future without it, which aids them in identifying and understanding their biases. They then design equitable solutions, such as policies, organizations, or tools, to address these biases and work toward an equitable future.

Finally, in Infrastructure, participants return to the present to craft antiracist infrastructures that will guide them to their preferred future. This section equips participants with tools to prototype modes of action that can help pave the way to the equitable future they imagined. We define infrastructures as purposeful combinations of resources to enable new choices and actions, suggesting three key categories under which these actions may be activated: policy, organization, and object. *Policies* are rules and guidelines to make decisions; *organizations* are groups of people who offer a particular service with a purpose; and *objects* are tools, technologies, devices, or other tangible things that enable a specific interaction.

We provided participants with worksheets for prototyping a policy or an organization, as well as hands-on building space for prototyping an

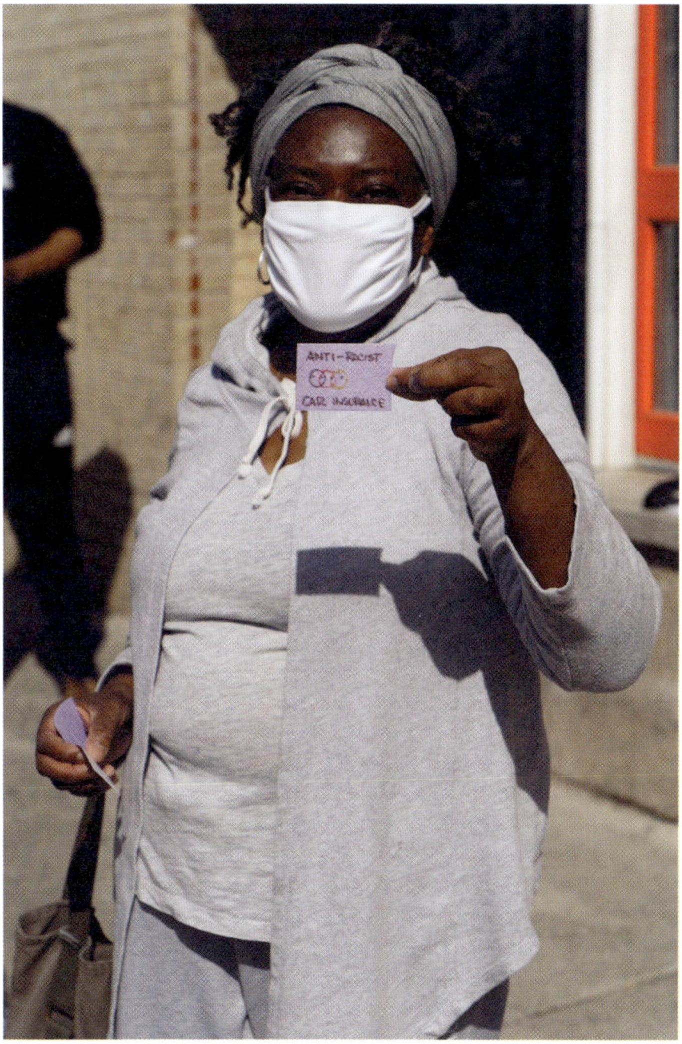

Art pop-up participant

object. These worksheets bring together the essential components of policies and organizations in an accessible format. We also developed two guidelines for structuring the pop-ups:

- **Make people comfortable.** Be mindful that participants are not always naturally equipped with skills and habits that would let them shape their preferred futures in the most effective way. Therefore, it is imperative to create a comfortable and inviting space. Think about the location, weather, and safety measures. Make sure that people are comfortable having hard conversations in your designated space. Play music in the background to create a more enjoyable experience.
- **Consider language.** Create room for people who can better express themselves in languages other than English. Provide translated worksheets and include a team member who can speak one of the native languages of the target audience. Be mindful that not all people will be able to engage with textual material. When this is the case, help people go through the activities by engaging them in discussion.

As participants identified moments when they had been affected by racism, the dominant word used to describe how they felt was "angry," but people also felt "disrespected," "ashamed," and "invisible."

Conversely, when participants imagined a future without racism, the primary word used to describe how they would feel was "happy," followed by "human," "valued," "empowered," and "safe." After experiencing the pop-up, participants were asked about their feelings around engaging with activities aimed at creating antiracist infrastructures, environments, and experiences. The overwhelming response was "possible."

In the wake of the challenges posed by the pandemic and the urgent need to address racial disparities, the Anti-Racist Design Community Pop-Up stands as a beacon of hope and transformative action. Through the power of design and creative placemaking, this initiative not only identifies instances of racism but also inspires a collective vision of an equitable future. It fosters unity, dialogue, and empowerment by combining a diverse assortment of experiences and perspectives to co-design antiracist infrastructures. By supporting local culinary entrepreneurs, especially Black and Brown business owners, the pop-up serves as a symbol of solidarity and inclusivity. It also grants participants the agency to craft their preferred futures. In doing so, it reshapes communities, reimagines what's possible, and reaffirms the potential for design to be a powerful force for positive change.

However, it's essential to understand that the Anti-Racist Design Community Pop-Up is not a solitary solution to the deeply entrenched issue of racism. Instead, it is a vital bottom-up initiative that creates a space for understanding and addressing the harm that racism inflicts on society. It facilitates meaningful conversations and amplifies voices that have long been marginalized.

As we move forward, we must remember that the journey toward a more equitable future is ongoing, requiring continuous dialogue, collaboration, and antiracist action(s). The overwhelming sense of possibility expressed by participants underscores the resilience and hope instilled by this initiative.

References

Deaton, J., Oladipo, G., and Vance, A. (2020, September 30). "Mapping the Disparities of Chicago's Unequal Pandemic." Bloomberg. Retrieved August 14, 2024, from https://www.bloomberg.com/news/articles/2020-09-30/mapping-the-disparities-of-chicago-s-unequal-pandemic

3.3 Case Study: Call and Response | Equitable Design Framework

Team: Omari Souza; Gabriela Disarli, Graduate Candidate, Texas State University; Dillion Sorensen, Graduate Candidate, Texas State University; Leslie Harris, Graduate Candidate, Texas State University

Chicago, Illinois, Fall 2018

Call-and-response and master narratives are two ideas that intersect in the study of design. The first term characterizes African American oral traditions that decenter ideas about objectivity that can often infiltrate art and design in destructive ways. The second term shapes the actual history of design, especially as it centers on Bauhaus—a German artistic movement originating in the Bauhaus art school, which operated from 1919 to 1933. The artists and designers associated with the school are known for their design innovations and embrace of both craft and mass production. We'll examine how both ideas come to bear in the Call and Response | Equitable Design Framework project.

Call-and-Response: An Interactive and Communal Approach

Call-and-response is a critical method rooted in African American oral traditions. It fosters an interactive and process-oriented approach to storytelling and music making, wherein participants engage in a back-and-forth exchange of words or phrases, akin to a game of catch. The interactive nature of call-and-response ensures that art remains meaningful and functional within the community, allowing stories and songs to change and grow with each performance. The practice values change over continuity and embraces multiplicity over codification (Sale 1992).

In "Call and Response as Critical Method: African-American Oral Traditions and *Beloved*" (1992), Maggie Sale emphasizes the importance of perspective and improvisation in African American oral traditions, challenging the ideas found in master narratives—master versions of history that present authoritative and seemingly objective accounts, often overlooking diverse perspectives and interpretations

Sale asserts that Toni Morrison's novel *Beloved* is an exemplary embodiment of call-and-response principles. The novel's narrative structure mirrors the communal nature of oral storytelling, with characters interacting in ways that reflect call-and-response patterns.

In Morrison's novel, oral storytelling is important in keeping African and African American traditions alive, helping the community heal, and giving people power and agency. It helps the characters deal with their painful pasts and stand up against unfair treatment. Storytelling also helps people understand each other better, especially in complicated situations (Yale National Initiative 2008).

A touching example of the power of storytelling in *Beloved* happens in a place called the Clearing, where Baby Suggs, a kind of community leader, holds gatherings. She invites people who were once enslaved to share their feelings and take back control over their lives. Baby Suggs tells them to laugh, cry, and dance, using stories to help heal their deep wounds and remind them of their value. These meetings in which everyone shares their stories provide a way to fight back against the cruel treatment they faced and to feel human together (Yale National Initiative 2008).

Morrison encourages reader participation by leaving specific stories open-ended, inviting the reader to engage in the narrative process and contribute their interpretations. By doing so, she challenges the notion of an objective master narrative and, instead, embraces diversity and subjectivity in the formation and telling of histories (Sale 1992).

Master Narratives: Dominant Histories and Perspectives

The phrase *master narrative* comes from literary and cultural theory, referring to dominant versions of history that claim objectivity and universality. A master narrative is a dominant cultural story or ideology that shapes how people understand the world and their place in it (Kleeblatt 1998). It often reflects the perspectives and values of the dominant group in society, influencing how history, identity, and social norms are perceived and maintained. These narratives often disregard marginalized perspectives and homogenize historical events. In contrast, works like *Beloved* aim to disrupt master narratives by acknowledging the subjective nature of storytelling and embracing a diversity of perspectives—all while revealing the inherent fiction in all historical accounts and highlighting the role of the storyteller in shaping a narrative (Sale 1992, 46).

It's important to consider the ways in which master narratives have shaped the history of design. One example lies in the Bauhaus movement, which emerged in Germany in the early twentieth century. It was first envisioned by the German architect Walter Gropius as a way of bringing together novel art and design (Metropolitan Museum of Art, n.d.). It included workshops for metalworking, cabinetmaking, weaving, pottery, typography, and wall painting (Metropolitan Museum of Art, n.d.). These workshops focused on designs that could be mass-produced, which had a big impact on modern architecture, furniture, textiles, and graphic design (Metropolitan Museum of Art, n.d.). Bauhaus embraced industrialization and the aesthetics of machinery, departing from traditional craftsmanship. This movement sought to create a style compatible with the rapidly growing industrialization of the time, emphasizing industry-based design styles. However, the master narrative that elevates the Bauhaus movement often overlooks other design approaches and perspectives (Sale 1992).

The Bauhaus movement is vital to the history of art and design. It changed how buildings, furniture, and even everyday objects were perceived, as well as how they looked and functioned. Bauhaus focused on making things simple, functional, and modern. Its ideas spread all over the world, influencing how cities are planned, how houses are built, and even how chairs are designed. Imagine if all the art and design around you followed similar rules—that's how powerful Bauhaus was in shaping the design of the modern world.

Many see Bauhaus as a kind of master narrative because its ideas became the standard for modern design. It's a major chapter in the history that everyone learns about in art classes. But some also criticize Bauhaus for focusing too much on industrial ideas and not enough on different cultures or rationales of making art. All the same, Bauhaus remains a key part of how we understand modern art and design today.

The Maker's Manifesto

The Call and Response: Equitable Design Framework project, showcased at Texas State University's JC Mitte Building in San Marcos, Texas, during the fall of 2018, was an interactive exhibit developed by a team that included myself as professor, along with three student leaders (all of them graduate candidates) who assisted in guiding the project. The project aimed to explore how not only experts with formal training but also everyday people could shape design movements.

The project creatively used the atrium window grid at the JC Mitte Building to engage the community in the design process, inviting diverse voices to influence design outcomes. The artists placed questions on vinyl over the existing panels between windows and invited viewers to respond to the questions through Post-it notes placed in empty window squares. The project aimed to foster a dialogue between makers and those traditionally seen as consumers—individuals affected by the outcomes of design artifacts, services, and experiences. By encouraging nonprofessionals to participate, the project disrupted traditional design norms, advocating for socially and environmentally responsible practices while prioritizing inclusivity, continuous evolution, and the rejection of dominant, singular design narratives.

The questions that were posed included inquiries about what it means to be a maker, the responsibility of makers, and the goals that makers should ideally have. The design team

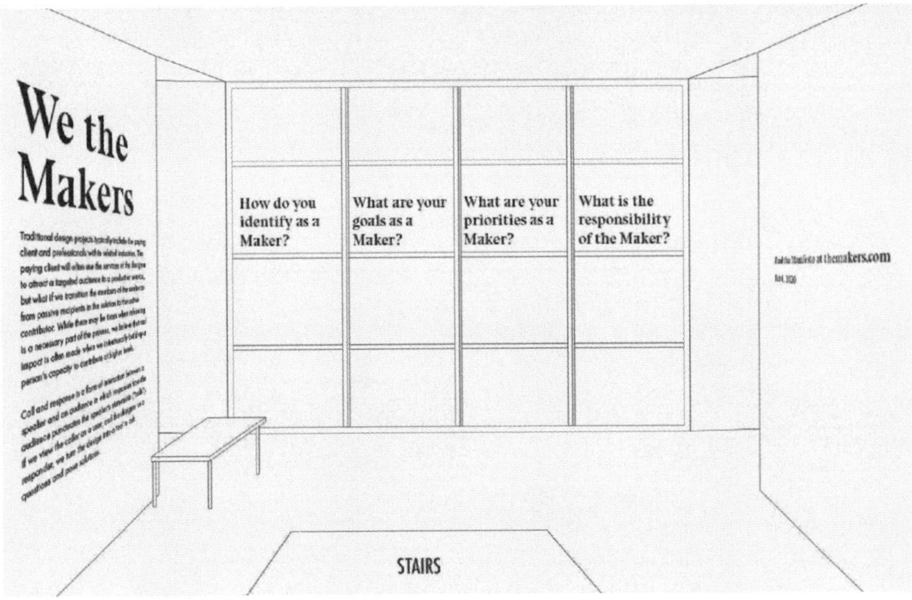

Exhibition mock-up. Before installing the interactive exhibit, the students created a digital mock-up to assess the available space and anticipate how users might interact with the installation within that environment.

View of the atrium installation in the JC Mitte Building at Texas State University

welcomed contributions from individuals regardless of age, gender identity, race, education, or occupation to create a call-and-response experience that would not be dependent on a master narrative from a single teller.

The survey explored the core identities, aspirations, responsibilities, and guiding priorities of both the makers and the viewers, who were all encouraged to participate and share their perspectives. Significantly, feedback focused on shifting priorities from profit margins to address broader issues like promoting sustainability, benefiting the environment, and supporting marginalized communities.

By incorporating various perspectives, the Maker's Manifesto successfully challenged the dominant design model, advocating for socially and environmentally responsible practices and emphasizing a profound desire on the part of the design team to align design with the greater good.

The Call and Response | Equitable Design Framework project expanded on principles of co-design, celebrating change over continuity or permanence and embracing diversity in both problem-solving and design. Inviting audience responses without strict designer guidance dismantled many of the hierarchical structures prevalent in traditional design. It established a partnership-oriented approach, transforming the audience into active contributors and sharing power in the design process. Inspired by African American oral traditions, this interactive method challenged traditional master narratives, such as Bauhaus and Swiss philosophies of design.

Through this inclusive and dynamic process, the Call and Response | Equitable Design Framework project fundamentally reshaped how both students and participants viewed design. By involving a diverse range of voices, the project demonstrated the transformative power of inclusivity in creating more equitable design solutions. It challenged the top-down approach to design by empowering individuals who are typically seen as consumers—those affected by design outcomes—to become co-creators in the process. This experience not only broadened participants' understanding of design as a collaborative and evolving practice but also provided a valuable framework that can be leveraged to develop more socially responsible and inclusive design solutions in the future.

References

Kleeblatt, N. (1998). "Master Narratives/Minority Artists." *Art Journal* 57, no. 3: 29–35.

Yale National Initiative. (2008, February 12). "12.02.08: Beloved: A Case Study in Storytelling Analysis." Yale National Initiative. Retrieved June 24, 2024, from https://teachers.yale.edu/curriculum/viewer/initiative_12.02.08_u

3.4 Case Study: WoodhillUpNext Transformation Plan

Cuyahoga Metropolitan Housing Authority

Cleveland, Ohio, 2018

Indigo Bishop leads an engaging session focused on community development at Woodhill Residence.

The Woodhill Homes public housing estate in Cleveland, Ohio, has a storied history that dates back to its construction in 1939 as a Works Progress Administration urban renewal project. Even in its early years, Woodhill Homes was ahead of its time, adorned with historical public art pieces that were celebrated by the community. However, over the decades, Woodhill Homes and its surrounding neighborhood faced challenges due to disinvestment and neglect. Aging infrastructure, crime, and social barriers created a sense of isolation among the residents, who lived with deteriorating housing conditions, outdated designs, and limited accessibility for those with mobility challenges.

In the midst of these challenges, the Buckeye-Woodhill neighborhood, where Woodhill Homes is located, is less than two miles south of University Circle, home to world-renowned institutions such as the Cleveland Clinic, University Hospitals, and Case Western Reserve University. Recognizing the potential for positive change and building on the strength of the surrounding neighborhoods, the city of Cleveland began investing

Woodhill community members and stakeholders, led by Indigo Bishop, participate in conversations about potential neighborhood development plans.

heavily in the Buckeye-Woodhill area. This investment aimed to generate momentum while honoring the legacy and desires of long-standing community residents.

In 2018, the Cuyahoga Metropolitan Housing Authority (CMHA) was awarded a $350,000 Choice Neighborhoods Planning Grant to develop the WoodhillUpNext Transformation Plan, aimed at revitalizing the Woodhill neighborhood, improving housing conditions, and reducing poverty. Under the leadership of Indigo Bishop, a Choice Neighborhood Administrator, CMHA took a community-centered approach, involving residents directly in the planning process—an intentional departure from traditional, top-down planning methods. This effort eventually secured a $35 million federal grant to implement the plan, with CMHA not only overseeing the redevelopment but also providing ongoing social services to support residents during the transition. The project underscores CMHA's enduring commitment to creating safe, affordable housing and enhancing the quality of life for the communities it serves.

The CMHA started involving residents in the planning process by inviting individuals from the neighborhood, including those identified by residents as potential leaders, to be "ambassadors." These ambassadors played a significant role in shaping the

Woodhill community members come together for a vibrant block party, celebrating milestones in the transformation plan while fostering connections and neighborhood pride.

future of Woodhill Homes and the surrounding community by collaborating directly with the planning team. Leadership roles were selected through a multistep process that began with recommendations from the community center manager and case workers. The recommended individuals were then asked to suggest other active community members, leading to direct outreach and engagement with potential leaders, allowing the community to choose from those who volunteered.

The ambassador program aimed to invest in community members and build their leadership skills. Over two years, the CMHA supported the ambassadors' growth through leadership development, educational opportunities, and tours to other mixed-income housing facilities. The CMHA ensured the ambassadors' active participation and representation of the community's voice by providing stipends and support.

While the community ambassadors were instrumental in fostering trust within the neighborhood, the CMHA still faced challenges due to historical issues between the community and external institutions. Many community members had experienced past attempts at neighborhood planning that yielded little or no tangible results, so some were skeptical that the current project would lead to meaningful change. Past attempts to improve the Woodhill community usually didn't involve the people who lived there and tackled only small problems instead of looking at the bigger picture. They might have fixed a few houses or added some lights, but

Residents explore redevelopment areas during a community walk, gaining firsthand insights into planned improvements and sharing their feedback with the planning team.

they didn't do enough to make the neighborhood safer or more welcoming.

Because they didn't listen to what the community needed and didn't have a long-term plan, the organizers of earlier projects didn't succeed in making real, lasting changes. When designers seek to engage with marginalized communities, it is essential to consider their historical interactions with institutions and well-intentioned individuals. If these past experiences have resulted in harm, neglect, or disregard for the community's concerns, it can lead to lingering negative emotions and deep-seated mistrust. Overcoming these obstacles is crucial for making meaningful collaborative progress.

Rumors of large institutions like Case Western Reserve University or the Cleveland Clinic buying the Woodhill Homes and displacing residents added to existing racialized mistrust. In the case of Cleveland, the expansion of significant entities like Case Western Reserve University and the Cleveland Clinic has contributed to gentrification in numerous communities. Thus, these institutions have the reputation of being disruptors of Black spaces—a problematic pattern that has persisted for several decades (Elrod, n.d.). One significant example highlighting this issue is the story of Winston Willis. A renowned African American entrepreneur, Willis rose to prominence in 1960s Cleveland. Originally from Detroit, he became a millionaire overnight after winning a substantial sum in a pool game. Willis invested his winnings in businesses, becoming a significant force in Cleveland's economic and social landscape (Carrasco 2024).

His enterprises included the Jazz Temple, a popular entertainment venue that showcased jazz legends and attracted diverse audiences. Despite racial discrimination and adversity, he sought to achieve economic prosperity and create opportunities for Cleveland's African American community. His version of the American Dream encompassed breaking barriers and overcoming racial segregation, challenging prevailing systems of inequality, and demonstrating that success could be achieved regardless of race or social background.

Throughout his entrepreneurial journey, Willis experienced numerous racially motivated acts of violence aimed at intimidating and silencing him, including frequent telephone threats, incidents of arson, and the delivery of explosive packages to his businesses. The bombings at his integrated music club, the Towne Casino, further exemplified the racial tensions and violence that were so prevalent in Cleveland's Euclid–East 105th area.

Willis found himself entangled in numerous legal battles due to his fearless confrontation of racial discrimination and his refusal to be silenced by powerful adversaries. His outspokenness against racism, through billboards and other means, attracted hostility from the local government and judiciary. As an African American entrepreneur with successful businesses and land holdings, Willis was seen as a threat by influential entities who were responsible for planning

Residents, stakeholders, community organizers, and architects convene to exchange ideas and collaborate on the WoodhillUpNext Transformation Plan, fostering a sense of equality and shared purpose.

urban-renewal projects. The mistreatment of Willis encompassed a network of other institutions. As research by Cleveland writer and race educator Ajah Hales has revealed, the County Recorder's office, Cleveland City Hall, the Cleveland Clinic, and even the city's Museum of Contemporary Art each played a role in the egregious actions against him (Saks 2022). Moreover, influential law firms and municipal officials with vested interests in urban renewal projects contributed to the targeted harassment and legal battles that Willis had to endure. He faced court cases, illegal seizures of his properties, and relentless harassment, all driven by institutional racism and corruption.

Willis's experience is a heart-wrenching example of the racial discrimination that continues to engender mistrust among minority groups in Cleveland toward various institutions. As Hales asserts, the involvement of powerful entities such as the Cleveland Police Department, local courts, high-profile law firms, and the Cleveland Clinic in illegally seizing Willis's properties sheds light on the ways in which systemic racism often manifested during that period (Hales 2022). The alarming lack of records detailing the transfer of his land further amplifies the reasons for the community's mistrust.

To this day, the impact of Willis's mistreatment and the subsequent erasure of his legacy resonates deeply within the Black communities of Cleveland. A collective memory of injustice and institutional betrayal can significantly influence how current generations perceive and engage with civic institutions. Therefore, acknowledging the historical experiences of marginalized communities is paramount when seeking meaningful engagement in the present day.

To that end, the CMHA prioritized building relationships and transparency across the community. The CMHA dedicated time to engaging with the district, investing in their leaders, and providing opportunities for open dialogue and feedback. The ambassador program was one crucial link between the planning team and the neighborhood residents. Inconveniencing themselves for the sake of the community was another vital approach CMHA officials took to build trust. They scheduled meetings at times most convenient for the residents, even if it meant negotiating for the community center to stay open late. By making the planning process accessible and considering the residents' needs above all else, the CMHA demonstrated its commitment to addressing community concerns and priorities.

The CMHA learned valuable lessons from community members throughout the engagement process. The residents informed the CMHA about the low literacy rates in the area, which led to a shift in communication strategies. Instead of relying solely on flyers, the CMHA focused on word-of-mouth communication and direct engagement.

One of the most significant successes came from the ambassador-led initiative to organize a Sip & Paint event. Initially skeptical about its potential impact, the CMHA supported the idea, and the event was a huge success. It brought together sixty residents, offering a unique opportunity for the planning team to engage with them in an informal setting, and to dispel rumors while sharing information about the transformation plan.

The WoodhillUpNext Transformation Plan's success, evidenced by a $35 million grant awarded by the US Department of Housing and Urban Development, elicits even more hope for a brighter future.

The project entailed a lot of important changes in the aftermath of talking with the community. CMHA officials fixed old and broken houses to make them safe and pleasant to live in. To make the neighborhood safer, they added better streetlights and security cameras, and worked proactively with the police. They built new parks and community centers where people can gather and make friends. For those who use wheelchairs or who have trouble walking, they added ramps and elevators, and made doorways wider. All these changes resulted in a neighborhood that was safer, friendlier, and more accessible.

Since its inception in 2018, the transformation of the Woodhill community remains on track, steadily progressing toward a revitalized future with new housing, retail stores, recreation facilities, and an early- childhood education center. Cleveland's Ward 6 councilperson, Blaine Griffin, views this as a critical

Four kids from the Woodhill community shine at a lively block party, bringing neighbors together to celebrate milestones in the transformation plan while building connections and fostering community pride.

initiative to shift the neighborhood's trajectory and restore vibrancy to a historically underserved area. While this redevelopment is an ongoing effort, requiring sustained dedication and partnership, the project continues to align with its original goals. Maintaining the principles of trust, inclusivity, and attentiveness to community needs will be essential as this vision unfolds into tangible, lasting change for Woodhill.

By learning from past mistakes and addressing historical grievances, institutions like the CMHA can continue building bridges with marginalized communities. Through such transformative approaches, we can move beyond ingrained legacies of mistrust and work to literally and figuratively build a society in which every community's concerns are valued, heard, and sufficiently addressed.

References

Carrasco, A. W. (2024, February 19). "Black History Month Spotlight on Winston Willis: A Forgotten Local Hero." Medium. Retrieved June 28, 2024, from https://aundra-willis.medium.com/black-history-month-spotlight-781adbcea44d

Elrod, J. (n.d.). "Gentrification, Revitalization, and Relocation." *Encyclopedia of Cleveland History*. Case Western Reserve University. Retrieved June 28, 2024, from https://case.edu/ech/articles/g/gentrification-revitalization-and-relocation

Hales, A. (2022, May 31). "The Downfall of Winston Willis: Searching for a Miracle in Cleveland." NPR. Retrieved August 27, 2024, from https://www.ideastream.org/news/2022-05-31/the-downfall-of-winston-willis-searching-for-a-miracle-in-cleveland-part-ii

Saks, N. (2022, May 30). "Searching for a Miracle in Cleveland: The Story of Winston Willis." WBUR. Retrieved August 27, 2024, from https://www.wbur.org/hereandnow/2022/05/30/winston-willis-last-seen

3.5 Case Study: Design Activities to Map Positionality

Omari Souza

Denton, Texas, Fall 2023

During my tenure as a professor at the University of North Texas, I had the privilege of instructing a group of first-year user-experience (UX) designers. Many of these students were pursuing their graduate degrees as a way to either transition into new career paths or advance in their current UX roles. Their shared ambition was to ascend to leadership positions, so I created an exercise designed to foster self-reflection while enhancing their understanding of teamwork and the individuals they aimed to serve.

Our journey into our identities, upbringing, and life experiences united our diverse cohort in a quest to unravel how our distinctive backgrounds had shaped our worldviews. Our objective was not merely to comprehend one another but to harness our unique strengths, recognize our vulnerabilities, and eliminate (or at least have an increased awareness of and willingness to address, to the best of our ability) our blind spots / learning edges to foster effective collaboration.

Throughout the course, I conveyed to the students that we are immersed in intricately interconnected systems and artifacts thoughtfully designed to operate in concert. Systems thinking is a way to solve problems by looking at the whole system instead of just parts of it. This means understanding how different parts of the system interact with and affect each other.

For example, a house can be seen as an interconnected system. In a house, the structural components—the foundation, walls, and roof—are all connected. If one part is damaged, like a cracked foundation, it can affect the whole structure. Utilities like electricity, plumbing, and heating are also linked. If a pipe bursts, it can cause electrical problems or even generate mold. Energy efficiency in a house depends on how insulation, windows, doors, and heating systems work together. Poor insulation can make the heating system work harder and use more energy. The way people live in the house also matters. Their use of water and electricity, and how they take care of the house, affects its overall condition. Finally, the house interacts with its environment; weather affects heating needs and sunlight influences lighting within the house. Landscaping around the house can also affect factors like drainage and energy efficiency.

Similarly, our identities, affiliations with in-groups and out-groups, and geographical origins function as an interconnected system with influence on our approach to problem-solving, how we navigate the world, and the kinds of challenges we encounter. Just as a house's foundation, walls, and roof are its main structure, a person's background—such as their upbringing, culture, and family values—forms the base of who they are. If something big changes in this background, like a family breakup or a move to a new country, it can shake one's entire sense of self.

Social interactions are like a house's utilities, such as electrical wiring and plumbing. Friendships, family ties, and work relationships all influence each other. A fight with a friend might make family life or work more stressful, just as a burst pipe can cause electrical problems. Cultural identity works like a house's energy efficiency, involving language, traditions, and customs interacting with one another. If cultural practices clash, this can create struggles, similar to how poor insulation can strain a heating system.

A person's behavior and lifestyle, like diet and hobbies, affect their well-being, just as the ways people use water and electricity can influence a house's condition. Also, external factors, like social norms and media, have an impact on identity just as weather and landscaping affect a house. Changes in these factors can shape a person's sense of self. Understanding identity this way helps us see how different parts of our lives are connected. These differences present unique problem-solving opportunities when creating experiences for diverse audiences, and open doors to collaboration with individuals whose strengths complement our positional blind spots.

In one class exercise, I tasked students with creating journey maps depicting their experiences using a restroom at a concert venue. Students worked individually, culminating in a collective sharing session.

Male students typically listed three or four steps:

1. Walking to the bathroom
2. Choosing between a stall and a urinal
3. Using the bathroom
4. Washing their hands (a step often overlooked, representing a UX issue for another day)

Conversely, for female students, the process encompassed an additional five or more steps, which might include:

1. Waiting in line
2. Inspecting the bathroom stall to ensure secure locking and cleanliness
3. Finding a place to hang bags, if carried
4. Waiting in line for access to a sink.

The number of steps increased when additional factors were present, such as pregnancy, menstruation, or physical disabilities. Additionally, the choice of attire could influence the speed at which female students navigated the restroom experience.

I would then ask my male students whether they had known about the added complexities of the restroom experience for women, and none raised their hands. Subsequently, I asked how many believed they could design an equitable restroom experience for women without a woman advocating for herself in the design process. Again, none of the male students raised their hands. Conversely, when I posed the same question to the female students, they all raised their hands confidently, expressing their belief in their ability to design a satisfying experience for men, even in the absence of male representation.

This disparity could be attributed to the enduring patriarchal nature of Western society, wherein the experiences of able-bodied men take precedence, sparing them from concerns related to those whose identities diverge from the default/norm. It is crucial to clarify that this exercise was not intended to isolate male students but to shed light on the fact that all of us have aspects of our identity that have been prioritized or excluded. These prioritized facets of our identity can, at times, close our awareness to the obstacles faced by individuals whose identities have been marginalized.

I would then challenge the confidence of the female students in my class by adding additional identity markers to the same exercise. I would inquire as to whether they would feel equally confident designing for a male who is:

- Physically disabled
- Transgender
- Elderly

In response, most of the students would lower their hands, revealing the nuances and challenges associated with designing for individuals with diverse identities who are not often represented in conspicuous or meaningful ways.

Many individuals with marginalized identities find that their true selves and the challenges they encounter, even in the most basic of tasks, are often disregarded. This oversight can lead to significant impediments, particularly when the person responsible for designing experiences is unfamiliar with a marginalized individual's unique perspectives and ways of navigating the world. To effectively address this, designers must start their creative process by recognizing and acknowledging some of their own experiential blind spots / learning edges before embarking on the task of designing for individuals from different backgrounds.

Positionality Matrix: Mapping Our Perspectives

We initiated our exploration by selecting eight demographic categories: ability, age, education, gender, language (first spoken), race, religion, and socioeconomic class. Each category was further divided into

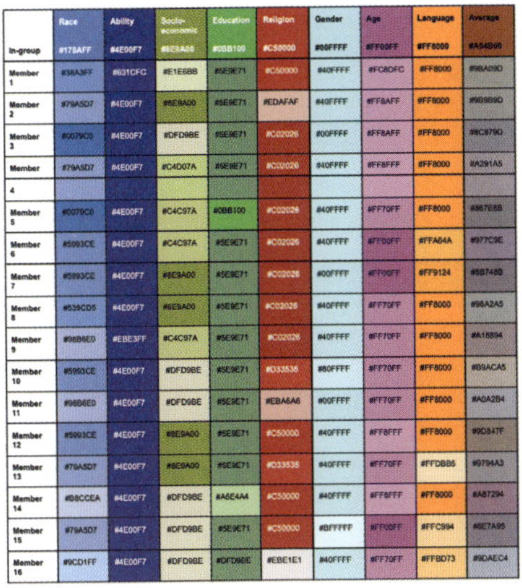

In-group	Race	Ability	Socio-economic	Education	Religion	Gender	Age	Language	Average
In-group	#178AFF	#4E00F7	#6E9A00	#0BB100	#C50000	#00FFFF	#FF00FF	#FF8000	#A54B90
Member 1	#38A3FF	#631CFC	#E1E6B8	#5E9E71	#C50000	#40FFFF	#FC8DFC	#FF8000	#9BA09D
Member 2	#79A5D7	#4E00F7	#8E9A00	#5E9E71	#EDAFAF	#40FFFF	#FF8AFF	#FF8000	#9B9B9D
Member 3	#0079C0	#4E00F7	#DFD9BE	#5E9E71	#C02026	#00FFFF	#FF8AFF	#FF8000	#8C879D
Member 4	#79A5D7	#4E00F7	#C4D07A	#5E9E71	#C02026	#40FFFF	#FF8FFF	#FF8000	#A291A5
Member 5	#0079C0	#4E00F7	#C4C97A	#0BB100	#C02026	#40FFFF	#FF70FF	#FF8000	#867E8B
Member 6	#5993CE	#4E00F7	#C4C97A	#5E9E71	#C02026	#40FFFF	#FF00FF	#FFA64A	#977C9E
Member 7	#5993CE	#4E00F7	#8E9A00	#5E9E71	#C02026	#00FFFF	#FF00FF	#FF9124	#8B7480
Member 8	#539CD5	#4E00F7	#6E9A00	#5E9E71	#C02026	#40FFFF	#FF70FF	#FF8000	#98A2A5
Member 9	#98B6E0	#EBE3FF	#C4C97A	#5E9E71	#C02026	#40FFFF	#FF70FF	#FF8000	#A18894
Member 10	#5993CE	#4E00F7	#DFD9BE	#5E9E71	#D33535	#80FFFF	#FF70FF	#FF8000	#B9ACA5
Member 11	#98B6E0	#4E00F7	#DFD9BE	#5E9E71	#EBA6A6	#00FFFF	#FF70FF	#FF8000	#A0A2B4
Member 12	#5993CE	#4E00F7	#8E9A00	#5E9E71	#C50000	#40FFFF	#FF8FFF	#FF8000	#9D847F
Member 13	#79A5D7	#4E00F7	#8E9A00	#5E9E71	#D33535	#40FFFF	#FF70FF	#FFDBB5	#9794A3
Member 14	#B8CCEA	#4E00F7	#DFD9BE	#A6E4A4	#C50000	#40FFFF	#FF8FFF	#FF8000	#A87294
Member 15	#79A5D7	#4E00F7	#DFD9BE	#5E9E71	#C50000	#BFFFFF	#FF00FF	#FFC994	#8E7A95
Member 16	#9CD1FF	#4E00F7	#DFD9BE	#DFD9BE	#EBE1E1	#40FFFF	#FF70FF	#FFBD73	#9DAEC4

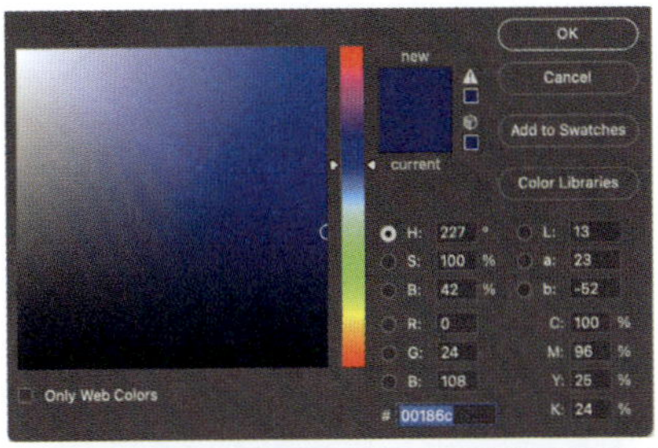

left: A positionality matrix visually maps social and demographic positions across categories like race, gender, and socioeconomic status, using colors to highlight intersections, differences, and power dynamics within a group.; top right: Initiating the design process, we selected eight demographic categories and assigned each a distinct color and saturation level, beginning with race, represented by blue. Participants identified their in-group or out-group status, and these were averaged into a positionality matrix, visually reflecting our collective perspectives across categories.; bottom right: In the second step of selecting CMYK designations, we divided the color value by the number of possible answers within each category, such as the seven racial options. Participants then multiplied this value by their specific identification, producing a unique hue that represented their positionality within that category.

in-groups and out-groups, each represented by distinct colors and saturation levels. Our first step was for each participant to identify their in-group or out-group status for each category. These individual identifications were then averaged to generate an average hue for each student, forming a comprehensive positionality matrix. This matrix visually displayed the alignment and disparities in our perspectives across demographic categories.

To establish colors for each category, we followed a systematic process. Initially, we assigned a specific color to each category. For example, we chose blue to represent the category of race. Once a color was chosen, we assigned it a number using its CMYK (Cyan, Magenta, Yellow, Key/Black) color model designation.

This designation was divided by the number of potential answers within that particular category. For instance, in the case of race, according to the American census, there are six possible answers (White, Black or African American, American Indian or Alaska Native, Asian, and Native Hawaiian or Other Pacific Islander). Although the census does not include Hispanic/Latino as a race, we added it as a seventh option.

Then, we multiplied the CMYK designation by the number related to our identification within that category. For instance, if someone identified as

American Indian or Alaska Native, they would multiply the CMYK designation by three, corresponding to the third option in the category. The resulting color, or hue, represented that person's positionality within that specific category.

To calculate the overall hue that mapped each individual's positionality, we added up all the CMYK designations across the chosen categories. This sum was then divided by the number of types included in the exercise. This systematic approach allowed us to visualize and quantify our positionality, offering insights into the alignment and divergence of perspectives across various demographic categories.

Visualizing the Collaborative Process

In this project, students worked together and learned about the differences between themselves and the people for whom they were designing. As they discovered more differences using a positionality matrix, they started seeking out classmates who had similarities with the group they were designing for.

For example, they shared similar articles to see if they understood them the same way. They gained new cultural insights that could affect how they created solutions. Students also asked their peers to help with visits, interviews, and focus groups, or to review their methods. This teamwork helped them understand more details and find any gaps in their knowledge.

As a student articulated:

> Our collaboration process was shaped by two primary factors: unfamiliarity and ambiguity. Initially, we were strangers to one another, and the lack of clarity regarding the exercise's objectives hindered our engagement. However, collaboration and engagement increased as we got to know each other and grasped the exercise's concepts.

Synthesizing Perspectives: Recognizing the Power of Differences

The "finding our hues" experience enriched students' comprehension of empathy-driven research while highlighting the shared aspects and distinctions defining our group. By applying the positionality matrix, students could visually grasp elements of their peers' identities they might not be familiar with, allowing them to strategically form teams to address the needs of specific demographics.

Our stories, experiences, and insights converge to shape a collective narrative that propels us toward the design of a more inclusive and compassionate world. Students in this class would later share that leveraging the methodology of viewing identity as an interconnected system helped develop self-awareness and empathy by allowing them to recognize how different aspects of their lives shape who they are. This approach improves teamwork, problem-solving, and inclusivity in design by encouraging appreciation of diverse perspectives and comprehensive solutions. It also fosters personal growth, resilience, and

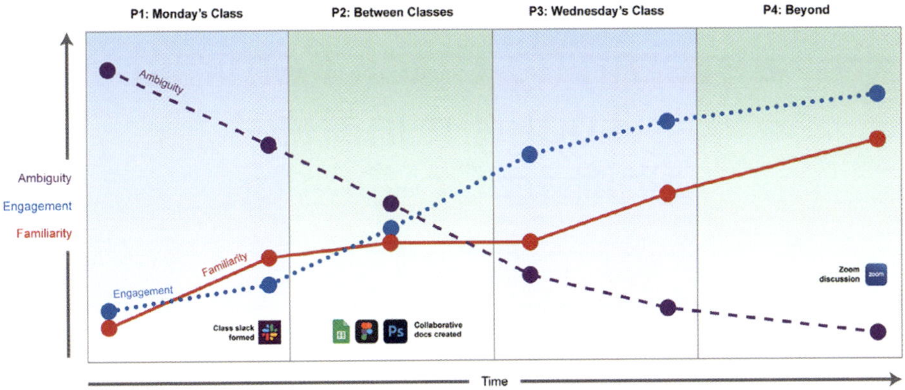

Category	Similarities
Ability	80% similar
Age	40% similar
Education	86% similar
Gender	67% similar
Language	73% similar
Race	33% similar
Religion	67% similar
Socio-economic class	40% similar

top: Visualizing the collaborative process; bottom: Chart illustrating the power of diverse perspectives

adaptability. In addition, it exemplifies the transformative potential of understanding our positions and harnessing that understanding to forge connections and meaningful dialogue that can inform our designs. This journey may be ongoing and imperfect, but we can continually improve our capacity to empathize and co-create through a dedication to lifelong learning.

3.6 Case Study: Leveraging Black Feminist Thought in the Shift to Co-Design

Yolanda A. Rankin

United States, 2017

In the design profession of the recent past, individual output and agency are often emphasized. In previous eras as designers, we may have idealized the image of the "rock star" solo designer. Corporate approaches to human-centered design often result in solutions that focus much less on collective efforts and impact. Today, there is a growing focus on design within communities. Sometimes this is design *for* communities, design *with* communities, design *by* communities, or creating communities of practice—especially among designers whose practices were more marginalized in previous eras.

It is essential that we differentiate between designing *for* communities and designing *with* communities, since moving from one of these paradigms to the other signifies a shift in power relations between the designer and the community.

Sharing my own positionality, I am a trained computer scientist who appreciates innovation and scientific advancements, having worked in the tech industry for several years. However, I advocate that people from all walks of life need to be the primary focus when we design, develop, and evaluate the efficacy of technology. This is not a trivial matter, since technology companies, particularly in the field of computing, have positioned white heterosexual men as the dominant group while relegating women, people of color, and those who do not identify as heterosexual or able-bodied to the outer fringes of the larger tech community (Harrington et al. 2022).

White heterosexual men enjoy the privilege of imagining, creating, building, and explaining technology, and they currently influence all aspects of design with no implicit limitations as to what is possible or what counts as innovation. In 2022, technology designers enjoyed membership in an exclusive club, with very selective criteria for who gets access and is deemed worthy of being recognized as an innovator. Those who live at the intersections of marginalized identities with regard to race, gender, class, ethnicity, sexuality, nationality, or ability often do not determine what constitutes design (O'Leary et al. 2019).

Within the field of human-computer interaction (HCI), practitioners emphasize people as the primary focus while positioning technology as the means for achieving a desired goal. Participatory design, co-design, and user-centered design techniques appear to be synonymous design approaches for enlisting targeted end users or consumers as collaborators. HCI scholarship argues that there are different degrees of participatory design dependent on the amount of collaboration among designers, informants, testers, and end users (Druin 1999). For example, testers provide feedback about how well a technology works and meets their expectations, and how it could be improved for a more positive user experience. This feedback informs modifications to the design of technology, but the testers do not determine which modifications will be made, nor are they responsible for implementing them. They influence the design of technology, but they are not positioned to be designers.

Despite the variations of user involvement in the design process, the field of HCI has struggled with establishing equitable design practices that engage historically excluded populations as equal partners and joint owners of technological innovations (Dombrowski 2017; Erete 2021; O'Leary et al. 2019; Rankin and Irish 2020). More recent HCI work has focused on redistributing power to position members of underserved communities as experts about their lived experiences, as well as capable designers, aligning with bell hooks's (2000) *design is for everybody* perspective.

This poses the question: If everybody is capable of doing design, then why doesn't everybody do it? The answer is complex because it points to the historical effects of racism, gender discrimination, xenophobia, and other forms of oppression that preclude historically marginalized populations from being recognized as contributors to design praxis. In addition, the answer involves examining power relations and the social context to understand how certain communities, particularly Black and Brown communities, have been perceived as irrelevant in technological innovation and less-than-desirable consumer markets (Erete et al. 2022).

Of course, this is a matter of perspective, which, again, points to who is disenfranchised for the sake of maintaining power and dictating the rules about who gets to design and who does not. The false narrative is one that depicts Black and Brown communities as being deficient while also lacking the intellect, resources, assets, and ingenuity to indulge in design thinking, let alone anything that would benefit the majority or dominant social groups. This viewpoint perpetuates racism and white supremacy, under the guise of rationalism and objectivity. It also represents the underlying rationale for designing for communities, which only perpetuates oppressive strategies that do not effectively address the specific contexts of those communities (Harrington et al. 2019).

In my own work, I strive to design with rather than for marginalized communities. In one project, I engaged Black women as co-designers and play-testers of a mobile game to facilitate learning Spanish vocabulary. Motivated by the lack of representation and the lack of inclusion of Black women in the gaming industry, I leveraged Black feminist epistemology, or Black women's ways of knowing, to draw attention to unique issues unaddressed within racial- or gender-focused movements that we as Black women encounter in our everyday lives. Patricia Hill Collins (2000) describes Black Feminist Thought as a critical social theory:

> For African-American women, the knowledge gained at intersecting oppression of race, class, and gender provides the stimulus for crafting and passing on the subjugated knowledge of Black women's critical social theory. As a historically oppressed group, U.S. Black women have produced social thought designed to oppose oppression.... It can take the form of poetry, music, essays, and the like—but the purpose of Black women's collective thought is distinctly different.... The need for such thought arises because African-American women as a group remain oppressed within a U.S. context characterized by injustice. (8–9)

In contrast to the initial theoretical foundation of feminism, which emphasized white women's liberation, Black Feminist Thought has been instrumental in the political, economic, and ideological advancement of Black women (Collins 2000). As an act of resistance to the marginalization of Black women, we dare to speak about the social inequalities and unjust design practices that exist within the gaming industry and subculture (Rankin and Han 2019).

Leveraging a sense of agency, I drew on Black Feminist Thought to create an opportunity for twenty-five Black women enrolled at an all-women's Historically Black College (HBC) in the United States to engage in the conceptualization phase of a game. Applying Black Feminist Thought as a critical framework for game design provides an alternative to traditional game design—one that uses the intersectional lens of race and gender to be more inclusive. As Black women intellectuals, we offer an insider perspective on how to meaningfully engage Black women as both producers (game designers) and consumers (informants) in the game-design process from beginning to end. Black Feminist Thought creates a platform whereby Black women in the game-design process can freely innovate and criticize the second language (L2) mobile-game prototype. *Second language* refers to a language that someone learns in addition to their native language. In this case, it refers to a mobile game made to help people learn and practice a language that is not their first language.

From the perspective of game designers, we identified an initial list of design specifications that aligned with Black women's lived experiences in the United States to motivate the design of the L2 game prototype. Leveraging the cultural practice of Black women engaging in dialogue while they work in the kitchen (Collins 2000), we deliberately chose the kitchen as the setting for the L2 mobile game, which promoted players' acquisition of food-related Spanish vocabulary. The context of socializing with others while preparing different Spanish dishes motivated the game title, *Bienvenido a Ma Cocina! (Welcome to My Kitchen!)*.

One Black woman in the design exercise was empowered to make a game character that looked like her: light skin with freckles, blonde hair, and brown eyes (Rankin and Irish 2020). Usually, Black women don't get the chance to celebrate how different and beautiful they are or to define themselves. This is a way to fight against the negative images of Black women in digital media. According to hooks (1992), Black women are often depicted in media through harmful stereotypes, which is unfair. She asserts that it's important to challenge these images in order to show Black women's authentic and varied experiences. This design exercise is a significant change from the usual way of making games, which often ignores Black people or uses old, unfair, limiting ideas about them.

From the perspective of Black women as players and informants in the game-design process, we provided insights into how to improve the design of L2 mobile games. For instance, the participants advocated for creating a more authentic game-play experience by including different facets of Spanish culture, such as music that is indigenous to a particular Spanish-speaking country. Though we engaged them as play-testers to elicit feedback about their game-play experiences, the Black women in our study recognized the need to respect the humanity, language, and culture of Spanish-speaking populations. This demonstrates how the Black Feminist Thought principle of social justice (Collins 2000) influenced the design of the L2 game to reflect the authenticity of real-life situations rooted in Spanish culture and the diversity of Spanish speakers as the context for game play.

In this way, designing for Black women cultivates an appreciation for other minoritized populations' perspectives of games and creates a positive game-play experience that appeals to a diverse group of players. If we as Black women game designers had taken the more traditional approach, where we acted as the experts in game design because of our training and proficiency in using game-design technology, we would have established power relations that positioned the Black women play-testers as subordinates, suppressing one group of Black women's ideas for the sake of our own egos. Using traditional design practices reinforces systems of power that privilege formally trained designers and oppress the creativity and ideas of Black women. Those who attempt to design *for* Black women neither intentionally redistribute power nor engage with us as collaborators who have an equal say throughout the design process. How often have Black women experienced such a scenario?

As this case study demonstrates, not only is it important for traditionally marginalized groups to experience their own power in the design process, but for those from dominant groups in society, it is essential to confront the concept of internalized dominance. This deeply ingrained perspective can manifest in the way we describe and judge the social practices, clothing, speech, and lifestyles of others. The narratives we construct through this lens often portray people as victims—flattened, one-dimensional characters lacking agency. Recognizing and challenging internalized dominance is a critical step toward more inclusive design and storytelling.

Conversely, for individuals who belong to marginalized groups, it is vital to remain vigilant against internalized oppression, which occurs when members of oppressed groups unwittingly perpetuate the narratives created by their oppressors. By embracing and telling their own stories, individuals can defy these damaging narratives and empower themselves.

As we navigate the intersection of design and storytelling, particularly in community settings, a restorative approach emerges as the path forward. This approach demands that the community's voice is heard at every stage of the design process. It encompasses community involvement in generating themes, as well as feedback on research processes tailored to community agendas, contextually appropriate ethics, and the acknowledgment of community partners. Additionally, it necessitates critiquing practices from a community lens and a nondominant cultural perspective, as well as ensuring accountability in research dissemination and post-project activities.

In the realm of community-engaged design practice, everyone must scrutinize their biases, whether they are insiders or outsiders. It is essential to consider how researchers interact within these communities and frame design and research questions from the community's point of view. The community's involvement in shaping research processes and outcomes is paramount, and the sharing of work with community members is a critical aspect of the process.

To adopt a truly restorative approach, it is essential to slow down, listen, and genuinely see people. In creating environments for co-design, encouraging participants to share their stories and experiences fosters collaborative knowledge generation. Sacrificial ideas (the initial suggestions people share in a group project to spark discussion and creativity, which act as stepping stones to better ideas) can serve as starting points for collaborative design processes, allowing for critique and reconstruction. Additionally, creating spaces in which honest feedback is welcomed ensures that the design process benefits from the community's collective wisdom.

Co-design is about building relationships and requires significant investment in building trust. It's a slow process. Speed is something that many of us have to unlearn. But can we slow down to honor the necessary aspects of relationship building? After all, effective co-design draws on empathetic skills that entail processes that aren't always aligned with "work" and goal-oriented activities; that is, sometimes we need food, drink, music, dance, and storytelling to create the right environment for collaboration.

Designers and researchers must ponder the implications of designing in the absence of considering historical context, systems, and exclusion. The essence of this inquiry lies in the question: How can we ensure that the individuals and communities most affected by the outcomes of our work are the ones in charge of influencing them?

References

Collins, P. H. (2000). *Black Feminist Thought: Knowledge, Consciousness, and the Politics of Empowerment*, 2nd ed. Routledge.

Dombrowski, L. (2017). "Examining the Role of Power in Co-Design." *Proceedings of the 2017 ACM Conference on Computer Supported Cooperative Work and Social Computing*, 1871–82. Retrieved August 28, 2024, from https://doi.org/10.1145/2998181.2998297

Druin, A. (1999). "Cooperative Inquiry: Developing New Technologies for Children with Children." *Proceedings of the SIGCHI Conference on Human Factors in Computing Systems*, 592–99. Retrieved August 28, 2024, from https://doi.org/10.1145/302979.303166

Erete, S. (2021). "Human-Computer Interaction for Development: Engaging Underserved Populations." *Interactions* 28, no. 2: 46–49. Retrieved August 28, 2024, from https://doi.org/10.1145/3448412

Erete, S., Rankin, Y. and Thomas, J. (2022). "Understanding the Role of Race in the Design and Use of Digital Games: A Critical Discourse Analysis." *Game Studies* 22, no. 1. Retrieved August 28, 2024, from http://gamestudies.org/2201/articles/erete_rankin_thomas

Harrington, C. N., Erete, S., and Piper, A. M. (2019). "Deconstructing Community-Based Collaborative Design: Towards More Equitable Participatory Design Engagements." *Proceedings of the ACM on Human-Computer Interaction* 3 (CSCW): 216. Retrieved August 28, 2024, from https://doi.org/10.1145/3359318

Harrington, C. N., Klassen, T. P., and Rankin, Y. A. (2022). "Technology and Social Justice: Examining the Role of Marginalized Communities in Shaping Digital Innovations." *Journal of Information Technology & Politics* 19, no. 2: 99–116. Retrieved August 28, 2024, from https://doi.org/10.1080/19331681.2022.2029771

hooks, b. (1992). "The Oppositional Gaze: Black Female Spectators." In *Black Looks: Race and Representation*, 115–31. South End Press.

hooks, b. (2000). *Feminism Is for Everybody: Passionate Politics*. South End Press.

O'Leary, K., Serrano, S., and Nassim, J. (2019). "Exploring Equity and Inclusion in Participatory Design: Theories, Practices, and Key Issues." *Proceedings of the ACM Conference on Designing Interactive Systems*, 931–43. Retrieved August 28, 2024, from https://doi.org/10.1145/3322276.3322363

Rankin, Y. A., and Han, S. (2019). "Games for Change: Designing Games for Social Impact with Marginalized Communities. *International Journal of Human-Computer Interaction* 35, no. 19: 1756–68. Retrieved August 28, 2024, from https://doi.org/10.1080/10447318.2019.1597573

Rankin, Y. A., and Irish, D. (2020). "Empowering Black Women in Game Design Through Black Feminist Thought." *Feminist Media Studies* 20, no. 6: 856–71. Retrieved August 28, 2024, from https://doi.org/10.1080/14680777.2020.1789443

3.7 Case Study: Reimagining Public-Benefits Applications

Civilla

Detroit, Michigan, 2016

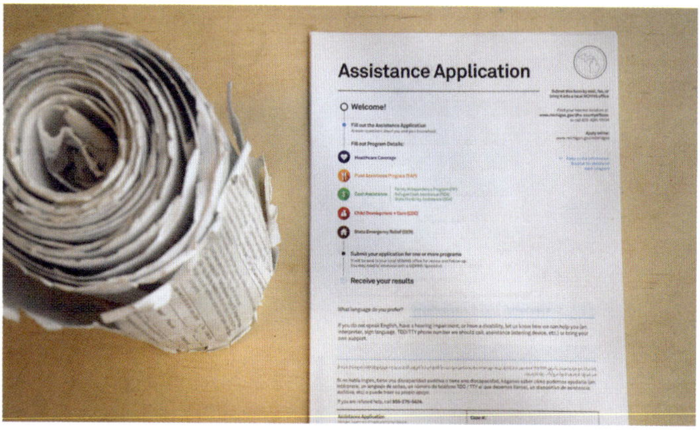

Civilla and MDHHS redesigned Michigan's public-benefits application process, creating a much shorter, more user-friendly application and an intuitive online portal, significantly improving access to essential services for millions of residents. The redesign also included comprehensive staff training and ensured compliance with all policy requirements, serving as a model for other states.

In 2015, in a dimly lit storage closet, Michael Brennan, cofounder and CEO of Civilla, pulled a daunting forty-plus-page benefits application from his back pocket with a bold aspiration to transform it. This extensive document was the Department of Human Services (DHS)-1171, the longest public-benefits application in the United States. With one thousand questions and eighteen hundred words, it posed a formidable barrier to more than 2.5 million Michigan residents each year.

Brennan first encountered this unwieldy document during his time at the United Way. He carried it as a stark reminder of the inefficiencies plaguing public institutions. His perspective began to shift when he learned about human-centered design from his longtime friend and mentor, Jim Hackett, former CEO of Steelcase. Inspired by this innovative approach, Brennan furthered his studies at the Hasso Plattner Institute of Design at Stanford University (the d.school). There, he met fellow visionaries Adam

Selzer and Lena Selzer. Together, they founded Civilla, united by a belief that public institutions could drive social change more effectively through human-centered design. Civilla, a nonprofit design studio based in Detroit, aims to revolutionize how public institutions address and overcome bottlenecks. Brennan and the Selzers envisioned helping these institutions return to their core mission of serving the community.

In 2016, the firm took on its first major challenge: redesigning the DHS-1171 application. This document, shaped by more than thirty years of process-oriented design, prioritized policy, lawsuits, and audits over the needs of applicants. Civilla saw this as a prime opportunity to demonstrate the transformative power of human-centered design, aiming to make the benefits application process more accessible and humane.

Civilla's work exemplifies the power of listening to marginalized communities and integrating their perspectives in order to drive innovation and create dialogue that leads to change and inclusivity. The founders of Civilla believe that the fastest and most effective way to scale positive change in society is by enhancing the institutions that serve the public. These institutions—designed to support safe, productive, and healthy lives—carry the weight of centuries of investment and infrastructure. Yet, in the modern world, they've often strayed from their original purpose, leading to a significant loss of public trust.

Rather than turning away from these struggling institutions, Civilla chooses to work alongside their leaders to strengthen and guide them toward meaningful change. They view public- serving institutions not as relics to be abandoned but as potential sites of innovation capable of balancing compassion with efficiency. By leveraging their deep foundations and extensive infrastructure, Civilla believes these institutions can be revitalized to better support the community.

Civilla's expertise spans several key areas. Its approach begins with user research and strategy, during which team members conduct thorough qualitative and quantitative research to understand the needs of the people who are served by institutions. This research helps identify the most significant opportunities for change.

Next, the team moves into service design, employing human-centered design principles to reshape services from end to end. This involves improving technology, business processes, policies, and operations to create more efficient and compassionate service-delivery systems.

When it comes to implementation, Civilla partners closely with institutions to navigate the path from concept to reality. Team members ensure that solutions remain focused on human needs throughout the implementation process. Moreover, capacity building is a crucial component of their work. They train individuals and teams in human-centered design to shift organizational cultures toward long-term innovation and efficiency.

The starting point for getting public benefits in Michigan was an application that was more than forty pages long. It contained more than one thousand questions and more than eighteen thousand words, making it the longest form of its kind in the country.

Civilla's project-development process is systematic and thorough, with four distinct phases. During discovery research, the team leads in-depth studies that place people's needs at the forefront. The insights gained during this phase help pinpoint the most significant opportunities for change. Next, in the design and testing phase, Civilla establishes goals based on the needs identified during research. Team members work in short, iterative sprints to design various viable solutions, testing each concept and refining it based on feedback. Once solutions are refined enough for real-world application, they move to the pilot phase. Here, new tools and processes are rolled out to small groups, allowing Civilla to gather feedback and measure impact before scaling solutions more broadly. Finally, the scaling phase involves preparing the organization for a full rollout. This critical step includes building readiness, securing buy-in, and facilitating extensive training, communication, and stakeholder engagement to ensure a successful and sustainable transition.

Through its comprehensive and compassionate approach, Civilla strives to transform public institutions

The Civilla team spent more than four thousand hours talking with people in their homes and offices, listening to the experiences of both residents and frontline staff. Through these conversations, they discovered that the DHS-1171 form was a major barrier for people trying to access the state's most important services.

into efficient, innovative entities that can meet communities' needs. By thoroughly researching, testing, and implementing thoughtful solutions, Civilla ensures that the changes introduced are sustainable and impactful, fostering renewed trust and functionality within public-serving institutions.

By engaging residents and frontline administrative staff in the design process, Civilla created a shorter, more user-friendly DHS-1171 application that significantly improved the application experience for millions of citizens. Civilla's transformation of Michigan's public-benefits application process was driven by a deep empathy for financially disadvantaged individuals. This journey began with extensive user research, during which Civilla's team members spent countless hours in residents' homes, immersing themselves in residents' experiences with the public-benefits system. By spending time in these environments, researchers gained valuable insights into users' challenges while completing the extensive forms. They identified specific bottlenecks and knowledge gaps that residents encountered. Many felt overwhelmed, describing the process as confusing, repetitive, and more focused on fraud prevention than anything else.

Civilla also engaged with frontline staff at the Michigan Department of Health and Human Services (MDHHS), recognizing the need for a holistic perspective. After six weeks of interviews with residents, Civilla realized that a key part of the story was missing: the frontline-staff experience. These staff members, who dealt with constant visits, phone calls, and error-filled applications due to the complex system, provided crucial insights into the problem's full scope.

Civilla's collaboration with MDHHS began in an unexpected way when Michael Brennan, Civilla's cofounder, reached out directly to the department with a cold call. Although Civilla had no prior connection with MDHHS, Brennan presented the studio's independent research findings, which were rooted in conversations with Michigan residents navigating the benefits application process. Driven by Civilla's mission to improve public services through human-centered design, this initial research was independently funded, showcasing Civilla's commitment to fostering meaningful change within public institutions. Brennan approached MDHHS with care, framing the conversation as a constructive exploration of user insights rather than a critique. This genuine, collaborative approach resonated with MDHHS leadership, prompting them to attend an introductory meeting at Civilla's office.

At the initial meeting, MDHHS leaders, dressed formally in suits and polished shoes, entered Civilla's humble storage space. Brennan carefully unrolled a forty-page scroll—the DHS-1171 form, an imposing benefits application—to demonstrate just how unwieldy and daunting it appeared to applicants. The scroll, stretched across the space, created a powerful visual that underscored the form's complexity and the psychological burden it imposed on applicants. With this backdrop, the Civilla team shared findings from their research

After nearly three years of redesign, a much shorter and faster application was introduced across Michigan in 2018, making it easier for millions of people to get the help they need and setting an example for other states to follow.

with Michigan residents, highlighting the form's overwhelming nature. For Terry Beurer, a longtime MDHHS leader with thirty-two years in the department, the scroll was a stark revelation; he had never seen the DHS-1171 presented in a way that exposed its daunting structure so vividly. This approach resonated with MDHHS leadership, leading them to commit to future sessions to explore further insights.

By involving both residents and administrative staff in the redesign process, Civilla developed a shorter, more user-friendly application. This transformation streamlined the process for millions of Michigan citizens—a testament to the project's success.

Through relationship building and an effort to understand the needs of marginalized people (whose feedback is seldom heeded in major decision-making processes that ultimately affect them), Civilla fostered buy-in from stakeholders and successfully implemented the redesigned application statewide.

3.8 Case Study: Disrupting Higher Education Through Antiracist Counterstorytelling and Alternative Futuring

Soniyah Robinson and Danielle Lake

Elon University, Elon, North Carolina, 2020

Biased: (Re)Designing for Equity and Social Justice is a university-wide, student-led design workshop series at Elon University (North Carolina) that infuses campus, local, and participant storytelling with equity-design practices. The series was imagined to create space for counterstories (i.e., stories that reveal hidden narratives, counternarratives, or narratives of resistance) and to encourage the design of antiracist practices across our campus communities. Participants learn about implicit bias and cycles of oppression, and share stories of social-justice activism. They also explore scholarship on critical race studies and equity-centered design, discussing work from bell hooks, Andrew Ibrahim, Bobbie Harro, Sasha Costanza-Chock, Josina Vink, the Creative Reaction Lab, and others. The series aims to shift the burden of antiracist design efforts from members of minoritized groups alone (Kernahan 2019). In addition to exploring the stories and counter-stories of others, participants reframe their own narratives and generate resistant and transformative future stories (Bell 2019) from which action-able opportunities can emerge.

The series is entirely student-led. It began in the spring of 2020, when students committed to social-justice activism expressed frustration with the disconnect between dominant narratives and lived realities. Their concerns sparked conversations that were hosted at various campus centers. These conversations ended up bringing together a range of stakeholders, including faculty and directors from the university's Center for Race, Ethnicity, and Diversity Education and the Center for Design Thinking.

The initial series in spring 2020 included three workshops:

1. **Biased: (Re)Designing for Equity and Social Justice** documents on- and off-campus stories of bias and helps participants explore, visualize, and discuss their own stories. After learning about on- and off-campus stories, participants map an experience of their own. In small groups, they talk about how they might disrupt these biases, exploring not just their initial ideas but also collaborative, ambitious, and even joyous ways they might intervene in these cycles. By the end of the session, participants commit to their next steps for addressing challenges that emerge from implicit biases.
2. **Designing for Liberation** infuses student facilitator narratives with research on cycles of oppression. We discuss equity-centered designer Josina Vink's work documenting how our effort to grow our own individual awareness of systems of oppression can generate collective awareness and collective action over time. We ask participants to consider how they might find opportunities to create and disrupt current systems and processes within our on- and off-campus communities. In the end, they explore together a range of prototypes for liberatory practices that press against the contextual constraints of their lives. At the end of this session, each participant commits to an action designed to disrupt cycles of oppression within their own life.
3. **Design Justice: Cultivating Anti-Racist Practices** explores the histories of the campus community more fully, integrating narratives from a recent history and memory report designed to share previously untold stories from Black students, faculty, staff, and community members. Participants map where they are in their antiracist journey and explore methods for continuing the work.

More than one hundred workshops have been offered through this series. Professors across academic departments, university administrators, and even off-campus community members (e.g., nonprofit organizations, local high schools, after-school programs, and regional government organizations) have requested these workshops.

To better understand the value and challenges of this series, we always ask participants to provide feedback. We created brief surveys that have helped us better understand the workshops' value and limitations. Feedback reinforced that the series increases their interest in equity-centered design strategies and provides them with ideas, resources, and strategies they plan to implement. These surveys also confirmed that what people most valued about the session was the opportunity to share their stories, engage in intergroup dialogue, and learn about antiracist design methods. We found that it was essential that session facilitators demonstrate an openness to sharing their experiences, which seemed to create space for workshop participants to do the same. Participant feedback also revealed that it was important for them to have the opportunity to visualize their thinking via design-thinking practices and to share their thoughts via intergroup dialogue. They consistently responded that they wanted more opportunities to interact, collaborate, and discuss.

We recommend that others interested in designing similar sessions hold space and time for sharing diverse stories. Based on our own experience, we also recommend sharing diverse resources (e.g., design-thinking tools and activities, books, podcasts, movies, centers, and classes) and creating "tangible takeaways" (i.e., tokens of their commitment to social justice, swag) for participants to carry with them throughout their social-justice journey.

To learn more, check out Elon's Center for Design Thinking or reach out to us at elonbydesign@elon.edu.

References

Kernahan, C. (2019). *Teaching About Race and Racism in the College Classroom: Notes from a White Professor.* West Virginia University Press.

Bell, L. A. (2019). *Storytelling for Social Justice: Connecting Narrative and the Arts in Antiracist Teaching* (2nd ed.). Routledge.

Conclusion

When I set out to write this book and seek out additional voices who would help to elucidate the power and importance of a restorative design framework, I purposely sought to expand our imagination and conceptualization around design and what it actually is.

Design's impact extends beyond mere functionality; it is also a powerful sociocultural tool. Consider, for instance, a dining table. A rectangular table with a designated head creates a clear hierarchy, centering certain individuals and establishing a social order. In contrast, a round dining table without a head promotes equality among diners by eliminating hierarchical seating positions. This simple design choice generates a slew of often unconsciously received narratives that can influence social dynamics and interpersonal interactions; this illustrates how design can guide our practices of being with each other and making meaning from our experiences.

Dining etiquette provides another example of design's pervasive, often unacknowledged, influence. Think about the rituals associated with serving meals and the artifacts central to these traditions. What messages do these artifacts communicate? How would these traditions be different without them? Consider, for example, the design of dining implements and the customs and assumptions surrounding their use—or their lack of use in cultures where people use their hands to eat. All these traditions play a crucial role in maintaining cultural continuity and shaping social behavior and ideas of propriety versus impropriety.

The essays in *Design Against Racism* have demonstrated that in Western societies, design is not just a tool of capitalism but an integral part of it. Design is used to craft products for consumption and to persuade consumers to purchase specific experiences and services. This strategic use of design aims to expand market share and drive economic growth. Companies invest heavily in design to differentiate their offerings and create desirable products that appeal to consumers' emotions and aspirations, thereby shaping the economic landscape. This becomes an obvious problem when design is deployed as a tool to maximize profits rather than to cultivate a communal experience that centers on justice and collective well-being (e.g., the design of green spaces in urban areas, or walkways and pathways that encourage connecting with nature and other people).

Design, therefore, is not merely about aesthetics or functionality; it is a fundamental force that shapes human experience, sociocultural practices, and economic systems. The essays in this book have sought to help us understand and consider the broader implications of design so that we can appreciate its role in guiding cultural evolution and influencing social hierarchies. Whether through the layout of a room, the form of a table, or the marketing of a product, design profoundly affects our lives and the world around us.

Throughout my academic journey, in both undergraduate and graduate studies, I frequently encountered the assertion that design, by nature, does no harm—or at least, should not. This perspective seems logical at first glance; how could the design of a logo, a chair, or a building possibly be harmful? However, this sentiment often serves to depoliticize design, presenting it as neutral and detached from social issues.

This assessment is misleading. Let's consider how design as practiced today functions as an extension of capitalism, and capitalism as a descendant of colonialism. It becomes clear that design often aligns with the interests of those who can afford it and reinforces the structures that sustain it. In this context, design does harm by perpetuating existing power dynamics and inequalities, often in inconspicuous ways.

For instance, take the chocolate and diamond industries, both notorious for their exploitative labor practices. The workers in these industries, including farmers and miners, often endure harsh conditions and inadequate compensation, while the final products generate substantial profits for multinational companies. Similarly, fashion brands frequently rely on sweatshop labor, and the production of electronic devices depends on conflict minerals like tin, tantalum, tungsten, and gold. Design plays a crucial role in marketing products from industries with exploitative labor practices by creating visually appealing packaging, crafting compelling brand stories, and designing immersive consumer experiences that distract from the harsh realities of their production. This strategic use of design enhances the desirability of these products while obscuring the unethical practices involved in their creation. The financial gains from these industries enable companies to expand their market influence while maintaining an oppressive status quo in the countries where these resources are sourced.

Design practices have long been embedded in the structures of capitalism. Traditional design serves the needs of capitalist production and consumption, often prioritizing short-term, profit-driven objectives. This leads to unsustainable models of production and consumption, where design drives consumer demand and economic growth, perpetuating capitalism's framework of infinite growth. The products and experiences created by designers not only fulfill market needs but also reinforce that system's foundational principles.

But we all know that capitalism faces a fundamental sustainability crisis. The system's demand for perpetual growth is untenable, given the finite nature of planetary resources. This relentless pursuit of growth leads to environmental destruction and resource depletion. Additionally, capitalism contributes to significant economic disparities, concentrating wealth and power in the hands of a few while creating economic precarity for too many. These challenges highlight the urgent need for rethinking the fundamental relationship between design and capitalism—for utilizing a restorative approach.

This global market expansion and cultural influence affect both consumers and producers, reinforcing economic and social disparities. A common saying I heard growing up is that tools often carry the spirit and ideologies of their creators. Unfortunately, contemporary design tends to romanticize Eurocentrism and white male perspectives, relegating other perspectives to the status of subcultures. This bias is evident in specific design outcomes and their failures. Consider the case of car accidents: Who is most frequently injured? The answer, which is not tied to driving stereotypes, is women. Car-safety tests have traditionally used crash-test dummies modeled after male anatomy. Consequently, women face higher risks of injury and fatalities, as well as greater costs related to recovery and therapy, because they are not equally represented in safety testing.

As a person of color, I frequently encounter practical challenges with everyday designs that fail to account for the diversity of users. Whether it's automatic faucets that struggle to recognize my skin tone, facial-recognition technology that inaccurately identifies people with darker skin, or the lack of hair-care products for textured hair in mainstream retail outlets, these experiences highlight how design often overlooks the needs of marginalized communities—which reinforces the importance of more inclusive and thoughtful design practices.

While design is often perceived as neutral and harmless, it is inextricably linked to the socioeconomic and political contexts in which it operates. By reinforcing existing power structures and biases, design can indeed do harm. At the same time, because it plays a crucial role in shaping cultural norms and directing flows of investment, labor, and resources, it can also be a site of necessary restoration and transformation. It has the potential to reorient us toward more sustainable and democratic ends.

As the essays in this book have demonstrated, design can help us to envision and materialize new ways of being in the world by contributing to broad and meaningful social change. In community-engaged design practice, which has been central to many of the practices addressed in this book that have envisioned the scope of a restorative design framework, designers must consider whether they are designing with or for a community, or if they are involved in a process that centers on design by the community.

These new relationships within the design process, when built with great intention, have the power to bring about changes in design methods and hierarchies. Co-design, or designing with, recognizes the diverse expertise among participants, acknowledging that lived experience and learned experience both hold value. In traditional design practices, learned experience tends to be prioritized over lived experience, so letting go of this bias is necessary when it comes to generating a collaborative process rooted in principles of restorative justice.

A restorative design framework necessarily elevates the voices and knowledge of individuals with lived experience, combining it with the expertise of those with learned experience to improve matters of common concern. It resembles a critical pedagogy approach, wherein knowledge is not confined to a single authority but is shared and co-created among all participants. In such an approach, diverse forms of expertise within the group are respected, fostering exciting opportunities for peer learning and collaboration.

A restorative framework emphasizes process as equal to outcome. While results are important, the unpredictability and unique trajectory of a restorative design process should be acknowledged. It may not unfold as initially expected, but it should always allow for organic growth and innovation.

The goal of co-creation, which is the very core of restorative design, is to promote wide participation and empower the beneficiaries of the design process to solve their own problems—which goes against the grain when it comes to histories of colonialism, extraction, saviorism, and the ways in which marginalized communities' concerns and ingenuity are routinely neglected.

I hope that the insights and perspectives shared throughout this book will resonate deeply with your own journey as a designer, educator, or storyteller. Restorative design is not just a methodology but a transformative approach that challenges us to rethink how we engage with the world around us. It calls for a deliberate and conscious effort to address the historical inequities and cultural erasures that have long shaped our field. By incorporating the principles of restorative design, you have the opportunity to create work that not only challenges the status quo but also contributes to healing and empowerment within marginalized communities.

I encourage you to critically examine your own practices, to question the biases and assumptions that may unconsciously guide your decisions, and to embrace a more inclusive and equitable approach to design. This book provides both the theoretical framework and practical examples to guide you in your own process, by demonstrating how design can be a powerful tool for social justice and cultural preservation. By engaging in community-driven and collaborative processes, you can help shape a future where design is a force for positive change—where it amplifies marginalized voices, reclaims cultural identities, and fosters a more just and inclusive society. Let this be an invitation to use your skills, creativity, and influence to build a more equitable world through the power of restorative design.

Acknowledgments

TO MY FAMILY—MY FOUNDATION, MY STRENGTH.
To my sons, Noah and Ezra—being your father is my greatest honor. May my journey inspire you to walk boldly in your truth.

To my mother, Mommy Jewel, and my father—your sacrifices, love, and wisdom have shaped me. I am because you are.

To my siblings; aunts Verna, Erica, Lisa, Monique, Tanya, Nisha, Jackie, Jennifer; and uncles Pete and Stephen—your unwavering support has been my anchor. To my cousins Jemar, Neville, Kimmie, and Trey—thank you for the laughter, memories, and lifelong bond.

TO MY COMMUNITY.
To the countless friends, mentors, and collaborators who have walked this journey with me—your belief, encouragement, and wisdom have fueled my purpose. To KenYata—your brilliance as a student and rising star gives me hope for the future.

TO THE EDUCATORS AND PEOPLE WHO INSPIRED MY CURIOSITY.
Alana Lomax, Aneya Raynor, and Aoife Mooney are followed by Brandi Greene, Camron Taylor, Charles Beckworth, and Charles Spencer. Curtis Stevenson, David Hart, David Middleton, and David Roll come next, along with Derrick Moore and Dominique Mueller. Duwain, Gretchen Caldwell Rinnert, and Heather Infantry are included, along with Jaime Kennedy, Jenn White Johnson, and Jessica Barness. Jillian Coorey and Joelle Williams appear alongside John Ferguson and Kelli Williams. Kevin Bethune, Larrie King, Laura Bishop, and Lauren Tate Baeza, leading to Lesley Ann Noel, PhD, Malissa Moore, and Marcus D. Taylor. Maurice Cherry, Michael Ewing, Michael Held, and Milan Drake are listed before Nate Williams and Ormond Brathwaite. Quinnton Harris, Rebecca Breuer, and Rod Wilson are also included. Sanda Katila, Sekou Cooke, and Sedric Travis precede Steve Johnson and Tanisha Coleman. Finally, Terresa Moses, Tim Mwangi, Tracey L. Moore, Tracey Moore, and Virgil Davis complete the list.

TO NIRMALA NATARAJ—THANK YOU FOR ALL YOU'VE DONE AND CONTRIBUTED.

TO MY FRATERNITY, KAPPA ALPHA PSI.
Your principles of achievement and service continue to inspire me to uplift others and leave a lasting impact.

TO ALL WHO HAVE SHAPED MY PATH—THIS JOURNEY IS NOT MINE ALONE.
THANK YOU.

WITH GRATITUDE,
OMARI SOUZA

About the Authors

OMARI SOUZA is an Assistant Professor of Communication Design at the University of North Texas. With a diverse background and wealth of experience, he has made significant contributions to various industries and academic institutions.

Omari's journey as a first-generation American began in the vibrant borough of the Bronx, New York. His cultural heritage traces back to his Jamaican roots, adding a unique perspective to his work and worldview.

Prior to his academic career, Omari held roles at esteemed organizations such as *VIBE* magazine, Capital One, Health Care Service Corporation (HCSC), CBS Radio, and Case Western Reserve University. These experiences gave him invaluable insights into media, broadcasting, and higher education. He is also a proud member of Kappa Alpha Psi, a historically Black fraternity dedicated to achievement, community service, and leadership development.

Omari cohosts the highly acclaimed minisode podcast, *The Design of Business | The Business of Design*. This engaging platform delves into the intricate workings of design within complex organizations, and how design influences decisions, products, and more. As a cohost, Omari brings together industry experts and designers from diverse fields to explore the impact of design on various aspects of business.

Recognizing the importance of representation and inclusivity in design, Omari is the founder of the State of Black Design conference. This groundbreaking conference aims to celebrate, promote, and amplify the voices and contributions of Black designers, fostering a more equitable and diverse design industry.

In his research pursuits, Omari focuses on methods of decolonizing design practices and conducting ethical research. His exploration of these critical areas challenges existing norms and strives to create a more inclusive and responsible design landscape. With his multifaceted background, Omari brings a wealth of knowledge and passion, and a commitment to positive change in communication design. His contributions and insights continue to shape the industry and inspire the next generation of designers.

ZARIAH CAMERON is a recent graduate of North Carolina A&T State University. She aims to cultivate a sense of community within her work and to amplify marginalized voices/stories. She recently became the first Equity Centered UX Strategist at Ally Financial, helping to drive an Inclusive Design methodology for the design organization.

GEORGE FOURLAS is a Senior Researcher with Security in Context. Formerly the SHIFT Endowed Associate Professor of Applied Ethics at Hampshire College, he has also held positions at Franklin and Marshall College, Worcester State University, the University of Oregon, and Globernance (Instituto de Gobernanza Democrática). He is a coeditor of *Radical Philosophy Review* and the Senior Managing Editor of Global Insecurity, the Security in Context blog. He is also a researcher with Capital One's MLXD team, where he focuses on responsible AI.

George's teaching and research take place at the intersection of social-political philosophy, applied ethics, critical race theory, conflict resolution, decolonial theory, and global studies. He draws on his international research and is eager to take students out of the classroom to more fully ground their studies in meaning-making encounters. He is also interested in the fine arts, martial arts, and being outside (especially in remote and isolated spaces). George wears many hats and a few belts—specifically, a second dan black belt in WTF/ITF tae kwon do and a purple belt in Brazilian Jiu Jitsu. Most of all, he appreciates spending time with his family.

SHAMIKA KLASSEN is a person who is passionate about people and technology. After graduating from Stanford University with a degree in African and African American studies in 2011, she served a year with AmeriCorps in New York City. She went on to study technology and ethics by developing technowomanism at Union Theological Seminary in the city of New York. There, she also created and developed the concept of a Tech Chaplain. She received her Master of Divinity from Union in 2017. She currently attends the University of Colorado, Boulder, as a doctoral student in the Department of Information Science, where she is studying technology, ethics, and social-justice issues.

DANIELLE LAKE is Director of Design Thinking and an Associate Professor at Elon University in Elon, North Carolina. Her teaching, research, and service explore the potential and the challenges of emergent, relational, place-based design projects for addressing wicked problems, building capacities, and transforming systems. The perspectives shared in her work are informed by her academic training as a feminist pragmatist philosopher and her lived experience as a white, settler, straight, cisgender, and able-bodied first-generation university professor situated at a private liberal-arts undergraduate institution within the southern United States. More about her work can be found at http://works.bepress.com/danielle_lake/.

CASSINI NAZIR is a designer of conversations, curricula, and interfaces. He is an Assistant Professor in the College of Visual Arts and Design at the University of North Texas, where he teaches classes in interaction design. His current research explores how curiosity can be meaningfully infused into design processes. Because curiosity is linguistically rooted in the notion of care, he explores ways that designers can also extend care to those for whom they build, as well as what they choose to build. In spring 2020, he was Designer-in-Residence for the SMU Master's in Design and Innovation (MADI) program. Prior to joining UNT, Cassini taught at the University of Texas at Dallas for ten years, where he directed two research labs. He was founding director of the Arts and Technology Usability Lab, which fosters collaborative research with community partners and offers experiential learning to students. With Roger Malina, he codirected ArtSciLab, a transdisciplinary research lab that helps the arts, science, and technology communities by pursuing initiatives of social urgency and cultural timeliness. His academic projects include collaborations with art historians, astronauts, biochemists, brain scientists, futurists, materials scientists, new-media artists, and a university press. He has worked with industry partners such as Toyota, Intuit, Sabre, DFW Airport, and projekt202.

LESLEY-ANN NOEL is an Afro-Trinidadian design educator, based in New Orleans, Louisiana. She practices design through emancipatory, critical, and antihegemonic lenses, focusing on equity, social justice, and the experiences of people who are often excluded from design research. She also attempts to promote greater critical awareness among designers and design students by introducing critical-theory concepts and vocabulary into the design studio (e.g., through the Designer's Critical Alphabet). Her research also highlights the work of designers outside Europe and North America as an act of decolonizing design. Her identity is shaped by her ethnic background as an Afro-Trinidadian; her experience as a daughter, sister, and mother; and her lived experiences in Trinidad and Tobago, Brazil, Tanzania, Uganda, and the United States.

YOLANDA A. RANKIN is an Assistant Professor in the School of Information at Florida State University. Her research interests include applying Black feminist epistemologies as critical frameworks for designing technology with underserved populations and developing strategies for broadening participation in K–16 computing education. A McKnight Fellow and a Woodrow Wilson Fellow, Yolanda has published more than forty peer-reviewed publications, including journal articles, conference papers, and book chapters. Prior to academia, she accumulated more than twelve years of industry experience while employed at IBM Research Lab–Almaden in San Jose, California, and Lucent Technologies Bell Labs in Naperville, Illinois. Yolanda completed her PhD in Computer Science at Northwestern University, her MA in Computer Science at Kent State University, and her BS in Mathematics at Tougaloo College, a Historically Black College in Jackson, Mississippi.

SONIYAH ROBINSON is a Design Thinking Catalyst and Social Justice Lead with Elon University's Center for Design Thinking. She also works as a project lead for the Black Entrepreneur Initiative at Elon and serves on the national Black Entrepreneur Initiative founding committee. Robinson is the founder and owner of Boundless Blackness, LLC, and centers her work on social-justice storytelling, equity through design thinking with a focus on human rights, and Black empowerment through entrepreneurship.